Call of the Cow Country

True stories by bronc buster Harry Webb
Cowboys . Indians . Outlaws . Will James . Butch Cassidy . Buffalo Bill
Mustangs . Coyotes . Bobcats . Lions

"DAYLIGHT" © J.N. SWANSON
THIS IS EARLY DAWN AND A SHAFT OF SUNLIGHT COMES THROUGH
THE WINDOW OF A ROCK BARN AND HITS THE BUTT OF THE COWBOY.
THERE'S DAYLIGHT BETWEEN HIM AND THE SADDLE AND ONLY THE
CHICKEN KNOWS WHAT KIND OF RIDE HE'S MAKING.

Call of the Cow Country
By Harry Webb

Publisher/Editor: C.J. Hadley
Designer & Illustrator: John Bardwell
Editorial Assistant: Ann Galli
Staff: Joyce Smith, Denyse Pellettieri White

Library of Congress Cataloging-in-Publication Data
Call of the Cow Country
By Harry Webb
ISBN 978-0-9744563-8-6
LCCN 2011911308

Publication of this book was made possible by generous donations from people who care about the American West.

No part of this book may be reproduced in any form or by any electronic or mechanical means, including information storage and retrieval systems, without written permission from the publisher, except by a reviewer who may quote passages in a review.

Published by Range Conservation Foundation, Carson City, Nevada, and RANGE magazine, with assistance from the Nevada Rangeland Resources Commission.

Special thanks to Buffalo Bill Historical Center in Cody, Wyoming, for help with show photography and to Jack Swanson for sharing his western paintings.

$35 U.S.A.
Printed in China
Copyright © 2011
Range Conservation Foundation
and RANGE magazine

The Stories

IN THIS PAINTING BY M.C. POULSEN, BUFFALO BILL LOOKS ABOUT THE SAME AS WHEN HARRY MET HIM AS A BRONC-RIDING KID, CRASHING THROUGH THE WINDOW OF THE CODY DRUGSTORE IN THE FALL OF 1909. HARRY LOOKS PRETTY MUCH THE WAY HE DID WHEN HE WAS HONORED BY THE NATIONAL COWBOY HALL OF FAME IN 1983.

The Art

Travels With Harry

Notes from the publisher, C.J. Hadley.

Nevada rancher Bud Hage wrote a story for me in 1978. It was called "Pine Mountain Storyteller." The star was Harry Webb, a Welsh miner's son who left home in Colorado when he was barely fifteen in search of his "North Star—Wyoming." He became a great cowboy, rode broncs for Buffalo Bill's Wild West Show, worked as a wrangler and extra for the Lubin Moving Picture Company in Philadelphia, broke horses for soldiers fighting in World War I, played fiddle for dances, and trapped rabid predators for the United States government. And then he did what he always dreamed of—built a cattle and sheep ranch south of Palisade, Nevada.

The story was a beauty and I told Bud, "I wish I could have met him."

Bud picked up the phone in my Nevada Magazine office and said, "Would you like to talk to him? He's in Los Angeles."

Harry had left his beloved high-desert ranch because the altitude was endangering his wife Kitty's life. He traded the ranch to a judge for an apartment building in Hollywood. It was a new, sea-level world for Harry, and a frightening one for the judge, who knew nothing of cows, horses, sheep, predators, rattlesnakes or open, lonely country. The judge lasted a few years and the once-beautiful ranch is now choked with sagebrush, but Harry was still in Southern California, minus the apartments.

Harry met Kitty in New York in 1910 and they were married for more than thirty years. She had a son, George, and Kitty and Harry had a son, Harry Junior. After Kitty died, Harry married Jane, who had a daughter named Bea, and that union lasted for another thirty years. He loved them absolutely and outlived them both.

When he got to California, Harry wrote true western tales for magazines and a novel called "Nuthin'," which Walt Disney Studios made into a movie in 1968. Starring Forrest Tucker and Ron

AFTER HARRY LEFT BUFFALO BILL, HE WORKED FOR THE LUBIN MOVING PICTURE COMPANY IN PHILADELPHIA. HE WRANGLED HORSES AND WORKED AS AN EXTRA. THIS PHOTO WAS TAKEN DURING "THE BATTLE OF SHILOH" IN 1912. "WE MADE SOME SILLY PICTURES. I SHOULD HAVE BEEN WRITING SCENARIOS INSTEAD OF PLAYING COWBOY." HE AND E.A. BRININSTOOL WROTE A POEM WHICH WAS PUBLISHED IN MOTION PICTURE MAGAZINE IN 1913. THEY EARNED TWO DOLLARS. NOTE: THE BLACK BOX AT THE START OF ALL STORIES INCLUDES HARRY WEBB'S CATTLE BRAND.

Howard, "A Boy Called Nuthin'" was the story of an urban boy visiting a western ranch. The boy was looking for cowboys, Indians and other "tough" characters he'd read about in Chicago. What he found was a ramshackle operation run by a sloppy character named Turkeyneck, who turned out to be his Uncle Tug. After many lessons learned, there was a Disneyesque happy ending.

In Bud Hage's story, he wrote: "It was probably inevitable that he would some-day have his stories in print, but Harry's start as a writer was almost accidental. He was reading a magazine one evening at the ranch. After finishing a feature story about the West, full of inaccuracies and distortions, he threw the magazine down and said, 'Hell! I can write a better story than that,' and promptly took up a pencil and paper and wrote a story about trapping bobcats. He mailed it to that same magazine and several weeks later received a check in the mail. The magazine accepted eight more of his stories without one rejection."

Thanks to Bud, Harry and I met that day by phone, and it wasn't long before I rode a dirt bike to Los Angeles to meet the old cowboy. ("Drive anything, ride anything, even a grizzly," he said that first day, "except that bloody, bloomin' motorcycle!") He was still handsome, articulate, vigorous, and we started writing letters. We talked often on the phone. At least weekly, envelopes filled with notes, pictures, and copies of stories he thought I might enjoy or like to publish (many of which had already appeared in other magazines) appeared in my mailbox. I ran some of the shorter stories in Nevada Magazine as "Horse Sense & Nonsense" (his title), but Harry always wanted a book.

In 1972, Harry won the Gold Spur for Western Literature for his short story, "Call of the Cow Country." In 1983, the National Cowboy Hall of Fame and Western Heritage Museum in Oklahoma City

HARRY WAS GIVEN THE TRUSTEES AWARD AT THE NATIONAL COWBOY HALL OF FAME IN OKLAHOMA CITY IN 1983. FROM LEFT: NEIGHBOR DOTTIE ZEDIKAR, GERRY WEAVER, HARRY, AND MASTER OF CEREMONIES DENNIS WEAVER BEHIND C. J. HADLEY. BELOW LEFT: CHRISTMAS IN NEVADA, 1981. NINETY-FOUR-YEAR-OLD HARRY RIDES CJ'S THIRTY-TWO-YEAR-OLD MUSTANG SWEETPEA. CJ'S ON QUARTER HORSE SLICK. HARRY WAS OPPOSED TO CJ'S BLACK HAT. "THOSE," HE SAID, "ARE WORN BY BAD GUYS." HE SAID ABOUT SWEETPEA: "JUST GOES TO SHOW WE MUSTANGS DEFY TIME. TOO BAD SWEETPEA CAN'T BE INDUCTED INTO THE COWBOY HALL OF FAME ALONG WITH ME." BELOW RIGHT: CROW INDIAN BEN MARROWBONE AND COWBOY HARRY WEBB, LAST SURVIVING MEMBERS OF THE BUFFALO BILL WILD WEST SHOW HONORED AT THE CODY RODEO IN 1983. THEY HELPED CELEBRATE THE ONE-HUNDREDTH ANNIVERSARY OF COLONEL CODY'S FIRST SHOW.

HARRY AND CJ IN TUJUNGA, CALIFORNIA, 1979. WHEN HARRY WAS HOSPITALIZED IN 1984, CJ FLEW DOWN TO VISIT. SHE WHEELED HIM AROUND FOR TWO DAYS AS HE CHEERED OTHER PATIENTS WITH HIS TRUE WESTERN TALES. HE "JOINED OLD SPOOK" THE NEXT DAY.

with two big fine saddle horses allotted him, George was out at the break of day and scanning the countryside for a Lawny, moving figure but having heard ~~the~~ the tales of many besides my own he was not so naieve as to believe he could ride around in hundreds of acres and bag a much-wanted killer lion. He was a couple miles from camp when a brownish movement down in a swale had him hit the ground with the safety off on his Hi-power savage. But it was a meandering coyote and he was out str...

me. George Vannoy, my stepson, the ...

but George loved Nevada ...

ABOVE: GEORGE VANNOY, HARRY'S STEPSON, WITH FRIEND IN ANGORA CHAPS AT THE BARN. GEORGE LOVED NEVADA BUT WED A SCHOOLTEACHER IN PENNSYLVANIA. HE WAS BACK HOME FOR A VISIT. AT TOP: HARRY USED TO TYPE HIS STORIES BUT IN LATER YEARS TOOK TO PENNING THEM ON YELLOW-LINED PAPER. "I'M TRYING TO GET EVERYTHING TO YOU," HE SAID. "SOME GOOD, SOME BAD, SOME WORSE. IT'S MURDER TO SIT AND WRITE A PIECE BUT SO MANY NEVADA HAPPENINGS COME MY WAY I HAD TO GET 'EM DOWN." RIGHT: HARRY WROTE A NOVEL CALLED "NUTHIN'" THAT WAS MADE INTO A MOVIE BY WALT DISNEY STUDIOS IN 1968. IT STARRED FORREST TUCKER AND RON HOWARD.

14 Sunland — Tujunga — La Crescenta
Sun Valley — Burbank, **Thursday, August 21, 1980**

FAMED TUJUNGA Western writer Harry Webb was the guest of honor last Thursday afternoon at a special showing of "A Boy Called Nuthin,' at Disney Studios in Burbank. The film was taken from Webb's book. Among those attending the showing was Caroline Hadley, editor of Nevada Magazine, who is publishing and gathering together Webb's stories of the Old West, drawn from his many years as a cowboy, rancher, and member of Buffalo Bill's Wild West Show. Among others attending the showing were Harry and Lois Billos, Dottie Zedikar and family, all of Tujunga, Bea and Frank Abbey from La Canada, and Bill and Lucy Colville. Photo above is still taken from the film, which starred Ronny Howard and Forrest Tucker. At left, is Harry Webb.

honored him with the Trustees Award and a copy of Charlie Russell's bronze, "In From the Night Herd." It was for "a lifetime contribution to the western heritage."

Nineteen-eighty-four was the one-hundredth anniversary of the first Wild West Show produced by soldier, scout, bison hunter, showman Colonel William Frederick Cody, who was born in Iowa Territory on February 26, 1846. Paul Fees, the curator of the Buffalo Bill Historical Center in Cody, Wyoming, invited Harry, the last surviving bronc rider from the show of 1910, and Ben Marrowbone, the last surviving Indian from the show of 1911, to appear at the centennial celebration. When that old cowboy and Indian walked into the arena—a glorious and perfect moment—about twenty thousand people in the stands dragged out handkerchiefs.

In our six years of close attention, I learned a lot about Harry. When he went riding with the "Elite 400" in New York City, the riding master wouldn't let him use his western saddle. "I sure felt silly! When I didn't rise and fall in the saddle when we were ordered to 'post,' Mr. Furst lost his temper, but the bigwigs liked my style and said, 'Why, he rides like he was glued to the saddle!'"

Harry said I rode like Bing Crosby, but equivocated quickly: "I was kidding when I told CJ she sat in the saddle just like Bing Crosby. Nobody but Bing Crosby could look that bad on a horse."

He also wrote, "When you ride that new horse of yours, be darn careful not to take off with a jackrabbit start. It is well to observe this rule any time as the gentlest horse, in a playful mood, often lights in crow-hopping."

He was a teacher, a listener, a friend, and despite the agony he went through in later years ("Jane and I are doing O.K. if we don't get down to details."), he always wrote with humor:

"While we were with Wyoming Bill's Wild West Show in 1914, I had a couple of silk shirts with dollar-size pearl buttons, but one day when half a dozen Seneca Indians went on a drunken strike and tried to bust up the show's performance, I wound up with nothing but the wristbands when the free-for-all fight was over."

When Charlie Russell visited Buffalo

Bill's Wild West Show in Madison Square Garden in 1910, he drew pictures for all the cowboys. Harry had his illustration for years, but it disappeared. "We didn't take care of them because there were so many," he said. "I regret that." But he did keep a poem:

"The West is dead, my friend
But writers hold the seed
And what they saw
Will live and grow
Again for those who read."
　　　C.M. RUSSELL, 1917

Harry holds that seed. He was generous with his work, and his stories and collections are in the University of Wyoming in Laramie, Garfield County Library in New Castle, Colorado (old magazines donated by Carl Osborn), and Gordon Yowell's Museum in Walla Walla, Washington (which has Harry's Buffalo Bill saddle, chaps, boots, spurs and trunk). Harry also sent material to college professor Gene Gressley in Wyoming to help with his work about the American West.

After Jane died in 1981, Harry and I traveled together to Cody, Wyoming, twice, and to the Cowboy Hall of Fame in Oklahoma City to pick up his award. He spent Christmas in Nevada with my family in 1981. I miss Harry, and I miss his letters. "I love you," he said at the end of each one, but he really loved us all.

Harry wrote an obit for one of his magazine editors, Rex Bundy of Pony Express magazine. "Rex may be gone from our midst," he said, "but time will be old before he is forgotten by his public. A prolific writer of historical events, he was a stickler for accuracy as well as being a friend to all mankind. Yes, Rex's pen is forever stilled but memory is long-lived. We will miss you, Rex."

Looks like Harry wrote his own obit, because it's perfect for him, too.

Harry was born in Colorado on November 7, 1887. He was 96 when he died on July 16, 1984. It's taken me twenty years to fulfill my promise to get his short stories published in a book, but I know he'll like it. I reckon he's up in heaven riding Old Spook, taking care of cattle, and making sure the predators don't take too many lambs. He'll pull on his white

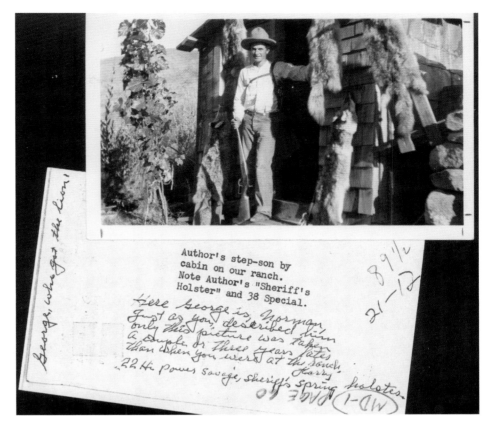

GEORGE AT THE CABIN ON THE WEBB RANCH. HE WEARS HARRY'S SHERIFF'S HOLSTER AND .38 SPECIAL AND HOLDS A .22 HIGH-POWER SAVAGE TO HELP HIS DAD RIDE THE TRAPLINES. THE NOTES ARE FROM THE BACK OF THE PHOTOGRAPH.

HARRY JUNIOR AT HIS DAD'S RANCH IN PINE VALLEY, NEVADA, WITH BIG HAT, COWBOY OUTFIT, TOY GUN IN HOLSTER AND DEAD BOBCAT.

hat, angora chaps and spurs and occasionally hang and rattle with a green colt.

The stories here are told in the language of the time—authentic and historically accurate. They cover love, hate, generosity, selfishness, murder, theft, insobriety, tenacity, foolishness, and other

peculiar human traits.

It's the American West. It's raw and real. And it's all Harry. ■

Call of the Cow Country

**There's something about big sky and a remuda of fine horses that makes a boy
go crazy with wanting it.**

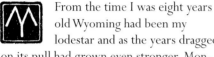From the time I was eight years old Wyoming had been my lodestar and as the years dragged on its pull had grown even stronger. Montana had its big cowboy outfits but it was to be many years before I realized it. I knew nothing but mines. First coal mines, then hard rock mines in Colorado.

From the day I was twelve until I was fifteen, my hands were either cupped around a shovel handle as I "mucked" in my father's hardrock tunnel, or swinging a double-jack for the old man. (My father was perhaps fifty, but to us kids he was the "old man.") And with every wooden-wheeled wheelbarrow of muck, or clank of the eight-pound sledgehammer, my thoughts were on the cow country of Wyoming.

There was a euphoric something in the state's very name that spelled romance, attracting me as the North Pole pulls the needle of a compass. My older brother Charley had never been one to hang around the old man after he was old enough to find work as the two just didn't jibe. He had written once in four years from Lander, Wyoming, saying he was "punching cows," and from that day on my lot became ever harder to bear. I vowed that I would find Charley in that far off land of my dreams and also become a cowboy.

My chance came one late November day in 1903, fifteen days after my fifteenth birthday. It was totally unexpected, too. The old man was drilling a "down-hole" and I was striking for him. I could swing either a single or double-jack all day and center the drill-head, but this time fantasy had me around the big herds of bawling cattle and the double-jack smashed the old man's hand.

Yowling a curse, he yanked out the drill and yelled, "'Arry, hi'll break your bloody neck for this!" He was Cornish so he always left off his aiches when they should be on and vice versa. The drill only whacked me once across the shoulder as we raced down the tunnel, then as I leaped off the dump it whizzed past my head. When the old man said he'd do this or that to any person, he usually made good his promise and if I hoped to ever be a cowboy, I had sense enough to know I would never attain my goal if I had a broken neck.

Our log home was on the west side of the Colorado Grand River below Red

> **From the day I was twelve until I was fifteen, my hands were either cupped around a shovel handle as I mucked in my father's hardrock tunnel, or swinging a double-jack for the old man. And with every wooden-wheeled wheelbarrow of muck, or clank of the eight-pound sledgehammer, my thoughts were on the cow country of Wyoming.**

Gorge Canyon and the mine was on the east side at the head of the mile-long gorge. We always walked a narrow trail up the west side of the river and crossed back and forth above the rapids in a homemade boat. To this day I'll never know why I didn't grab the boat and leave my irate old man stranded.

Working my way down the canyon through precipitous cliffs where the wild water churned directly below, I reached an old trapper's cabin directly across the river from ours. Old "Dad" Stanley talked many an hour that night trying to dissuade me

from my decision to take one of our horses and head for Wyoming.

"You damn kids runnin' off," he snapped, "makes me sick! Done the same though, myself. But after I growed up an' knew the heartbreak of havin' one o' my own run off, I've wished many a day an' night I'd o' stayed home another few years. Never saw 'em again. Heard long afterward, when it was too late, they'd needed me in their old age an' wondered a heap about me."

Although this talk made me feel bad, it didn't lessen my desire to head north.

"Some day," I told him, "when I get plenty of money and a fine outfit, I'll come back. The folks don't care about me anyway." That was the rebel in me talking.

The next morning I watched through a knothole until I saw the old man go up the canyon, then had Stanley row me across in his flat-bottomed boat. On reaching home, I found my two younger sisters and our kid brother hanging onto our crying mother and squalling bloody murder. I couldn't savvy why all the fuss about me being gone as I'd often gone over to old Stanley's beaver trapline and stayed overnight without letting my folks know.

But soon I found out it wasn't me they were all crying about. Our mother had entered a contest in *Comfort Magazine* and the winner would get a "free trip to the St. Louis World's Fair" the next year. She had found the seven faces in a bushy tree and the weekly mail carrier had brought a letter the day before saying she was a winner.

Mother was positive she could work the next month's puzzle but was boo-hooing because she didn't have a thing to wear, even though the fair was half a year hence.

Mother didn't try too hard to persuade

me not to leave, saying, "I don't much blame you, Harry. Your father's a brute, but I hate to see you running aimlessly all over the country like Charley. Tim Mugrage wants a boy to help with the work on his farm at twenty dollars a month, so you can soon buy yourself a horse and a saddle. A rolling stone gathers no moss, you know, so I think you should work near home and…"

"And neither does a sittin' hen lay eggs!" I shot back at her, my mind past the arguing point. "I'm going to take the three-year-old gelding and get away before the old man gets back." I'd asked the old man every week for a year to give me this bay colt and all I'd ever got out of him was a grunted, "We'll see."

Mother tearfully dug up two dollars she'd got for boarding Lee Miller, a prospector, and which she was hoarding for her trip to St. Louis. Seeing her and all the kids crying made it a tough decision and at that moment I almost weakened. But Wyoming was calling in a louder voice than my family's crying, so I rode away, wearing an old jacket of the old man's and with nothing but a bridle on Star. I didn't say goodbye. My throat was closed too tight.

I made good mileage that day and after spending seventy-five cents for a late dinner and horse feed in Steamboat Springs I realized, at that rate, my money wasn't going to

hold out for long. I began to see that once you left home it cost money to eat; especially with a horse to feed. Well, Star would have to eat even if I didn't! His were the legs that had to carry me to that golden mecca.

All I knew about my goal was that it lay far to the north, and I used the Big Dipper's two bottom bowl stars to keep me on my course. I traveled late that night reaching a spot on the Little Snake River just beyond a hamlet called Slater. I was searching for a spot where I might find grass for my horse. At that time of year grass was scarce, but a town meant my money would take wings in a hurry.

Fortunately, campfires loomed up and I found myself in a large camp of Gypsies. A Gypsy woman had once cured my mother's headache for fifty cents when we lived in Steamboat Springs and I'd admired Gypsies ever since. They were fine, honest people. These folks took a liking to me and picketed my horse inside a barbed-wire fence where the grass was tall, and where their horses were hobbled. (They had cut the wires.) Then they fixed a dandy supper and rustled up some blankets for me.

The next morning they had all the horses around the wagons and the women were cooking breakfast when I woke up. They were all so nice. I was hoping they, too, were going north so I could stay with them, but no

such luck. They were following the trail down to the Yampa River and maybe on to the Green River where they would winter.

After breakfast, a tall, hatchet-faced man with rings big as dollars dangling from his ears hit me up for a horse trade.

"We can't let a boy like you go bareback," he said. "You've got to have a saddle. Now we have a fine bay here and we'll let you have him and the saddle in exchange for your horse and five dollars. Your horse is a dead mate for that chestnut there and by having a mated team we can sell them. Otherwise, we wouldn't part with him for love or money."

I said I didn't have five dollars, but I might trade even. Their horse was a nice looking animal and I was chafed from riding bareback. That saddle, while not much to look at, was a big inducement.

"Oh let the boy have them for his horse and two dollars," a pretty woman said. "He's a nice boy and I want him to have a saddle to ride all that distance."

I hated to part with Star, but I thought it would look a lot better when I rode into a cow outfit asking for a job. "Well," I said, "if you'll throw in that harmonica you were playing last night, I'll give you a dollar and we'll call it a trade." After a lot of jabbering I didn't understand, she climbed in one of the covered wagons and came out with the harmonica.

I don't think I ever got more comfort out of anything than that saddle and especially the mouth harp. The bay was a dandy and all regrets and fears quickly vanished. I was as free as an eagle and when I wasn't galloping or trotting I had that harp in my mouth. I was cutting due north, no road, no nothing except the blue sky above me and vast rolling country ahead.

Several miles lay behind and I was playing "Blue Bell," the Spanish war song, and thinking that those Gypsies were either fine folks or crazy for parting with this horse, when suddenly the bay's head began jerking up and he fell over on his side, nearly breaking my leg. I was sure he was dead and mumbled, "Oh, Lordy God! Now what'll I do? I'm afoot with a saddle!" But as suddenly as he had fallen, he was on his feet as if nothing had happened.

I had gone several miles following a nice stream and was still shaking from my scare, so to calm myself I was trying to play "The Yellow Rose of Texas" when the bay reared straight up and fell over backwards. This time I wasn't so lucky, the saddle horn rammed my ribs, and for a moment I thought I was the one who was dead.

My horse was on his feet before I was able to get up and was walking away, dragging the reins off to one side, and every time I tried to catch him he would start trotting. My ribs hurt so bad I could scarcely breathe, let alone run, and it was some time before I could catch him. But I had learned one thing. At least I thought so. This blamed horse simply didn't like my brand of music! From then on the harmonica stayed in my pocket. I was going along humped over the bay's neck when up went his head and he dropped as if drained with one of the old man's sledgehammers.

This time I took stock of things. I had heard enough about horses eating the "loco weed" to know this critter was locoed about as bad as possible. Those Gypsies had known this, and instead of being the wonderful people I admired they were a band of crooks! I called down every curse on them I had ever heard and invented a few of my own.

That horse fell over backwards, on his side, or simply on his head so many times during the next few miles, I lost track. But I had learned to pile off whenever he began trembling or jerking his head. I had followed the stream until it suddenly bent to the east and although I hated to leave it, I knew my goal wasn't that direction. I had consumed gallons of creek water on account of being feverish, and to leave it worried me.

There was a wagon road leading off to the northwest, which meant little to me. I might be five or a hundred miles to any habitation at all it told me, but roads always led to some place and even though darkness was closing in, the road buoyed me up a bit. I was taking a last big drink, as no telling when I would see water again, when I heard the squeak and rattle of a wagon coming down the hill to the north.

When the man pulled up his four-horse team to the stream, I was never more glad to see a human. That is, so long as it wasn't a

Gypsy. All humped over, I led my horse to the wagon just as the man tossed the lines to the ground and climbed down a front wheel.

"What in Sam Hill yuh doin' out here?" he asked, but before I could answer he said, "What's the matter, yuh got a gut ache?" It didn't take long for me to groan out my trouble, where I was from, where I was going, and about my horse cutting his crazy didoes.

"Them goddamn Sicilians would skin their own mother if they could get a nickel for her hide!" he said. "But by God, you're in man's country now, and soon's I get unhitched, we'll see about fixing you up. Tie that sonovabitch to a wheel and lay down 'til I c'n git us organized."

In a jiffy the teams were unharnessed, hobbled, and he was rummaging in the jockey box below the footboard. "This'll knock the spots out of that fever," he said as he mixed something from a bottle with a little water. "Use it all the time for my horses. It's acronite. Freighters never go without it. 'Course with horses we sprinkle a batch o' pure quill on some paper an' ram it down their throats. Drink 'er down."

I had never heard of acronite and hesitated. I was wondering if he, too, was locoed and maybe this horse medicine would kill me dead.

"Down with 'er!" he demanded. "She's a smaller dose an' diluted."

"Tastes like Sweet Spirits of Nitre," I said once it was down.

"'Bout the same," he said, "only a hell of a lot potenter. Eat up your kidneys if I gave you a horse dose." In a few minutes instead of finding myself dead or my kidneys "eat up," I felt a lot better. It sure killed my fever and even my side didn't hurt like it had.

"I'm go'nta picket that bug-house horse o' yours so he can't run off and leave yuh. Then t'night, we'll tie him up an' let the bastard eat wagon-wheel hay." From that moment on I loved that rough, tough, bushy-whiskered man.

"Now before I start cookin' we'll have a look-see at them ribs. Well," he said, after feeling around, "they ain't busted." Going to the jockey box he came back with a bottle.

"What's that?" I asked, though not caring what it was.

"Mexican mustang liniment," he grunted, pouring out a palm-full and slapping it on my ribs and over my right kidney. "Horse sprains a tendon and we rub a batch o' this in. Burns the hide right off if we rub it too hard, but she sure knocks out a sprain. Take the hide off clear t'your insides if I rubbed 'er in. But we ain't rubbin' 'er in, just pattin' 'er on. Bet yuh'll feel better in two shakes of a wampus cat's tail."

"It's better already," I was happy to tell him, thinking if he was a specimen of Wyoming's folks I sure wasn't going to be homesick for my own for a long time to come.

Sitting around the campfire that night, I learned this creek was known as the Savory and his name was Rasmussen. He owned a homestead on this road halfway between the Savory and Rawlins. He was hauling a load of winter supplies to "some folks east of here. Husband got all smashed up when a stacker boom broke durin' hayin'. No, not particular a close friend, just a neighbor. 'Bout twenty-five miles from my shack t'Rawlins. You'll stop at my place tomorrow night. The old woman'll be powerful glad to see a new mug. Don't see many folks along this road."

I opened up and told him all about my old man being a Cousin Jack and me being a good miner myself. I also told him about my mother entering the World's Fair contest and how she was all ready to go and crying something awful because she didn't have a fit dress to wear. At this he sure laughed, but when I mentioned that I intended to get a job punching cows up around Lander, he looked pretty solemn for a minute. Then getting rid of a big cud of tobacco he said, "I wouldn't put too much stock in gettin' a cowboy job right off if I was you. You're a bit…"

Just then my horse slammed back on the halter rope, breaking the halter and falling over backwards.

"That's a god-awful poison, that loco weed," Rasmussen allowed, as he hurried to get another halter on the horse before it took off in the darkness. "'Tain't the weed itself. The weed's a mild narcotic, alright, and the horse gets just like these fellers they call morphine fiends. In the late fall, after

the plant's all et up, the horse paws out the roots. They're crazy for it an' if there's been enough plants around, the horse gits crazy as a loon. Never gits over it, either.

"I don't recommend unloadin' him on some poor sucker, but if you can make it to Rawlins without him killin' yuh, I'd advise just turning him loose an' catching a ride with some freighter. Lot's o' freighters 'tween Rawlins an' Lander. Well, reckon we best hit the blankets an' warm the ground fer a spell. I'm a light sleeper so whenever the worms start workin' in that critter's skull, I'll hear him an' see that yuh don't have t'pack your saddle from here t'Rawlins."

I won't attempt to record the number of times that handsome bay threw himself before I rode up to Rawlins' main street, but the moment I rode into a livery barn to inquire about freighters going north, the liveryman had his eyes on my horse.

"Nice lookin' nag you're riding, Bub," he said as he walked around my mount. "Steal him?"

"Nope," I said, mad at his remark. "Traded a chestnut sorrel for him." I started to ask about the freighters but he wasn't listening.

"Give you a good trade on him," he went on. "I see he's broke to harness and I've a dead match for him, blaze face and all."

Being broke to harness was news to me! Maybe my horse wasn't locoed after all. Maybe he just didn't like to be rode! But then he'd had one fit when tied up.

"What makes you think he's broke to harness?" I asked.

"These little gray collar marks, that's how. Sure you didn't high-grade him?" He saw I was getting madder by the second so he changed his tune. "Just fooling, Bub," he said, laughing. "Just wanted to get your dander up. Allus say something like that. Come here. I want to show you something."

I followed him through the barn to a big feedlot out back.

"See that dun-colored horse out there? That's the best saddler and cow horse that God ever built four legs on. But like I said, I need a mate for that bay there in the corner and I'll swap you the dun for yours. You can…"

I was thinking so fast I quit listening. The

Gypsies had given me the same talk about needing a mate for one of theirs so they'd have a matched span. On the other hand, this man wasn't a Gypsy and now that he'd got down to business he was a pretty nice fellow. I thought of Rasmussen's advice. I thought of getting to Lander in style. I did-

I rode away, wearing an old jacket of the old man's and with nothing but a bridle on Star. I didn't say goodbye. My throat was closed too tight.

n't have to think about being penniless. That part I knew.

"That dun won't buck will he? I'd have to have a gentle horse if I traded."

"Buck? Ha! That's rich! Listen, kid, you could explode a box of dynamite under him and he'd stay as decomposed as your grandma at a knittin' bee!"

"I reckon he would, alright," I said, having to laugh at his words. I'd heard my old man and prospectors talk "decomposed" stuff.

"If he's what you say he is," I said, thinking how Gypsies always demanded a little money to boot in a trade. "I might trade with you for ten dollars to boot. I know what my horse is and…"

"Ten dollars!" he exploded. "Listen, boy, you can buy most any horse in this whole damn country for ten dollars!"

"I'm broke," I said, "and if I part with my horse I've got to have some money."

"I'll go for five," he snarled, "and not a penny more! Besides, if you're broke, you'd still be broke wouldn't you, if we didn't trade?"

As dumb as I was, I could see the logic in that last remark but I still played Gypsy. "Seven dollars or no trade," I squeaked, itching for that five and praying my horse didn't throw a fit any second.

"Tell you what I'll do, young gobbler," he bargained, taking a look in my horse's mouth, "I'm so damn tired looking at that lousy cap you're wearing, I'll go for five dollars and there's a pretty good cowboy hat hanging there in the harness room I'll throw in for good measure."

Going in the harness room he came out with the hat and wedged it over my ears. "There, now you look halfway human."

I was so elated over the hat I couldn't speak. "And I'll throw in a good supper and breakfast at the restaurant," he added, "and you can sleep in the harness room. I'm tired of all this dickering!"

I guess he thought I wouldn't trade. Before I could get my wits together, he had unsaddled the bay and booted him out to the feed racks. I was glad of that, because I was in mortal fear my steed would kill the deal.

That night, with a big supper inside me, I should have slept like a pup, but sleep was the last thing on my mind. I'd had a look at myself in the restaurant mirror and to say I was pleased with my reflection would be an understatement. But there was something else that haunted me. I had discovered a pair of boots hanging among some of the horse collars and I'd wished I'd spied them before closing the horse deal.

In the morning, soon as it was light enough to see I had the dun saddled and, fearing this man may have unloaded some old outlaw on me, I was leading the saddled dun around the corral when the liveryman called from the stable door: "Dandy animal ain't he?"

"Yeh," I replied. "Only he steps around mighty funny. Like he wanted to buck or something."

"Prob'ly got a kick on the leg," he said. "Horses are always scrapping when they're feeding. Come on. We gotta go put on the nosebag ourselves."

At breakfast, I worked up the courage to mention the boots. Those I had to have, even if it meant parting with some or all of my money.

"If yuh can wear 'em," he said, "take 'em.

Prob'ly throwed away by some cowhand."

At that my appetite faded. With those boots, big hat and a good horse—not to mention my five dollars—I was in what my mother would call "seventh heaven."

The next morning we were no more out of the livery barn than Buck bogged his head and had me "hangin' an' rattlin'" before he quit bucking. But once we were out jogging along the freight road, my mind reflected on my good fortune. Lander, where the livery stable owner had said cowboys were "thicker than fiddlers in hell," lay but a hundred and fifty miles across the desert. A huge, blue sky above me and tranquility within, I forewent my desire for a while to hurry and played the mouth harp. When I finally kicked Buck (as I called him) into a gallop he seemed to stumble a lot, which I attributed, as the man had said, to being "kicked on a leg."

I took great pleasure in looking down at my shadow, adjusting my hat to various angles, and assuming a cowboy stance in the saddle. And whenever my mind returned to the locoed bay, I eased my conscience with the thought that maybe, just maybe, the horse was balky under saddle. One of my old man's horses would balk so bad at times with nothing but an empty buckboard she would throw herself over the tongue and it would take hours to get up some little rise. Buck, I found, was tough as whet leather harness and never seemed to tire, and I was several miles past the stage station when I overtook a jerkline team of ten all-white horses, two wagons, a feed cart, and a camp wagon. The driver, riding the near wheel-horse, said he was going to Lander and invit-

ed me to tie my horse on behind and travel with him. "Good bunk and plenty of grub in the camp wagon," he said, "and you'll be a heap of help to me."

His outfit only moved two or three miles an hour, so I declined his invitation. I was in a hurry to get to Lander, find my brother, and get to punching cows.

Shortly after passing the freighter I was surprised to see a cowboy-looking man limp onto the road from behind a long upthrust dyke of rocks that lined either side of the road for several hundred feet. He said he had done a lot of bronc busting in Montana but had been "wrangling horses at the stage station back down the road." He had got drunk and lost his wages in a poker game and was "hoofing it to the 71 Ranch on the Sweet Water," where he hoped to get a job breaking horses. A bronc had broken his leg in Montana was why he limped—so he said.

Karl was a comical fellow and we got real chummy and, on account of his bad leg, we took turns in riding and walking. He was an old-timer, maybe forty or so, and told a lot of hair-raising experiences which made the time pass quicker but slowed me down a lot getting to Lander and finding my brother Charley.

It was my turn to ride, as the run-over boots had worn blisters on my heels from walking and for no reason at all Buck stubbed his toe and all but tossed me over his head.

"Let me have a look at his feet," Karl said. "He may have a rock caught in his frog. Nope, nothin' wrong there."

I told him about Buck maybe getting a leg kicked in the corral so he felt and jabbed

Buck's legs.

"Solid as a rock," he reported, and began looking in Buck's eyes. "Oh ho!" he exclaimed. "How old did that jasper say this horse was?"

"About eight," I replied, as Karl was looking in Buck's mouth.

"Eighteen—or twenty-eight—would be a damn sight closer to it! Hasn't had a cup in a tooth for years and he's parrot-mouthed! Not only that, he's blind as a bat. Kid, you've been took with a capital T."

I got off and looked, expecting to see no eyes at all, but Buck's eyes were a bit scummed over. "He's still a good horse," I said by way of consoling myself.

"Darn good," Karl said. "Been a real cow horse in his day."

This softened my remorse over passing off my locoed horse on someone I'd thought was such a nice man. I now fervently hoped the bay was locoed and would get worse by the minute!

"You can't trust nobody any more," Karl commiserated as we went along. "Well, you're at least five bucks ahead of the deal, anyway. And from the looks of the sky off there we'll need some of that five to get under cover tonight. Sunshine in this damn country one minute and a blizzard chops your face into pieces the next! We sure don't want to get caught out tonight!"

A strong wind had sprung up from the north and I said, "What'll we do Karl? It's getting pretty late."

"Well," he said, "there's a stage station in that big pass there. That's Crook's Gap and I'd say it's about four miles. So I reckon one of us better jog along after a bit and see about us stopping. We can sleep in the barn, so that won't bother us. It's the horse feed. Some of these stations run short of hay except for the team changes. Hay's usually a dollar a flake, but I know where I worked they wouldn't let you have an ounce for five dollars sometimes. Meals are only four bits, but we have to do some tall talking for horse feed. Lots of freighters stop there and may want some feed too."

Some time later—Karl was riding and the sky had darkened and the wind swept our voices away—he yelled, "She's getting worse by the second, so maybe one of us better hightail it on ahead and see what luck we have."

"I can walk better than you," I said, "so

you go. You know more about these people than I do."

"Might be a good plan at that," he said. He had gone but a few yards when he trotted back. "Maybe I best take that five along. Money talks louder than my mouth, even in this damn wind."

"Good thing you thought of it!" I shouted back and dug out my cherished greenback. The awful wind took my breath away and it was snowing so hard I couldn't see more than a few feet. My heels hurt so bad I had to sit down and bandage the blisters with torn pieces of my bandanna. It seemed I had walked a lot farther than four miles, where Karl had said the station was, but still no station.

As I stumbled along, my thoughts lingered on what Karl had said about us better not being caught in a blizzard at night and I began getting panicky, running against the icy blast and falling down. Then when I had despaired of ever reaching the station, I heard dogs barking and there was a light but a few feet away. A young woman and her son ran the station, but my joy quickly curdled when she told me no rider had stopped there.

"Fred," she asked, "did anyone on a horse stop at the barn?"

"No'm," the boy said, "but I saw a man gallop by about an hour or two ago." At that I was downcast and I could only falter through my predicament.

"Well, don't you worry," the lady said. "There will be stages and teams going to Lander and you're welcome to stay here as

long as you want to. But I know one thing, whoever that man was, he'll never have any luck in this world and surely none in the next! He'll suffer for a mean trick like this. The Lord will see to that!"

I hoped he'd suffer, but there was little consolation in what happened to Karl now or after he was dead. My outfit was gone and I had but a few nickels to my name. That night a stage stopped to change teams and while I was helping Fred hurry with four fresh horses, I was so fascinated with the two big headlights on the Concord coach I forgot all about my loss.

"Oh, yes," Fred said, "they drive straight through from Lander to Rawlins and the same back to Lander."

The storm lasted all night and until the evening of the next day, and when my freighter friend pulled in I hurried to tell him my troubles and accept his offer of taking me with him. How I wish I could remember that station lady's name, because it wasn't until we were camped at the Sweet Water Crossing that I discovered she had slipped two dollar bills in the inside of my old overall jacket.

The freighter (a Mr. Selfrige or Sellers, something like that) said, "I'll bet there's something about this river they never taught you in school."

I told him I'd never even heard of the Sweet Water until Karl mentioned getting a job there.

"Well, sir," he said, "I'm going to tell you something that few folks know and can hardly believe after they do know it. But the head of this river and the Big Sandy River both head from the same spring. It's on a divide in the Wind River Mountains. The Sweet Water goes on to the Atlantic Ocean and the Big Sandy goes to the Pacific. Now what do you know about that?"

I didn't know anything about it and could only say, "Jiminy Cricket! Is that right?"

"A fact," he said. He knew lots of things. He told me he would bet me his jerkline horse against a hole in a donut that this Karl was one of the Hole in the Wall gang and that his real name was Tom O'Day. "I heard in Rawlins, O'Day had been seen around town. Probably looking over a bank for the gang to rob."

"Karl wouldn't be a bank robber," I said, "even if he did steal my horse. He had no money and said he'd been working at a stage station."

"That's the way they work. Rob a bank or hold up a stage, then they cache the money, scatter out and work a while at cow punching, or even shoveling hay until things cool down. That throws off suspicion."

"But why would he take my horse and five dollars?" I wanted to know. It didn't sound like good sense to me.

"'Cause he wanted to get back to his hideout in the Big Horn Mountains damned quick. That's why!"

Well, sense or no sense, and no matter if he was O'Day or Karl or whoever, he'd sure put the kibosh on me riding into Lander in grand style like I'd pictured myself doing.

It was a lucky thing I had the two dollars, because no one in Lander knew where my brother was. Some said he had taken off for

Colorado, others thought he was down in the Lost Cabin country breaking horses for the Wimsey and Johnson outfit.

No matter, he wasn't in Lander, I was on my own, and instead of being a cowboy riding the range I worked at everything from washing whiskey bottles in Bill and Joe Lannigan's Saloon to pearl diving in the Chinese restaurant. First time I'd known washing kettles and pans was called pearl diving. The Chinese owner was a fine man and owned a ranch on the Sweet Water. I sent my mother a post card saying I was fine and had a job "diving for pearls." Guess when she got that card she thought bats had invaded my belfry.

Some weeks at this and I graduated to

I was usually going around limping and sporting a peeled-up face from being thrown, kicked and tromped on, but 'practice makes perfect' someone had said and I sure got plenty of that.

jobs in Ed Farlow's and Welch's livery stables. By then I was acquainted with several cowboys from the various outfits all over the country and especially from the Big Horn Basin where the really big cow empires were.

I had also made friends with a lot of fine town kids about my age and older. Their dads owned saloons, stores or livery stables and those kids were wild and woolly and great bronc riders. Lee and Lon Welch (their mother ran the Cottage Hotel right near Mr. Welch's big livery barn), Ad St. John, Stub Farlow and Brocky Jones were the best bronc riders of any of the town kids. They would run a herd of wild Indian horses (the Shoshone Reservation lay just a short distance north of town) and ride them all day long. Then there were dozens of hard-bucking horses around the livery stables to ride. And the harder they bucked and the meaner they were, the louder those kids would let out their war-whoops. Talk about bronc riders!

Freckle-faced Brocky Jones was my hero. He'd chop a horse up with his spurs as he

yelled "Powder River! A mile wide and an inch deep!" Brocky drank like a lumberjack but was a barrel of fun.

It wasn't long until they had me tackling the broncs and although I'd ridden pigs, calves, and bucking burros down home, I found riding a squalling bronc was something of another class. Sometimes I made a fair ride, but mostly I hit the ground. The kids would tell me I was doing fine, so I'd spit out a gob of corral manure, tuck my shirttail back in, and repeat the performance. As Brocky remarked weeks later, "If we'd give Harry two-bits every time he got piled, he could buy himself the best ranch in Lander Valley!"

I was usually going around limping and sporting a peeled-up face from being thrown, kicked and tromped on, but "practice makes perfect" someone had said and I sure got plenty of that.

By spring, I was riding the snakiest broncs we could dig up and barring nothing. Of course, like Brocky and the rest, I occasionally bit the mud, but it wasn't my habit any more and one day when I made a ride on a big brown gelding Peeky St. John said, "By God you can outride your brother Charley forty times over!" This accolade coming from one of the state's finest contest riders convinced me I was ready for the cow outfits.

I had made very little money during the winter, but once spring and fine weather came, it seemed the town had more money than Mr. Carter had liver pills. Long-line freighters, stage drivers, cowhands, sheepherders and hundreds of soldiers from Fort Washakie all but poured money in the gutter. In fact, any day, it was nothing to pick up silver or bills in front of a saloon and there were lots of saloons. The funny thing was, jobs went begging because no one would work. Everybody had too much money. Everyone, that is, except yours truly.

Ranchers would hurry up and down sidewalks and in saloons offering three dollars a day for men to clean ditches or build fence only to find no takers. A man came up to me and said, "What's got into all you goddamn loafers and parasites, anyway? Here I'm offering four dollars a day and board for somebody to shovel last year's sand out of my ditches but not a damn mother's son of you will take a job!"

"Show me the job," I said. "I've swung a

double-jack and shoveled muck in mines, so your job is a first cousin of mine."

I'd learned from my bronc-riding friends to talk tough. I'd also seen enough to know if I expected to hit up a cattle baron for a job, I damn well better have a horse and saddle between my legs.

The job was right at the south end of town, across the Popo Agie River, and I'd only been working a week when one day my long-lost brother came riding along the ditch. I didn't know the whiskered stranger at first, but after crying a bit I managed to get down to sensible talk. He'd been breaking horses for George Wimsey down by the Lost Cabin alright, but had to quit.

"Well, you didn't try very damn hard to find me!" he said, when I told him somebody said he might be down there or in Colorado. He had a fine horse outfit, angora chaps and all; even a big six-shooter and cartridge belt buckled on. That made me more determined than ever to work on this ditch or anything else until I could have the same things. I thought maybe he had lots of money and was going to help me out when he asked, "How you fixed for money, kid?"

"Fixed pretty good," I said, then quickly added, "but I can sure use some more!"

"Who the hell can't!" he grumbled. "I'm about broke, so I'll have to borrow five or ten from you."

He didn't admit it, but I figured he was a drinker or a gambler. But I was sure of one thing—he could pull all my teeth out with his fingers easier than he could wheedle me out of a penny. My clothes were ragged but I was saving for a horse and a saddle even if I had to go naked like that Godiva woman I'd seen the picture of.

I talked Charley into taking a job on this ditch, which he didn't like doing. I didn't fancy it either but that was beside the point. By the end of May, I had bought a fine saddle horse and saddle from a drunken cowboy who had gone broke in a saloon and said he was "shedding this blasted country forever!" His home was in Rapid City, South Dakota, so he hopped a stage for Rawlins.

Charley spent his money as fast as he made it, even though I talked myself blue in the face. Every day or two he would want to borrow five dollars and said he'd pay it right back. But he didn't know all the hell I'd gone through to get to Lander. Oh, he knew alright, but just wasn't interested. But I decided I wouldn't trust him any more than I would trust a Gypsy. Yes, or that Rawlins liveryman, or Karl whatever his name was. So Charley went on shoveling the ditch!

On a beautiful day about the last of May he threw down his shovel and said, "To hell with this! Any damn fool can dig ditch! How'd you like to go down to the Big Horn Basin with me? The Dickie Brothers have several broncs they want broken and I hear Colonel Torrey at the M Bar is hiring a lot of cowboys, so if I don't take the Dickey job we'll go to the M Bar. There ought to be some little job you could handle. It's a cinch you couldn't ride a bronc and the horses with roundup wagons are snuffy, too, so…"

"The hell I can't ride a bronc!" I cut in, knowing my wild and woolly brother would soon get the biggest surprise of his twenty-one years.

As we rode out of Lander the next morning, I thought it was the most beautiful day of my life. But I suppose its beauty was greatly enhanced by knowing the fulfillment of a mining kid's dream and destiny lay but seventy-five miles due north. ■

"Riders of the San Joaquin" © J.N. Swanson

Cowboy jobs were pretty much the same all over the West. These are Californios, also known as vaqueros. Their horses are all in different phases of training. The bit on the horse on the left is a spade, the one on the right is a hackamore. There are braided rawhide bosals, reins and lariats and some twisted hair ropes called mecates. These vaqueros are taking a break from gathering cattle in the high country to the west of the Sierra Nevada.

Cowboy Life, Good, Bad, and Plain Hell

Yes, the old grind would start all over again and we, to the last man, would be happy to be a part of it.

 When Johnnie's teacher asked him to define a "cowboy," Johnnie's definition was clear-cut. "A cowboy," he said, "is a cowherder who wears a big hat, a six-shooter and spurs, and not very bright."

Had Johnnie been "bright," he should have added that no job required more stamina, patience and versatility than cowboying in the old days. Yet there was a romantic ring to the very word that kept the ranges crawling with this breed. They came in all sizes and temperaments. As alike as peas for jokes and ornery tricks, yet each with individual qualities.

One who stood out above the others like a privy on a knoll was George Brown. George was not only a top cowboy and bronc buster, he was the best nighthawk in Wyoming's Big Horn Basin and perhaps the state. George could read a horse's mind. Some might think a cavvy of roundup horses would stay put in a swale full of knee-high grass. Not so. They prefer high ground, be they grass heavy or lean.

Knowing this, George could take a two-hundred-horse cavvy out at sundown and have them in the one-rope, quarter-acre corral at daybreak without one being missing. And being in demand, he was as independent as a hog on ice. If he chose to do something, he did it. If he didn't want to do some certain thing, he was like a mule. You could stomp his head in and he'd still balk.

George had nighthawked with the M Bar wagon three summers straight and since he didn't fancy cowboying in fifty-below-zero winters, our boss, George Pennoyer, let this lanky cowhand toast his shins around the ranch all winter so he would have him handy come roundup time in May. But just two days before the

wagon was to roll, Brown up and hired out to nighthawk for the T.A., simply because he was offered fifty dollars a month instead of the forty-five the M Bar paid for hawking. A dirty trick? Sure.

But he wasn't a mile on his way when he met John Sales, the Padlock cow boss, and by the time they had stopped to augur and roll smokes, Sales had said, "To hell with the T.A.! I'll give you fifty-five to hawk for me. I'm startin' our wagon tomorrow and still haven't found me a nighthawk. What say?"

"You got yourself a nighthawk, John," George said. "I've got me a girl over in Meeteetse and we plan on hitchin' up soon's I get a little money ahead. I done blowed in my summer's wages last fall or we'd be workin' in double harness right now, so your fifty-five talks my language."

They were well on their way in the opposite direction to the Padlock when Sales let it be known the Padlock had sold all its cattle to a Montana outfit and were going in the sheep business. "Yessir," Sales said, "we're gathering everything as fast as possible and…"

"Whoa," Brown cut in, "you mean old J.P.'s gonta run sheep?"

"Yep. No more Padlock. It'll be the J.P. Rothwell Sheep Company. With the Padlock runnin' thirty thousand cows an' the M Bar a hundred-thousand more and Uncle Sam making these big outfits tear down miles of fences around land they don't own, not countin' the nesters that's closin' in, J.P. says he's callin' it quits."

"That lets me out then!" Brown said. "I don't hawk for no lousy outfit that sells their cows an' goes in for sheep!"

"Hell's fire, George," Sales all but begged. "I'm in a fix! You can't quit on me like this."

"The hell I can't," Brown snapped. "I done quit two jobs this mornin' t'go with your wagon an' now I'm quittin' you. Why the hell didn't you tell me right off the bat about ol' J.P.? That's a dirty Injun trick, John. Now it's so late I'll have to head back to the M Bar an' get a fresh start in the mornin'. Adios, goodbye an' so long!"

"Oh, oh," Pennoyer said as we were loading up the mess stove on its rack. "Look who's coming. Looks like our nighthawk changed his mind."

As Brown unstrapped his bed and shoved it to the ground, Pennoyer was giving him the dog eye. "What happened, Brown? Change your mind?"

"Nope," Brown said. "Just took me another furlough, is all." Then he proceeded to tell us of Sales' fifty-five a month and of the Padlock going into the sheep business.

"Knew a month ago about their deal," Pennoyer grunted. "That's why we're cutting down. Old Mizzoo's going to spay for us this summer. We're spaying every she calf and shipping two-year-old heifers along with the steers this year. You going with T.A. or with us?"

Brown's answer was short. "That depends."

"Depends on what?" Pennoyer asked, bristling.

"On if I get fifty-five this summer. Hawks is scarcer'n hen's teeth so wages have gone up."

"Not here," Pennoyer snapped. "And this thing of outfits going in the auction business regarding wages had better be nipped in the bud! But I'll go for fifty 'til this wage business is back on a sensible basis."

"Fifty-five," Brown bargained, "or I'm

off to the T.A. come mornin'." Pennoyer knew he was stumped, at least temporarily, because a good nighthawk was as essential as a roundup cook.

"All right, Brown. But by God I'll put the quietus on wages next year!" Pennoyer was all but foaming at the mouth over having to give in to Brown's blackmail.

Pennoyer didn't know it, but due to Colonel Torrey, he had a surprise coming. Old and paunchy Torrey had sold the M Bar to The Rocky Mountain Cattle Company the year before. He retained the use of one dwelling and some of the corrals until he could round up, break and dispose of a thousand or more of his Morgan and Hackney horses. The Colonel was ambling toward his corrals and, thinking Brown just another cowhand looking for a job, called him over.

"My good man," the Colonel addressed him, "you are the very one I need and need badly. I want you to start breaking horses for me at once."

"You got a corral full o' bronc riders now," George laughed, "so why any more."

"I need all I can get," Torrey puffed. "I have three riders running horses and only five bronc busters. This is the last summer I have use of the corrals so I am paying sixty dollars a month for bronc riders."

"Sixty dollars!" George exclaimed. "The hell of it if there's a hop-toad in the soap so far as me bustin' broncs for you or anybody else. I'm gittin' hitched this fall but unless I give up my ridin' broncs, my girl and her mother says I can peddle my talk somewheres else. She don't want no stove-up bronc buster on her hands, an' a two-dozen-year-old hand don't git a sixteen-year-old wife ever' day."

"My good man," puffed the Colonel, "in that case it gives me great pleasure to hear of one of you cowboys taking a wife and quitting your wild ways. Now my good man [the Colonel being from Tennessee and very religious drove all his riders to hitting up the lug with that "My good man" palaver], it so happens that the man at my big corrals across the mountain has quit. So you can have that job. There is

a cabin there and you will only be required to watch for herds coming in, so you can attend the gates and keep the corrals repaired. I paid fifty dollars a month to that other man but since you plan on making something of yourself I shall pay you sixty and…"

"'Nuf said," Brown cut in. "I know the setup at that horse camp so I'll take the job. But it bein' a sort of lonesome country over there, I'm headin' for Meeteetse an' grab me that long-haired pardner for company while she's in the notion." Any of the conversation we cowhands hadn't overheard was plentifully elaborated on by George as we readied the chuck and bed

wagons for rolling out the next day.

Naturally, Pennoyer was orie-eyed at both Brown and Colonel Torrey and, to the Colonel's horror, cussed them up one side and down the other. That evening though, through a streak of good or bad luck (depending on how you looked at it), two young fellows rode in and asked to see the proprietor. That "proprietor" remark told us they were greenhorns.

"I'm the ramrod here, if that's what you mean," Pennoyer said. "You ever nighthawk?"

The fuzzy-faced youths looked at each other then one asked, "What's that?"

"Night herding the cavvy," they were told.

"Oh, I can do that," one replied, "but unless we both can go to work I won't take the job."

"I'll put you both on," Pennoyer said. "Turn your horses in that corral over there

and get busy heaving them sacks of oats in that wagon by the granary."

"You gone loco, George?" Bud Bridges asked. "That punk'll lose every damn horse on us!"

"I'll put both of 'em on the job," Pennoyer replied, "until I can find a real one. And as for Brown, I'll see that he never gets a nighthawk job in this whole damn country! It's getting so you can't trust a man's word any farther than you could throw a bull by the tail!"

That afternoon, a string of howling riders arrived with sixty-five of the cavvy horses from the Pitchfork (one of the out-

A BUSTED-UP BRONC BUSTER, 1904. NOTE DUST AT LEFT WHERE BRONC HIT THE GROUND BEFORE UNLOADING HIS RIDER. THIS WAS AT THE THERMOPOLIS "BUCKING CONTEST," PRE-RODEO DAYS. THE BRONCS WITHOUT THE FLANK STRAP COULD REALLY GET CROOKED. NO EIGHT-SECOND GUN!

fit's ranches on the Greybull and run by George "Kidney Foot" Merrill). During the afternoon, many local "reps" and those from the T.A., the Double Circle, the Antler and the Bay State outfit in the Ten Sleep country across the Big Horn, began pulling in. This added thirty more horses to the cavvy, bringing the number of men with the wagon to eighteen, not counting Ernie Purdy, the day-horse wrangler, the two so-called nighthawks, Old Mizzoo the spayer, or Bill "Slippery" Sloud, the cook.

There never was a more beautiful morning than that of May 8, 1908, and probably never a more colorful sight than those four-horse wagons, the long cavvy, and the laughing, singing bunch of riders in white shirts and vests. Adding something new to Wyoming cowboying were the two Mexican sombreros Gaspipe Mullison and I wore.

Just for the hell of it, we had sent ten dollars to a firm in Mesilla Park, New Mexico, for these high-crowned, bushel-sized, saucer-brimmed monstrosities adorned with a couple pounds of gold and silver braid. When we left our Stetsons at the ranch, we didn't know the downright hell our fancy headgear would eventually dish out.

There is something about roundup time that defies description, and as our outfit strung up Owl Creek headed for the high range to our west, we were in a gala mood. Sunshine, a big sky above and the smell of virgin grass makes the forty-dollar-a-month cowhand oblivious to the months of eighteen-hour, seven-days-a-week that lay ahead.

Pennoyer had said we would camp that night on the crown of the Owl Creek range and start circle-riding between the Muddy and the Big Wind. So with two days of doing nothing but moving along ahead of us, we were as frisky and playful as only cowboys can be. Old Bud Bridges and Sam Cremer were warbling a song that had truth as well as poetic value: *Just a little sunshine, just a little rain, just a little happiness, just a little pain.*

Some cowhand had devised an easy tune to the famous four-panel sketch and words that hung in every saloon. These scenes showed a cowboy on day-herd on a sunshiny day, then with his slicker on in a downpour. The third panel showed him with a beautiful dancehall girl on his lap and the fourth panel—well, the reader will have to visualize the cowhand standing by his mount some weeks later, his face twisted up as though he'd been forced to eat a mouthful of nails.

On the west slope of the Owl Creek mountains, the new cook tent had only been guyed down at the four corners and our rolled-out beds were scattered about. Saddles, chaps, spurs and other gear lay wherever a rider had unsaddled his mount. Joe Grammar, an old hand, had gone with the two nighthawks to show them a spot where the cavvy would be less likely to get away. "An' don't by God fall asleep!" he warned them. "Let 'em scatter enough so they can feed but keep your eyes peeled for any that's sneakin' off. Them that belongs to the reps will try to get away and head for their home range, so watch 'em every minute."

We didn't know the downright hell our fancy headgear would eventually dish out.

With millions of brilliant stars overhead and the soft tinkle of several horse bells coming half a mile through the night we were soon lulled to sleep.

It was perhaps two o'clock in the morning when we were roused by yells, curses, banging utensils and a howling blizzard. The cook and the others were yelling, "Grab holt o' this tent!" As the big tent flopped and ballooned in the wind that all but knocked us down, all hands rushed to help. But we were too late. With a boom like an underground explosion the tent pulled the four pegs and almost took the cook and Pad Holloman with it as it sailed off in the howling darkness.

There being nothing we could do about the tent until morning, we didn't try to find our boots and overalls that had lain besides our beds, and got as comfortable as possible in our wind-rumpled, snow-wet blankets and soogans.

By daylight the howling wind had eased, allowing over a foot of snow to blanket all our scattered belongings. It was a dismal sight and task as we dug about for our Levi's, boots and vests. The cook and the Bay State rep were the only ones who had brought a coat. While the horse wrangler and cook managed to get a fire going in the big roundup stove, minus its pipes which had gone with the wind, others rolled and strapped their wet beds. Only those who have experienced it know the job of trying to get new, wet boots over wet socks.

"Wonder if our damn hats blowed away!" Gaspipe said. Fortunately, they hadn't but before the month was over we were wishing to hell they had. One had lodged in the spokes of the bed wagon and the other had been snagged by a dead tree branch nearby. Lash Hinton's hat and that of Pad Holloman's were goners.

But more disconcerting was the fact that there was no sound of the cavvy coming in. "If them lunk-heads would get here with the horses," Pennoyer blustered, "we'd be able to scout for that damned tent! Lucky thing Joe went with 'em last night or we'd be in a damn sight worse fix than we are. We at least got *one* horse."

As we shivered in snow to our knees eating breakfast, with snowflakes the size of chicken feathers still falling, Joe Grammar said, "As soon as I git this grub et I'm taking off to look for them two jaspers. It's a leadpipe cinch that somethin's wrong. They've probably lost the whole damn cavvy."

After Joe had left, we scattered out in the direction the tent had gone. Through the pure white mountain, it would be a miracle if we spotted the white tent. But around noon, the tent was found hanging from a fire-killed tree a quarter-mile across a deep canyon. It was a job for the two who found the snagged and ripped tent to lug it back to camp.

One of the tree joints of the stovepipe had been found and after most of the rips had been mended with twine and set up, Gaspipe, with a perverted sense of humor, allowed that "Outside of bein' about as waterproof as this damn hat of mine she's as good as new!"

And still no horses. It was nearing sundown, if there had been a sun to go down, when Joe and our nighthawks came in with the cavvy. They had lost only a dozen or so of the reps' horses but becoming lost themselves had followed the main herd to the lower country thinking the horses were leading them back to the wagon. Instead, Joe had picked up their trail. Lash Hinton's string was leading them back to the Double Circle on the Wind River and Joe had overtaken them ten miles from our camp.

"By God," Pennoyer said, "let's get off this mountain as fast as we can get hitched up."

"What about serving supper?" the neophyte nighthawks wondered. "We're almost starved to death."

"We ain't giving a tinker's damn if you're plum entirely and totally starved t'death!" Pad Holloman shouted. "We're headin' for a climate that suits our duds."

Once we were down in the 'dobie flats we were no better off. Down there it was raining as if the ocean had turned upside down and it never let up for two weeks. By the end of the first week, though, the two nighthawks had, as they said, "enough cowboying to do us the rest of our lives."

Bob Long, an ex-sailor but a real cowhand, volunteered to nighthawk until one could be found. Some of the riders with big strings whacked up their mounts with the reps whose horses had gotten away, but Gaspipe and I weren't so lucky. We each had bronc strings of ten each and if anyone thinks it's fun having a bucking contest at all times of the day down a rain-washed butte, or stampeding and tumbling into a wash on you, he better have his head examined.

Under ordinary circumstances it would have been bad enough, but with those sombreros on we were dealt seven kinds of hell. The leather chin thongs we had added to hold them on choked us black in the face when a bronc went crazy from our billowing slickers and stampeded until he rolled into washes full of wild water which was an everyday occurrence.

Emil "Red Dog" Rothwell, repping for his dad, H.P., somewhat alleviated our misery by trading a fat thousand-pound steer to a homesteader (who survived peddling whiskey to the Indians) for a gallon of two-dollar whiskey. In a way it sort of boomeranged on us, though. Paul Derkhorn, a Bay State rep, and Red Dog got in a fight and wound up pulling their guns.

When several jumped in and were wrestling the guns away our boss got a .45 slug through his right foot. That stopped the fight but they vowed to kill each other come daylight, so Pennoyer took charge of their shootin' irons until they sobered up. The argument had started over having to hold all Padlock cattle. Only for them there would be no standing night guard until the beef roundup started. Wet beds and standing guard didn't make for good fellowship it seemed.

Lash Hinton said, "One good thing, as long as she rains I won't be too discomfited, but if the sun ever shines again I'm sure up skunk creek without a paddle or compass."

Lash had been as bald as a doorknob for ten years even though "Sagebrush Bill" Hilcher offered Lash his hat days later. Sam Cremer said, "I've heard that by cutting the crown out of a hat so the sun can fertilize the hair roots it will grow hair. And now that the sun's shinin' again, it's a good time to try it."

With a hat on, Lash was a handsome fellow, but without hair or a hat his ears appeared as long as a mule's. But being a vain chap, Lash said he'd try the sun treatment. We thought nothing of it until the next day when we came in off the circle

We shivered in snow to our knees eating breakfast, with snowflakes the size of chicken feathers still falling.

and found Lash under the bed wagon where Pennoyer lay recuperating from the gunshot wound.

Lash was in moaning, raving delirium and Pennoyer was kept busy keeping wet gunnysacks on Lash's head. None of us had ever seen anything like that. In fact, we'd never seen *anything* swollen like that unless it was a dead cow or maybe a poisoned coyote. The scalp was as red as if held in the branding fire and water under it puffed up like a huge bladder.

The wagon was then working the Wind River about ten miles from the Double Circle ranch so the next morning, with Lash raving like a maniac, his bed was rolled out in the bed wagon and Ross Sheppard headed across the hills with him for the Double Circle. On returning, Ross said Lash would never pull through, but it just shows the stuff cowpunchers are molded from. We saw him a little over a year later and he had a head of black hair that would have done justice to an Ethiopian. Lash was real proud of it but said he sure as hell wouldn't recommend sunshine as a hair restorer.

After working the upper Muddy and

the Wind River up as far as Tea-Pot Butte, the wagon swung back along the west and south base of the Owl Creek range and we camped one day about five miles from Colonel Torrey's horse camp near Stagner Mountain. We had maybe eight hundred head in the roundup and were just finishing branding and spaying when George Brown rode up. (Old Mizzoo got thirty-five cents a head up to seven thousand spayed, and twenty-five cents for all over that.)

All hands were wondering what sort of greeting Pennoyer would have for Brown as he still bellyached about the low-down trick the cowboy had dealt him. It didn't take long to find out. Pennoyer, Pad Holloman and Joe Grammar, all top calf ropers, were doing the roping for three sets of us wrestlers, and as Pennoyer skidded a calf to the fire, Brown said, "Hi, George. How's she coming?"

"Making out first rate!" Pennoyer snapped, giving Brown a mean look.

"Didn't think you were," returned Brown with a big laugh. "From what I been hearin', I 'llowed you'd have t'fold up without me a nighthawkin' for you. But if you'll quit giving me the dog eye, I've got some news for you. But why that right hoof in a sling?" Pennoyer's right foot was wrapped in burlap.

"Cow run a horn through it," Pennoyer lied, "and the best news you can bring is to get to hell back to your gate-tending."

"Oh, hell," Brown laughed, "I promoted myself. I got Sweetheart doin' the gate work an' I'm chasin' horses. Talked Old Fuddy Duddy into giving her a job so now we get double pay. Yessir, we've got 'er made now, an' not countin' setbacks I'll get me fifty or so cows this fall for a taw an' in no time I'll be a big cattleman like you."

"That the good news you fetched?" Pennoyer flung over his shoulder as he started for the herd.

"Hell no. You know Frenchy what's his name. Outside o' me he's the best nighthawk in seven states an' he's lookin' for a job."

"Thought Frenchy was hawking for the Angler Outfit," Pennoyer said, pulling up.

"Got his neck bowed an' up an' quits all I know. So when I run acrost him, I thought of you."

"Where's he at now?" Pennoyer growled.

"Up t'the corral sparkin' my pretty squaw," Brown said. "An' speakin' of pretty things, Gaspipe, how much for that Mexican bonnet you're hiding under?"

"You can have it for your Stetson and five dollars," Gaspipe replied. He'd threatened to toss the cumbersome hat in the branding fire an hour before.

"She's a trade," Brown said, "but you'll have t'come up t'the camp for the five. Now, George, what about Frenchy?"

"I'll ride up this evening, so you tell Frenchy to stay put."

"Don't worry," Brown called, riding away. "The way he's actin' around my golden-topped wife he'll stay put."

"I'd have swapped him mine," I said to Gaspipe, "for that hat and sure wouldn't have wanted any loot, either."

"You'll never get rich runnin' your own goods down," Gaspipe snickered.

That evening Pennoyer, Gaspipe and I rode up to the horse camp to see Frenchy, get the five dollars and especially to see Brown's wife. We had heard about this sixteen-year-old Mormon girl George bragged about "hitching up with," but had thought it was just a joke.

After we'd all said hello to Frenchy, a handsome little booger, George got around to the introductions. "Fellers, this is Sweetheart," he said all puffed up. "Ain't she a lollapaloozer?"

Sweetheart was a golden-haired lollapaloozer and no mistake, but shy as a young Shoshone squaw. While we hunkered on our bootheels swapping talk she sat curled in a cowhide-bottomed chair, and when she wasn't trying to pull down the hem of her faded skirt she was playing with her bare toes. She seldom looked up, but when she did she had a smile that fitted her winsome face.

"Oh," Brown said, by way of apologizing for her toe picking, "I've got a lot o' learnin' t'do on Sweetheart, yet. But I'm workin' on her. Got her so's she can boil a pot o' java without burnin' it up an' when I git her broke in to where she'll wear shoes when we got company I'll be right proud of her. I sent to C.H. Hyer for a nice pair o' boots for her an' if she won't wear 'em I'll wear 'em out over her pretty head. She's the dumbest thing God ever

put a head on, but I'll get her smartened up in time."

"I do too wear shoes," she said meekly, "but some horses ran over me at the corral and smashed both my feet and I'm trying to get them well so I can wear the boots when they come."

We felt sorry for this girl as we envied her tough six-foot husband and Pennoyer said, "You take care of them feet, Sweetheart, and pay no attention to us. Look at me. I been wearing a gunnysack boot for two weeks so I know how a foot can hurt. You put plenty of liniment on 'em,

When several jumped in and were wrestling the guns away, our boss got a .45 slug through his right foot.

George, or she won't wear a boot all summer."

"Liniment we ain't got," George said. "Had a jug over to the corral but some Injuns found it an' thought it was fire water. Downed the last drop."

"I'll send one of the boys up with some I got," Pennoyer offered. "It's that Mexican mustang liniment for horses but it sure kept me from having to take my foot to the doctor."

"You do that," Brown said, "because if she pulls another stunt like the other day she'll need liniment on her noggin'. I'd run a wild bunch a good twenty miles an' when I had 'em at the corral instead o' bein' there t'open the gate she's here in the wigwam readin' about that damned Chip O' The Flyin' U Feller. We hold some gentle horses in the corral for decoys an' from now on Sweetheart better be Johnnie-at-the-rat-hole or she'll find herself traded off."

It was midnight when Frenchy went to the corrals to get his horses and, now that we had a nighthawk who understood nighthawking as George Brown did, we knew Pennoyer wouldn't put the old whammy on him as he had threatened.

As we were leaving, Brown thought of something else important. "Oh, say! Yuh know what this attle brain did to my hat?

She wanted it for herself so she trimmed off every last bit o' gold an' silver braid on it! Now it's no more'n a thirty-cent straw bonnet. So I'm wondering if you'll sell me yourn."

"Well," I hedged, "I hate to part with it, but I'll let you have it for five dollars."

"Dig out another five, Sweetheart," George called. "I've bought me another hat. An' by God don't you dare go whittlin' on it, either! Just t'show yuh what I'm up against learnin' Sweetheart a few things," he continued, "the day after I fetched her here I told her t'clean up the place an' she burned up my chaps because she thought they were an old pair o' pants with the seat wore out. Talk about a numbskull, she's it!"

A week later, the wagon was camped directly across the Wind River from Shoshoni and four of us—Bud Bridges, Sam Cremer, Bob Long and I—decided to ride into town for "supplies." To do this we had to go up the river several miles to a bridge as the Big Wind was a mighty river even in low water. Now, in late June, it was a fearsome body of silt, uprooted willows and floating cottonwoods.

By midnight, Bob was drunk as a hoot owl so we headed for camp. Behind his cantle he had tied a flour sack filled with Levi's, two cartons of Bull Durham and twelve pair of sox for a dollar that were advertised with a funny ditty: *The longer you wear 'em the stronger they get, and put 'em in the water and they'll never get wet.*

Bob was carrying a gallon demijohn of bar whiskey and perhaps all would have gone well if Cremer and Bud hadn't started shooting up the town which fetched the new town marshal emptying his .45 at us. As we spurred away in the darkness Bob went the wrong direction and, before anyone could stop him, his horse had leapt off the high bank into the river a hundred yards west.

The next day we searched both sides of the river even though we felt it was useless, as a few hundred yards below where he had disappeared the river plunged down into sheer-walled rapids. So we may as well get back to work.

We worked Stanger Mountain and moved down along the river below the canyon a mile above Thermopolis. Once through the canyon, the Wind River became the Big Horn. We were cutting out the cows and calves (many now belonging to distant outfits) and the Padlock stuff when Frenchy came tearing out to the herd and we knew something terrible had happened to rout the nighthawk out of his bed under the bed wagon. Frenchy murdered the King's English at best, but now his garbled words had us gathering around.

"Iffen I ain't seen a ghost," he sputtered, "it's Bob Long!"

"Where at?" the riders, as excited as Frenchy, asked.

"Over to the wagon!" Frenchy yelled. "He just rode in!"

Leaving the herd, several of us hightailed it to the wagon. There wasn't any doubt about it. There sat Bob explaining his experience to the cook. A horse from Bert Emery's livery stable stood hip-shot nearby with a new saddle on him. Bob had no idea how or when he got into a house and didn't remember anything until he heard awful screams and saw a young woman dash out of a door.

"Me layin' there in her fancy bed with my chaps an' boots an' spurs on an' covered with mud must o' been a scary sight, alright," Bob said. "What was worse, that damn demijohn was in the bed too. Her husband come in with a wagon spoke ready to brain me but I talked fast an' he calmed down a bit. They were a couple young nesters who'd got a piece of land there at the head of the canyon when the reservation was throwed open for settlement. They'd been on a week's visit up in Lander and I guess it was sort of a surprise findin' me in their bed. I'll say one thing, I never want another spree like that one!"

During Bob's three or four days in that bed he half emptied the demijohn, astounding us by being able to swim with a finger crooked through the ear of a heavy bottle. "Oh, hell. That creek's nothin'! I swum for an hour once draggin' a buddy when I was in the Navy after we capsized our boat." To our knowledge his horse and outfit were never found.

That afternoon, the chuck and bed wagons had loaded up on supplies in Thermopolis and we were headed out of town when we noticed smoke and flames boiling out of a two-story house and saw belongings of every description being carried out, or tossed out of the windows.

It being Fourth of July and firecrackers exploding everywhere, something had no doubt set the building on fire. Naturally, an hour's heavy drinking had the cowhands in a gay mood so just for the hell of it we exercised the rule of "losers weepers, finders keepers." Sam Cremer rode out of town shaded by a beautiful

IT TOOK A LOT OF WORK FOR HARRY TO GET HIS OWN RANCH IN PINE VALLEY. HE TRAPPED PREDATORS FOR THE GOVERNMENT, MUSTANGED, AND RAN CATTLE ON THE HIGH DESERT. THIS IS HARRY AND SON. NOTE HARRY'S BRAND ON GATE.

pink parasol from a baby buggy while I packed something far more sensible: a big pillow with a six-inch border of blue lace on the sham.

A cowboy's headrest is usually his timothy-sack "warbag" of shirts, sox and odds and ends, but *never* a real pillow, and for the next few weeks that beautiful pillow

About a foot of a two-foot snake showed itself and with a yell of 'rattlesnake!' I threw the pillow among the snoring riders' beds.

(growing greasier by the day) was constantly being purloined by some cowhand. But there came a night when I wished some smart aleck besides me had it.

We were camped near a little alkali creek in the Blue Ridges south of Greybull River and on coming off second guard this full-moon windy night, I crawled back in bed only to have a greasewood bush at my head keep bothering me. Pulling tarp and bedding back I yanked off some of the bush, but the wiggling against my pillow still disturbed me so more of the bush was yanked out and I lay back again. No good.

"Damn that bush," I grunted and jackknifed on my heels. Pulling the bedding back in my lap, I dug out the bush to the last root. Carefully folding the blankets back, I took the pillow from my lap and as I did, I thought it seemed mighty heavy for a pillow even with a pound or two of scalp grease and dirt on it. As I felt for it, about a foot of a two-foot rattlesnake showed itself and with a yell of "Rattlesnake!" I threw the pillow among the snoring riders' beds, dumping out not one, but *two* big rattlers that had crawled between the sham and the pillow while I was on two hours' guard.

This had everyone, including Slippery Sloud, climbing wagon wheels and calling me everything but my name. And as the buzzing snakes coiled on or in beds, Eddie Ilg managed to get his gun and began blasting away at them with the end result that Pennoyer's blankets were set on fire besides stampeding the night herd a quarter-mile away. That ended all sleep that night as everyone searched his bed for more snakes. It also ended any hankering for that fancy pillow, including me.

It also was the end of cowpunching in Wyoming for old Joe Grammar. On pulling his boots on, Joe had to dislodge a rattler from a boot. With a yell he said, "That's all, fellers! Chasin' longhorns through cat claw bushes run me out of Texas but, by God, it was a picnic compared to sleepin' with rattlers an' havin' 'em in your boots! I'm quittin'!" Joe had "quit" a dozen times in two years but this time he made good his threat. After breakfast, he saddled up and headed back for Texas and the longhorns.

To show the hardiness of this breed of cattle, one day in August I was sent to ride a lone spring several miles from any other water. On coming to the spring, which was no more than a mud hole in a draw, a lone, sleek, buckskin cow with three-foot horns snorted and dashed out only a few feet from me. As plain as if painted on was a Moccasin brand that covered half her side.

I gave chase for the simple reason there were no other critters at the spring and she was headed in the direction of the roundup. After a couple miles, on coming to the brink of a long, steep slate-rock slide, I saw the cow had raced down the other side and was running in a different direction than I wanted to go.

When I reached the roundup ground I told of seeing this beautiful animal and got laughed at. "You been seein' things that ain't," Bud Bridges said. "There ain't been a Moccasin critter in this country for ten years or more! Old Otto Franc shipped some up from Texas years and years ago but what wasn't shipped died off long ago." Others agreed with Bud and only that two circle riders came in and told of seeing this cow and trying without success to head her into their bunch I would have been tagged as locoed or an awful liar.

By August, the beef roundup started, and although there would still be many calves we had missed, Old Mizzoo tallied up and went on his way. While we cowhands earned $120, Mizzoo had collected a bit over $3,000. "That," said a cowhand, "shows the difference between a hard *job* and a soft *occupation*."

Beef prices were way up: four-year-old steers were bringing four-and-a-half cents a pound in Omaha and heifers three cents, so the outfit's owners, Merrill, Phelps and Pennoyer, decided to put out a second roundup wagon, with Matt Brown running the northern one and shipping

from Cody or Basin.

By that time, the railroad cutting through the North Western at Shoshoni had reached Worland, so Pennoyer's wagon would ship out of there. To take advantage of market and save the trouble of working out the heifers at the railroad, Pennoyer got the idea of holding separate herds. That way we could load out two trains and be on our way by two o'clock in the afternoon. A fine idea, but we had several night stampedes and the ensuing milling of two thousand panicky heifers and steers knocked plenty pounds off them.

Our boss was still determined to ship around two thousand head every ten days so after breakfast, just out of Worland, the wagons would head back to the range. Then as soon as the trains were loaded, we would grab a quick preordered dinner of ham and eggs at the only restaurant in town and hightail it to where the wagons would camp for the night, gathering beef on the way.

Unfortunately, even though the two pigtailed Chinese would promise to have "dinna leddy" the instant we got there, they never started cooking until we were at the tables. Three times they had delayed us a good hour (at the chuck wagon a cowhand had to be downright lazy if he took over ten minutes to lay away a big meal) and time now being of the essence Pennoyer said, "From now on I'm holding the wagons right here until after we eat, then we won't lose any time."

The fourth time to the shipping pens when the first trainload had pulled out for the main line at Billings, Red Dog Rothwell and I were sent up to town to fetch a couple dozen bottles of beer for the sweating crew. At that time the town consisted of exactly six buildings. "You know somethin'?" Red Dog said. "Let's play a joke on them Chinks!" Our joke meant ordering twenty-three dinners of ham and eggs and hot biscuits. "And," Red Dog warned, "if that grub ain't right here on the table at two o'clock sharp you won't get paid because we have t'hurry. Savvy?"

Red Dog was mean looking at best and his words brought their heads bobbling. "He be leddy," one assured us. "He slavvy cowboy allus hully."

Ten days later at the shipping pens, a brakeman said to Pennoyer. "You fellows

sure raised hell and put a block under it that other trip."

"How come?" Pennoyer asked. Red Dog and I hadn't mentioned our stunt to a soul.

"You damn soon will," the brakie said, "if you go near those Chinamen!"

"We don't owe the Chinamen a red cent," Pennoyer snapped.

"Owe 'em for a couple dozen platters of ham and eggs is all! Some of your outfit ordered a batch of meals ready at a certain minute and nobody showed up to eat it. They're layin' for you guys with a pair of cleavers," the brakeman warned. From then on, whoever went for a beer made himself scarce in the Chinamen's end of town.

August 24 was a red-letter day for us. The wagon was camped beside the meandering flat creek in Big Buffalo Basin and we were on circle in the hills west of the basin when the worst cloudburst in the memory of any rider hit us. In a few minutes water six inches deep was moving off every flat into the head of the narrow basin and Pennoyer said to me, "Maybe you better jog down to the wagon and if it looks bad get any riders who have come into the roundup ground and pull the wagons to higher ground."

By the time I got to the cliffs at the head of the basin a mountain of water was carrying every movable object with it. Trees, sagebrush and mud rolled towards our camp half a mile below. As bad luck would have it, not a rider was visible and as I raced to the wagons I found the nighthawk asleep and the cook busy at his stove. With a yell, I roused them with, "Let's try to pull these wagons away! There's a wall of water fifteen feet deep right behind me!"

"To hell with a little water," Slippery said. "I was here first."

"By God," Frenchy said, "I hear it comin'! Hook onto the bed wagon and let's see if we can move it!" Only that I was riding the smallest horse in my string we might have moved the wagon but not being able to budge it we began carrying bedrolls, and anything we could grab, to higher ground.

The flood was rolling under the wagons by then, and out of breath from running with beds, we turned to help Slippery. But he, in one of his "ringy spells," wouldn't budge. He was standing in water near to his knees lifting lids and peering in various pots and kettles. When the water rose to the oven a geyser of steam blew the door open and he calmly climbed on the wagon seat. "Let 'er all blow to 'ell for all I care," he giggled.

We knew the big broiler held half a flour sack of suet pudding (called "spotted dog" or "a sonovabitch in the sack") and as Frenchy grabbed this by its ears and as I was lifting a five-gallon pot of simmering fruit, a second wave of water hit the top of the stove causing an explosion of steam that sent us staggering blindly through waist-deep water with our burdens.

Riders from the roundup ground at the east end of the basin and one of the day herders came dashing in, their ropes ready. But though they managed to pull the chuck wagon to higher ground, the damage was already done. Every sack and box of food in both wagons was destroyed by the flood that rose through the wagon beds. A hind quarter of beef in canvas under the wagon had been swept away, as was the cook tent and stove.

"Damned if I know now which is the worst," Pad Holloman said. "A blizzard, a month's steady rain, or a cloudburst! First I lose my hat an' now I lose my bed with my spare shirt in it! On this damn outfit a man ain't got much use for a bed but I sure hate losin' my shirt."

"Lucky somebody saved that sonovabitch in the sack and them prunes," Sagebrush Bill gloomily said as we scraped the last bite from the empty broilers.

"Yeah," Ross Shepard lamented, looking out over a sea of mud, "but look at me! I filed a homestead on this basin this spring and intended building me a cabin right where them wagons set. But Uncle Sam can sure as hell have it back now." A few years later, Ross's words came back to mock him. He had relinquished his right when Buffalo Basin became one of Wyoming's major oil fields.

The bed wagon was sent down to Grass Creek Ranch (one of the outfit's many ranches where the reps' herds were being held) for what supplies old John Payne, the caretaker, could part with and the beef roundup moved along.

"Come hard, go easy," Frenchy cursed. His rope corral had been torn to shreds by rolling trees and brush.

By the middle of September we were gathering the last shipment for the year, which, with the herds Brown's wagon had shipped, would cut the outfit's cattle down as they planned to do. Twenty-eight-thousand steers and heifers had gone to Omaha's stockyards with one more shipment to go.

Our final roundup was at Kester Springs, so named after Curt Kester, a cowboy homesteader. Curt had ridden home one night from the T.A. wagon and caught his neighbor friend in bed with his wife. The butt of Kester's .45 left his neighbor wearing a silver plate for a skull the rest of his half-witted life. Curt, badly disillusioned, simply rode off for a new range minus Mrs. Kester, and the home-

Cowboying was a hell of a way of life any way you looked at it.

stead was abandoned to the elements.

We had finished working the herd and were eating supper when George Brown and his wife came by in a buckboard. The "Howdy's" exchanged, Pennoyer said, "Well, Sweetheart, so you finally got homesick for mama and are going for a visit, huh?"

"Not prezcly," Brown answered for her. "Yuh see, I got her broke to where she's a pretty fair grub slinger an' at least wears her boots. But no matter how hard I worked on her I'll be damned if I could learn her t'comb her hair or wash her ears. So I'm taking her home an' I'm gonta tell her mother either you learn her t'clean up once in a while or she don't come back! A man don't prezcly need a wife but somehow I wouldn't trade her for all Old Torrey's horses if she'd just scrub up. So I'll come back and look her over in a couple of months an' maybe I'll take her back, an' maybe I won't. It's up t'her an' her old lady now."

Once we were back to the ranch and the wagons put away for that season, we riders had a few days' breathing spell until we would be combing the range, branding any big calves we had missed during the summer. Once that job was over, we, to a man, vowed this would be our last year punching cows! I'd had one of my string get kettled off one day when the bolt in my stirrup broke and he bucked over a twenty-foot cutbank and landed upside down on me. With several ribs broken from my breastbone I'd only been fit to pilot the wagon during the last ten days of the beef shipment so I reckoned I'd head for Colorado and look up my folks before they died off on me.

Cowboying was a hell of a way of life any way you looked at it. We were in the wrong business, and that was for damn sure! Bud Bridges said he thought he'd get a job tending bar. Slippery Sloud had put all his money into four houses in Thermopolis which rent alone would pay off. He "wouldn't cook again for Jesus Christ," he vowed, "let alone put in twenty hours a day with a damned roundup wagon!"

Bob Long thought he'd go back in the Navy, or better yet, the Army. There was the life! Ross Sheppard guessed he'd buy himself "a ball-peen hammer and a pair of pinchers and open a watch repair shop."

"Well, I know one thing," Gaspipe emphatically declared. "If that lousy George Brown sheds that pretty wife o' his, I'm buildin' a loop on her an' I don't mean maybe! I'll get me a little homestead an'…"

"I done got me a claim staked out on her," Frenchy piped up, "so just lay off. But no matter what happens, this is my last year at nighthawkin'."

Right then, we griped on everything in a cowboy's life. The chillblains of winter and the long, miserable rains of spring; the ornery broncs that brought aching bones, not to mention the sweat and wariness and nightguard duty that left few hours for sleep! Yes, by God, we'd had it, or so we vowed at this time.

We were unaware that deep within us lay a dormant compulsion ready to surface when spring—glorious spring—with its sunshine and irresistible odor of greenery smote us. Let May roll around and there was an indefinable enchantment in the very word "cowboying" that would send us yipping behind the chuck wagon as it rolled up Owl Creek. Yes, the old grind would start all over again and we, to the last man, would be happy to be a part of it. ■

The Indomitable Dude

The eccentric German Otto Franc was an unlikely cattle baron, but he and his Pitchfork Ranch in Wyoming became legends.

 Otto Franc was a slight-built, blue-eyed German and a stickler for perfection and neatness even to the appearance of the ranch he founded. Otto was born in Germany in 1846 and went in the cattle business in the Big Horn Basin in 1879. Being a rank dude, the seasoned cattle barons said, "That German won't be around long. He'll be belly up in jig time." But instead of going belly up, Otto Franc's "Pitchfork" became one of the Big Horn Basin's major cow outfits.

Settling on the cream of all land along the Greybull River, he persuaded his eastern brothers to back him in the cattle business. In those days, the finest grass grew tall as far as the eye could reach, so with funds from his brothers he went to Montana in 1879 and brought a herd of fine-grade cattle to his chosen spot and thus the Pitchfork Ranch and its pitchfork cattle brand began to make history.

Otto Franc was soon to be a name to conjure with for he made a success of a business that was as alien to him as a stiff-bosomed shirt would be to a hog. But in those days one didn't have to be a born cowman to survive. Cattle rustling hadn't hit that part of Wyoming as yet and with more grass than there were cattle, no outfit needed a hay meadow. All that was necessary was a log headquarters and a cattle brand.

Years later, whenever the Pitchfork was mentioned, George Merrill, who then owned the ranch, told us how Otto had come to choose such a name and brand for his outfit. Otto said he had picked up a weathered pitchfork near Red Lodge, Montana, and brought it along with his cattle. The day he reached his cabin, an old cattleman came by and seeing the dudish dressed German with the pitchfork laughed and said, "What the hell is the idea of that thing? You intend to farm or run cattle?"

"I don't know," Otto answered, "but I thought it might come in handy."

"Yeah," laughed the cattleman, "it might. You could punch your few cows around with it."

Still laughing, the man went his way and left Otto scratching his head. Finally Otto said to himself and the roaring river, "Everybody has a mark on his cattle it seems, so why not me with a pitchfork? That man don't know it but someday he will see pitchforks scattered all over the Big Horn Basin."

And, Merrill said, "That foresighted dude not only meant an implement, but also his cattle. It wasn't long until there were twenty thousand Pitchfork cattle. We old hands hadn't brains enough to start growing hay, but Otto had, and the winter of 1886 left us with nothing but a sad experience. The next spring any place where there was cottonwood shelter along a creek or river you could have walked on nothing but carcasses for miles. Otto? Oh, he lost some, but nothing like all the rest of us."

I came to the basin two years too late to know Otto Franc, but the stories told to us cowhands by old Colonel Torrey and George Merrill (better known as Kidney Foot) let us understand the eccentricities of Otto in his later years. He and another legendary cattleman, Josh Dean, were close friends but there all similarity ended. Otto, though not a woman-hater, shied away from marriage while Dean to his dying day married any female who would have him—getting most through *Heart & Hand* magazine.

Both believed in getting every ounce of work out of their ranch hands and cowboys but while Old Josh would work a horse until it fell down, Otto pampered his fine breed of saddle and work stock with a passion. Not only did he have the best work stock money could buy but he was a fanatic on beautifying his ranch until the Pitchfork became the showplace in all the Basin and had been the first to intro-duce the growing of hay on a large scale.

After the winter of '86, Otto vowed he would have two years cutting of hay in stacks for every hoof he owned and in this he never varied. It was a pattern other stockmen saw logic in and soon followed. Otto was also the first cowman to hit on the idea of having his cowboys do ranch work whenever there was a lull in riding work—an idea that died with the suddenness of being born.

The Pitchfork was fast becoming the finest timothy and alfalfa meadows of any in northern Wyoming and, wanting to enlarge this acreage, Otto drove into Meeteetse and brought back a load of grubhoes. He told the cowboys, "Boys, down beyond that round hill there's a couple hundred acres of beautiful, level land I want to put into hay. I know it is rich soil because the sagebrush is five feet tall on it. So you boys take this wagon and go down there and start grubbing out all that brush. My ranch hands will go with you."

"Listen, Mr. Franc," Henry Spikens said, "we're cowboys! We didn't plant that damn sagebrush an' by God we ain't goin' t'dig it up!" Otto didn't want to lose his cowboys so gave up and hired a lot more ranch hands. "Two years later," Merrill told us, "that two-hundred acres had timothy grass three feet high on it."

It seems, though, Otto liked to sit on his porch and let his eyes enjoy his broad meadow and a hill set squarely in the center of it cutting off his view. The more Otto viewed the hill the more he detested it. The hill had to go! Otto sent two men with four-horse teams and two wagons each to Cody for heavy plows, slips, and wheel-scrapers and the outfit was soon ready to start removing the hill. "I want that hill dumped in the river," he said, "and not a stone left on my meadow."

As the work proceeded, Otto would sit for hours on his porch with field glasses to his eyes watching the offensive hill being lowered by the swarm of men and teams.

It was a Herculean job and no rancher except the vain German would have undertaken it. As indicated before, Otto had the finest teams in the country and doted on their being handled with "kid gloves," so to speak. Then one afternoon, as the hill had lowered to where he could see the meadows beyond, Otto sat with his field glasses when something occurred that Otto or half of Wyoming never forgot!

A plowman left his team to go to the water barrel for a drink and the team started moving away. Dropping his dipper, the driver raced to catch his team but a scraper driver was already on the run yelling "Whoa!" but the abandoned scraper team started and with others dropping their lines and joining in the chase the inevitable happened.

Plow and scraper teams were running in every direction with the implements leaping in the air and coming down on the teams' rumps or chopping hind legs to pieces. With tendons cut, teams were falling in a tangled mess. This was too much for Otto and with a cry of *Mein Gott!* he rushed in the house. Hearing the commotion the cook went to Otto's bedroom and found his employer with his head under the covers sobbing.

Several horses that had legs broken or tendons severed had to be shot and only that Otto couldn't stand the sight of blood he would have shot the teamster who had left his team while getting a drink of water. Needless to say, that put the kibosh on hill-moving for some time.

Another incident Kidney Foot delighted in telling us took place on the Pitchfork in 1899. A big slump came in beef prices just as Otto was ready to start the herd to the railroad at Cody. Instead, he had his cowboys bring the beef to the ranch until prices got better.

Otto had a section of bluegrass pasture on Franc's Fork, named after its owner and, still determined to revolutionize

cowboying, he thought to put the idle punchers doing granger work. "Boys," he said one day at noon, "beef prices are so low I may not ship for a couple of weeks and being as hay hands are scarce I want you to ride down to that east meadow and help with the haying. My foreman there will show you what to do."

The cowboys saddled up and went to the meadow. "Glad you're here," the foreman told them. "Take some of these pitchforks and help load those wagons. Looks

like bad weather coming and I want to get that hay in the stack as soon as possible. I gotta jump on my horse and go to the house a minute but you boys know what to do."

Instead of leaving their horses and getting pitchforks the fellows rode off and were soon tossing overhand loops on haycocks, taking their dallies and heading for the stack. Otto had been watching through his glasses and the foreman was met by a screaming maniac and sent back on a run. Seeing the riders pull up to the stack with but a few straws left in their loops brought a yell from the foreman.

"Christ almighty, fellows!" he yowled. "Whadda you think you're doin'? Now I'll have to have the whole damn meadow raked again! I told you to grab pitchforks!"

"Anything we can't do on a horse," he was told, "we ain't doin'!" It was twenty years before any big outfit dared to ask its cowhands to do ranch work. But the "handwriting was on the wall" and eventually the era of straight cowboying was over.

Merrill told us many incidents in Otto Franc's days on the Pitchfork and being as he had worked for Otto after first coming to Wyoming with a trail herd, few knew Otto better than Kidney Foot. Otto was not only a keen cattleman but along with his big outfit he branched out in all diversified directions early in his career. He founded a town on the Greybull. There being no post office nearer than Lander, some ninety-odd miles to the south, and Billings, Montana, far to the north, he brought pressure on the government and had a post office established at a homesteader's place and named it Otto, with the homesteader's wife as postmaster.

One amusing incident Kidney Foot liked to relate concerned his longtime friend Josh Dean, who Otto had persuaded to take the job of carrying mail from Lander. One day when the mail was a day late, Josh rode in "sick as a colicky horse" and a near-empty demijohn dangling from the saddle horn. But he was not too sick to be eagerly overflowing with the details of a hanging he had witnessed in Lander.

"Never mind the hanging," Otto fumed. "You know I can't stand gruesome news! Where's the mail?"

For a moment Josh had a blank look on his face. "Lord God," he finally groaned, "I plumb forgot to bring it." Folks around Meeteetse, in fact all over the basin, liked to say, "From that day until he died, ol' Josh never drank anything but Adam's Ale"—water.

But the writer happens to know differently. In 1912, a Philadelphia paper ran an article on a certain Josh Dean who had come East to check on a young lady who had promised to marry him providing he sent $500 to cover her "debts" and train fare to Cody.

"I've paid out money for these so-called debts, clothes and train fare four times," Josh had told the reporter. "But this time, by crackey, they better have money for duds an' train fare or they ain't hookin' ol' Josh."

I went to Josh's hotel to renew my acquaintance with this master "tall yarn teller" and found him keeping company with several bottles of scotch and fizz water. "Thought you didn't drink," I remarked, "so what happened? More woman trouble?"

"Woman trouble's got nothin' t'do with it," he replied. "I just don't drink likker out of a trough like I used to. This is merely t'wet my whistle now and then."

Getting back to Otto Franc: Although Otto had befriended and financed many a homesteader he, like most big cattlemen, had made a few enemies and in his later years appeared to be expecting to be done in by one of them. Whether this threat was real or if Otto was getting queer and imagined it, no one could say. But according to Kidney Foot Merrill, Otto kept an arsenal of guns handy and went to bed with a six-shooter under his pillow.

Then on a November evening in 1903, Otto was found lying dead by a barbwire fence, his discharged shotgun hanging on a wire. And therein lies a mystery. No one was more familiar with firearms than Otto or more careful in handling them. So it seems incongruous that he would drag a shotgun or rifle through a wire fence. Also there was doubt as to how a shotgun could discharge at such close range and only one pellet pierce his body. He had been found by ranch hands and carried to the house and in those days the authorities

No one was more familiar with firearms than Otto, or more careful in handling them.

knew nothing of ballistics and cared less. Just another dead man and it was pronounced "an accident."

Otto Franc's remains lie in Meeteetse, the town he helped to bring into being and watched through its growing pains during a period when a few bad actors ruled the town and their smoking six-shooters brought it a modicum of fame.

It was said Otto Franc did more for the little man and the Big Horn Basin contiguous with his domain than any other person. Yet, no great shaft rises there to commemorate this great man's grave, such as was erected in memory of Josh Dean whose only claim to fame was a penchant for marrying and his raw humor and stories that no one could distinguish between truth and a whopping lie.

After Otto's demise, three cattlemen—George Phelps, George Merrill, and George Pennoyer—gobbled up the Pitchfork, Z Bar T, LU, Grass Creek Ranch, Colonel Torrey's M Bar and Basin Ranch under the title of The Rocky Mountain Cattle Company. With a book count of 130,000 head of cattle, it was truly the kingpin of all outfits in the basin if not the state.

Some say the increased bands of sheep tolled the death knell for this monster outfit while others declared the 1906 law prohibiting a fence on public lands ruined them. It was a known fact that every ranch had thousands of acres of public domain under fence and after arrests for this offense crept westward from Nebraska, The Rocky Mountain Cattle Company found homesteaders in the center of meadows and wholesale wire-rolling and post-pulling took place from the M Bar on Owl Creek to the Pitchfork on the Greybull.

While all these put a crimp in these ranches and contributed to the cutting down of the company's vast herds, they had foreseen coming events and were ready for them. Like most big outfits they had their cowboys file homesteads, have a few blankets and tinware in a ten-by-twelve shack and "prove up," then sell for a mere pittance to the outfit. In 1907, 1908 and 1909 the roundup wagon I was with had a spayer along and Old Mizzoo spayed nine thousand heifer calves at fifteen cents a calf and we shipped ten thousand two-year-old heifers along with almost twice that number of three- and four-year-old steers.

So while lowering the cattle number, they had title to homesteaded and ranch land for fifty miles. Then lo and behold, the richest oil pools in the state were discovered right on the company's holdings and the three owners became so rich overnight they no longer cared about cattle—except as a hobby.

The Pitchfork was sold to Charles Beldon, whose true to life cattle scenes appeared on every calendar the Blackleg Serum Company put out as well as in most high-class periodicals. The Merrills moved to the old M Bar, Phelps retained his Z Bar T, and Pennoyer bought a small cattle ranch on the Big Wind River near Crowheart Butte. Thus ended an empire that had evolved from the idea of two "dude" cattlemen—Colonel Jay Torrey and Otto Franc. ∎

The Outlaw

Old Joe Wagner was a drunk, but not a liar.

This story was related to Fred McGee and me in 1906 by old Joe Wagner, who shortly afterwards became my brother's father-in-law. Fred and I were waiting at the Wagner ranch (a short distance from Lander's main street) for my brother Charley to get back from the George Wimsey ranch near Lost Cabin where he had gone to collect some bronc-breaking wages.

Five or six years prior to our meeting Mr. Wagner had been a fairly prosperous rancher, but when his wife died it started Joe down the skids of no return. He took to drink and drank and drank and borrowed on his ranch from month to month and year to year until the ranch was plastered to the hilt with mortgages. It didn't appear to bother this bulb-nosed, puffy-faced German though. He had his bottle and moved his old bench as he followed the shade around and was happy.

The setup there filled Fred and me with pity as there were two lovely teenage daughters whom we knew wanted to invite us to have supper with them. But from the whispers to their dad when he was in, we heard one say, "Please, Papa, don't drink any more while we have company." It was evident there was little if any food in the house.

We put our minds in gear and when Fred had a chance he said, "Lorraine, we've got to stick around until Charley pulls in so Harry and I better go get some supper and then come back."

Lorraine looked at her sister then said, "We'd love to have you eat supper here but Papa or I haven't been to the store lately. But if you don't mind the little we have, you are more than welcome."

"Sounds fine," Fred lied. "We've been eatin' bachelor grub [another lie] for a spell so some girl-cooked grub would go mighty good. But if there's anything you're short of, I wish you'd take this money and gallop to the store." Handing her a ten-dollar gold piece, he added, "Get plenty while you're at it. We might be eatin' several meals here." Lorraine

seemed embarrassed but, with money, she was soon galloping off on the one horse Joe hadn't drunk up.

"Yessir," Joe said as he resumed his bench seat, "this dag-blasted banker knows he's taking the food right out of my girls' mouths but a lot he cares! 'Minds me of a case that happened here several years back. A young woman—seems I recollect her name was Eggeers or Eggerson, something like that—and her husband had mortgaged the ranch so's to plant a big apple orchard. Then his luck ran out and he got killed by a runaway team. Left her with two little kids and owing four thousand dollars. But a lot that skinflint banker cared. I could tell you his name, he's dead now, but his kids are still living right here in town and even though their father would steal the coppers off his dead brother's eyes, them kids are fine upstanding folks!"

For a moment, Joe took time for a bit of thinking. "I know what that poor woman must have gone through, after getting a notice the banker was coming out the next day with a notary and unless she had every cent to clear that four-thousand-dollar loan he was foreclosing.

"But just to show how things can happen, a fellow rides along that day and stops at her ranch for a bite to eat and rest his horse. During the talk, while the fellow was having fun with the two little girls, it was natural for her to tell him her troubles. After listening a while, this fellow went out to his horse and come back with a handful of hundred-dollar bills. 'Now you take this,' he says, 'and when your banker comes out you pay him every blasted cent and be mighty sure you get a

HE SAVED A WOMAN'S RANCH FROM A SKINFLINT BANKER. WHO WAS HE?

paper showing he's paid in full. Then later you go to the courthouse and have that mortgage cleared.'

"I can't say what that poor woman thought or all that was said, but we heard she did plenty crying. Huh? Oh sure, the banker and his witness showed up in his buggy but he got the jolt of his life, not that he wasn't glad to get the money but he couldn't figure out how she could raise so much money all at once and she wouldn't tell him. I've had a dozen foreclosure notices from Old Noble but I guess he don't want my ranch as bad as that other banker did because we're still here."

Fred and I pondered this and also the story Joe had related. "Did that fellow," Fred finally asked, "ever get his four thousand back from Mrs. What's-her-name?"

"That's the queer part of it. When the banker and his friend were on their way back to town a robber waylaid them and took every blasted cent they had!"

"Good!" Fred and I chorused. "Served that bird right!"

"Sure did," Joe chuckled. "But the best part was when Mrs. Eggers or—pshaw, beats all how a person can forget names—gets a letter telling her to forget the loan, that she didn't owe him a penny. And you know who that letter was from?"

"How the hell would we know?" Fred said.

"Butch Cassidy, that's who," Joe said, "and you fellows are just like him." Those last words gave Fred and me grist for a lot of thought.

"Maybe," Fred said, as we rode away the next morning, "it was just old Joe's way of sayin' he appreciated that money I donated." ■

Buffalo Bill, The Man

If it hadn't been for a roan horse that was scared of snakes, I probably would never have seen Buffalo Bill Cody—let alone work for him.

 We had finished loading a forty-car train of four-year-old steers in Cody, Wyoming, and The Galloping Swede said, "Lord, God, fellers, I'm so dry I'm spitting sparks! Where at's th' nearest saloon?"

Like most of us, this was his first trip into Cody, but we allowed that The Galloping Swede had nothing on us. (I'd nicknamed the Swede that because he didn't seem to know a horse had any other gait but running.)

"Follow me," said George "Gaspipe" Mullison, socking in the spurs, an' I'll lead yuh to th' Holy Grail an' the last one there buys th' drinks." Gaspipe was a runty cuss but big on the talk and maintained the Holy Grail was what books referred to as the Wailing Wall.

We hit the main street running (if Cody had another street nobody knew about it) and that was when my roan set off the fireworks. The dusty street was full of loops of baling wire tossed out of livery barns. One of these flopped up in front of my horse and he lit halfway across the street with his nose under his tail. He was the "sun-fishing" bellering type of bucker and no matter if you were in the rim rocks, just let a crooked stick or piece of wire wiggle near him and Mr. Cowboy better be set for a ride. I had been told a rattlesnake had struck him in the jaw while he was grazing and the fangs not coming loose, the roan had gone crazy, tossing the big rattler about until it was finally flung loose to be killed by the horse-wrangler.

Anyway, between the roan doing his thing and me whooping like a Comanche, we were stirring up the dust and the natives when the roan landed on the board sidewalk and plowed through the plate-glass window of the Campbell Drug Store.

I had time to see two Indian skulls grinning at me from among the display of jewelry before throwing up my arm to protect my face. Then the horse and I were upside down among plate glass, rings, watches and broken perfume bottles. Some of the cowhands got my eccentric mount and me outside where I was decorating the landscape with spouting blood when the druggist took over with a mixture of hell-fired stuff he said was "new-skin," which years later I learned was collodion. Makes no difference, anyway. Blood didn't stand a chance under several layers of that fiery goop.

Somebody ran up with a flask of whiskey which I was lowering when a white-goateed giant pushed through the crowd and in a booming voice said, "What you trying to do, cowboy, commit suicide?" I told him I guessed I wasn't hurt too bad, only my head felt like it belonged to somebody else.

"Well," he said, "that was a good ride you made while it lasted and I'll give you a job in my show next spring if you want it."

At the moment I didn't know what he meant by "show" but mustered voice enough to ask, "What show?" If I'd hit him in the face with my hat he couldn't have reacted more violently.

"What the blazes show do you suppose?" he all but shouted. "My show, of course! Buffalo Bill's Wild West."

Taking a card from a fancy billfold, he continued: "Write to Johnny for a contract. Sixty a month and I'll see you in New York in April." Just like that. As if it was a foregone conclusion I'd turn handsprings over such an offer.

A well-dressed dude (we cowhands always catalogued big-city folks as dudes) addressed my would-be employer: "Colonel, wouldn't it be a good idea to have the doctor look this boy over? I'll foot the bill."

"Coddle these fellows," the Colonel said, "and they're spoiled rotten. He'll get messed up worse than that before he rides some of the broncs in my show. But if you want to foot any bill, take a look at the way he wrecked Mr. Campbell's store."

It was winter before we learned the name of the gentleman who had offered to "foot the bill" if I was taken to a doctor. He was the famous "Bet-You-a-Million-Gates."

He had won this sobriquet when he and another "plunger" stood looking up at two pigeons on the cornice of a New York building. "I'll bet you a million dollars," Gates is supposed to have said, "that the gray one flies away before the white one does."

Be that as it may, I was more interested in Buffalo Bill's offer than I was in Gates and the pigeons. Here I had worked near Cody and heard of Colonel Cody for a couple of years without ever associating him with my boyhood hero, Buffalo Bill. I had avidly read perhaps a thousand ten-cent Buffalo Bill books by Ned Buntline, but no mention had ever been made of him as a showman. He always killed Indians.

Back at the M Bar ranch, we cowhands discussed the idea of me going with any Wild West Show. First came the dread of getting so far from our own little world, and secondly Buffalo Bill's intimation that getting one's throat cut and his head torn off was as nothing compared to the everyday mayhem those show horses could dish up.

"I wouldn't work for that old S.O.B.," a hand put in, "if he paid me a thousand a month! He seemed to think just because he's Buffalo Bill he c'n Lord it over everybody!" Others were in hearty agreement.

Those show broncs came in for judgment, too. They were a "foreign" commodity so far as our knowledge went. We had thumbed and twisted that card with Johnny Baker's New York address until it was near pulp with everyone trying to dissuade me. That was with the exception of Gaspipe who said he'd go, too, if we could both get contracts, all of which brought howls and jibes.

"If I can't set anything that old bastard can toss at me," Gaspipe bragged. "I c'n always come back here and look poor cows in the behind in forty-below blizzards at forty per!"

The upshot of it was that in February 1910, Gaspipe and I were studying our contracts and a letter stating we were to be in Rushville, Nebraska, by April 14, so as to be picked up by the midnight train bringing

Indian agent Billy McCuen and his Indians from Pine Ridge, South Dakota.

Did I say contract? Death warrant would be more like it. There were so many "clauses" and parties of the first and second part that in legal jargon meant if we got our necks broken we would have to pay our own funeral expenses. The party of the first part could assess "fines" (total pay and "holdback" of five bucks a week to be paid at close of the show) for any of the following "infractions": drinking, swearing, fighting, ogling girls, missing a performance, conducting or participating in "collections" (to get some fired cowpuncher back home), conducting raffles, failure to ride, or refusing to ride, any bronc assigned by the chief of cowboys, etc., etc.

"Hell's fire!" old Pad Holloman exclaimed. "This party of the second part ain't got as much rights as a skunk at a banquet. A feller might as well be dead to start with. I wouldn't sign that thing if they held a gun to my head."

A week in trying to work cattle we had gathered along the Wind River (so the hungry Shoshone and Arapaho Indians wouldn't eat them) and trying to fight them over the Owl Creek range through three feet of snow and the sky full of sundogs to tell them it was from forty to fifty degrees below zero, can be a powerful persuader, so Gaspipe and I affixed our John Hancock to our contracts and mailed them, and from that moment on we worried. We worried at work and in the bunkhouse. We'd be one hell of a long way from home and supposin' we got bucked off or fired for some other reason? And no money? According to those contracts, we could lie maimed or dead and Buffalo Bill wouldn't lift a hand to help us or ship our bodies back home. A bleak outlook, alright!

"Well," I said, by way of bolstering our morale, "Buffalo Bill knows me and seems to like me, so I think we'll be Hunky Dory."

"Yeah," Gaspipe concurred, "you stand pretty high with the ol' booger alright. But in case one of us gets fired, the other one quits. Savvy?"

"You damn tootin'!" came my promise.

Those months, from the time our contracts were mailed until we quit the M Bar, were the longest any human ever had to endure. At least for me they would have been, had it not been for a streak of good luck (which some prefer to call fate) meeting me head-on. We cowhands had been gathering up bulls so they could all be shoved into the Big Buffalo Basin until spring, where the winter grass reached a critter's knees. I had picked up half a dozen at ranches along the Big Horn and was cussing and fighting them up the Owl Creek road towards the home ranch when this so-called fate took over—Buffalo Bill and the fate that was destined to change my life forever and amen.

When we landed in Rushville, Nebraska, the afternoon of April 10, we wished to hell we hadn't been in such a rush to get there. We were surrounded by half a dozen others who had jumped the gun. Also, it was plain to see that half of them had an inflated idea of their bronc riding ability and Gaspipe and I wondered if they had studied any of those clauses.

The one (though swank) hotel in the little town charged two dollars a day for board and room, and for four long days it was up to Gaspipe and me to accept promises and foot the bill for these drones.

The hotel owner had a steadfast rule that "Gentlemen must wear coats in the dining room," so the hostelry's manager had to rustle up a dozen or so coats, as most of the cowboys only wore vests. Wearing coats of every style, color and fit, it was no wonder other diners eyed us as though we were a band of half-witted freaks and we were glad when McCuen with his Injuns rolled into Rushville.

Counting papooses and squaws, there were over a hundred Indians in the chair car which, along with a baggage car filled with teepee poles, bundles of their canvas and

HARRY WEBB WITH PHOTO OF BUFFALO BILL, CA. 1980. THE SHOWMAN CARED MORE ABOUT HIS COWBOYS AND INDIANS THAN HE CARED TO ADMIT.

hide coverings and a couple dozen yelping dogs, would be hooked onto whatever trains we had to transfer to and go straight through to the East.

In Omaha, a young beauty boarded the train and (although Gaspipe and I were unaware that such could happen) later on darn nigh busted up our long friendship. But, first, a woman rushed her daughter aboard and made us cowpunchers promise to look after her and protect her. Well, it was evident the mother need have no fears on that score. Any one of us would have fought a buzz saw over the girl and give it twenty turns the start. "I'm leaving her in your hands," she said, crying.

Arlene Palmer was the cutest, sweetest sixteen-year-old God ever molded. And being a lover of horses and a good rider, she was also on her way to the show to ride with the Russian Cossacks, a dangerous job and one requiring more skill than us mere bronc-stompers possessed. No wonder the mother had placed her under our big, strong wings.

When a man came through the car tapping a musical dingus with a little hammer, we saw folks getting up and Gaspipe said, "That must be the supper gong. Let's get Arlene and take her with us and go hang on the nose bags." But before we got to where Arlene sat, a well-dressed, paunchy, fatherly looking man had her in tow. It wasn't long until we were glad it was him instead of us who had latched onto her. She ate a four-dollar meal and our funds (thanks to our dead-broke comrades) had fast been depleted.

But getting back to the young, blonde beauty who had attracted our attention. Long before we reached Chicago, Gaspipe was escorting her on tours through the Indians' cars, showing her the Indian paraphernalia and dogs in their baggage car, and on into the baggage car where our saddles, chaps and spurs were. Gaspipe had beautiful silver-mounted spurs and bridle and I guess that turned the fair one's head to putty and her heart to mush.

But Gaspipe had it just as bad. From then on, he close-herded that damsel as if he was afraid one of us might get her in our loop. We couldn't figure the queer quirks of human nature. Here, with a batch of handsome he-men to choose from, she had fallen for a runt. Of course, she wouldn't have weighed over a hundred pounds herself if

she'd been drug out of the river with all her clothes on.

Anyway, from then on, day or night, Gaspipe put in his time up forward with Eva. I'd at least got that much information out of him. Along about midnight, Gaspipe came back so droopy-eyed he could hardly see. "I've just got to get a bit of shut-eye," he mumbled, "so I wish you'd go up and keep Eva company for a spell. But don't forget to come wake me up before we reach Pittsburgh. We'll be there in less'n two hours and I want to see her off th' train."

I'd had oodles of sleep, so couldn't think of a better chore than girl-sitting. Right away she confided that she was head-over-heels in love with "George." But it being so sudden, she wondered if she was taking the right step. She was married to a doctor but planned on divorcing him and marrying my cowboy friend. "You and George are such close friends," she said, "that I…" Seeing me holding my head in both hands, she broke off the love talk and wanted to know what was wrong, as if I'd had a stroke or something.

"My God, girl," I said in a moaning voice, "if you weren't so beautiful and sweet and innocent, I'd say hop to it. But I can't let you destroy your life." Looking around as if for prying ears I leaned close. "That lowdown blatherskite evidently didn't tell you he was wanted in Wyoming for horse stealing and killing a sheriff. If you hook up with him, in no time a-tall, you'll be a widow! Once they get him he'll have a rope around his neck an' dancin' on air."

Oh, I laid it on plenty thick. Reaching in her handbag, she took out Gaspipe's picture, tore it to bits and dropped the pieces down behind the radiator. On the Pittsburgh platform, she clung to me and all but ate me up with kisses, as she thanked me for saving her from that "monster."

I was on the way back to our car when I met Gaspipe. "We ought to be gettin' t'Pittsburgh, hadn't we?" he said. When I told him Eva never wanted to see him again he wouldn't believe it. Didn't take long to convince him though when he saw his picture torn to chips. I never saw a man so discombooberated in my life, so I told him what I'd done.

"Look, Gaspipe," I said. "You and me's been buddies a long time and I knowed if you got hitched, it'd bust us up for all time, so…"

Gaspipe was only half my size but he called me some choice names before starting a wallop down by his heel that sent me in a woman's lap. Everybody was yelling and screaming and we had the aisle littered with junk before I laid him low, which I hated to do. It was weeks before he even spoke to me again.

The fairgrounds in Trenton, which was the show's winter quarters, was a sight to behold when we arrived on a beautiful noonday. Such an aggregation of gold-leafed wagons, big tops, horses, circus performers, cooks, waiters and canvas men was beyond even the wildest dreams of us Wyoming bronc-stompers. Only one of our twenty or more, Ben Brown, had ever so much as seen a Wild West Show. We had seen and competed in Frontier Days at Cheyenne but never any such organization as was gathered here for a week's rehearsal before the opening in Madison Square Garden. Buffalo Bill and Pawnee Bill shows had merged and was now billed as "Buffalo Bill's Wild West & Pawnee Bill's Far East."

Johnny Baker, arena director and a foster son of Buffalo Bill, lost no time getting into rehearsal, drilling us from morning 'til night, and in three days had the cowboys, cowgirls and Indians pretty well whipped into presentable shape for the intricate serpentine numbers. Between these acts, he ran the Cossack troupe through their act.

Most of the Cossacks were old troupers and needed little drilling, but on account of three new members, Arlene Palmer included, they had to go through the grind several times a day. Arlene was the only girl member and we cowboys shook in our boots watching that beautiful little creature in Cossack dress doing headstands and leg-drags from that high saddle. Some of their mounts were also new at the game and would try to kick the rider's head off in those leg-drags.

On the fourth day, Cy Compton, chief of cowboys, had three of the bucking string brought out. "Stick your hull on him, Webb," he told me, "and ride him out."

We had sized up the bucking string in the stables and pronounced them "mean lookers," and when I screwed down in the saddle, I was shaking in my boots. But I made out far better than I thought I would.

"Bring the blue mare here," Cy ordered. I rode that bellering, twisting she-devil and

Vigo was my mount in Buffalo Bill's show, until Old Barney hooked his insides out the night we left Santa Barbara, California, in 1910.

when the third one was led over, I began to wonder, "Why the hell, me?" We knew many of the twenty-seven cowboys would be eliminated down to around twenty, and I said to myself, "So the bastards are trying to get me out, huh?"

Cy told me not to fan the buckers with my hat (the bronc riders custom), but to rear back on both reins as the horses went higher and made a better showing that way.

By that time, I was so mad I was ready to head back to the range. "What the hell's the idea?" I demanded.

"See those two cameras there?" Cy said, pointing. "They're taking pictures for the lithographs." He then told me that Gail Downing, one of Buffalo Bill's best hands the past three years (who lived in Cody and would join the show later on) had written

him boosting my bronc riding ability to the sky. I didn't know Gail, and where he got his misinformation I had no idea, unless he had spied me breaking into Campbell's Drug Store. Anyway, Cy's explanation quelled my hostility.

So far Buffalo Bill had not been around, as he left all rehearsals to Johnny Baker and it wasn't until opening night that I saw him. There had been three full dress rehearsals that day and when the night show went on, Madison Square Garden was bulging at the seams and thousands were turned away.

It was ironic that tragedy should strike us when the announcer introduced "The Congress of Rough Riders of the World!" The curtain was whipped back and with leather-lunged whoops, we poured into the arena four abreast. A lead horse stumbled and

went down with twenty or more horses trampling the rider. Of course, nothing must interfere with an act, and it was many minutes before we knew Ben Brown of Chugwater, Wyoming, had been carted away unconscious. "Bad concussion and five ribs broken," we were told.

Now what? According to those contracts, Ben was in more than one hell of a fix! But we needn't have worried. Colonel Cody paid the doctor's and hospital bill and Ben's wages went on until he was back in the saddle four months later.

During the forty minutes that the Far East acts performed, Cy assigned the buckers we were to ride and briefed us on any dangerous habits they had whereby the rider could be badly hurt. "The Colonel wants a wild show tonight, boys," he said, "and I'm putting out our best horses. So ride 'em high, wide and handsome."

Twelve of us were to ride, with helpers snubbing the horses until the rider was all set. The act, supposedly, was to consume only twelve minutes, so we were told to work fast. I had drawn Blue Dog, a chunky blue-gray, and Cy said he would hold for me as Blue Dog had to be thrown after being saddled and mounted while down. Otherwise, he would throw himself over backward.

I was the first to ride and with Buffalo Bill on his big white Isham standing near, I figured he recognized me and was watching to see how I performed in the arena. Cy tossed the long lead rope around Blue Dog's front legs and he went down. "Now," Cy said, "when you get about fifty feet from the barrier down there, you quit him and get away fast. Don't ride him until he stops or he'll be on you and bat your brains out. He killed a fellow that way."

"Christ!" I said. "I can't quit a horse while he's bucking. I either ride 'em or get bucked off." I was scareder than a pregnant fox in a forest fire.

"You do as I say," Cy told me. "I don't want to see you get hurt." Wondering just how I was going to quit Blue Dog while he was still bucking, I stepped over his left side and felt for a stirrup. When Cy threw the rope down, Blue Dog shot up like a skyrocket. I seemed to be doing a good job of riding but how to quit him had me worried. He was going high and crooked and nearing the four-foot-high cloth barrier when I hit the

WILD WEST INDIANS AND COW BO

Left to right, plus Indians: Seated by girl, Indian Agent Billy McCuen. Cowboys: Smoky Warner, Font Hitchcock, Carl Downing, "Gaspipe" Mullison looking over Carl's shoulder, Harry Webb (white shirt),

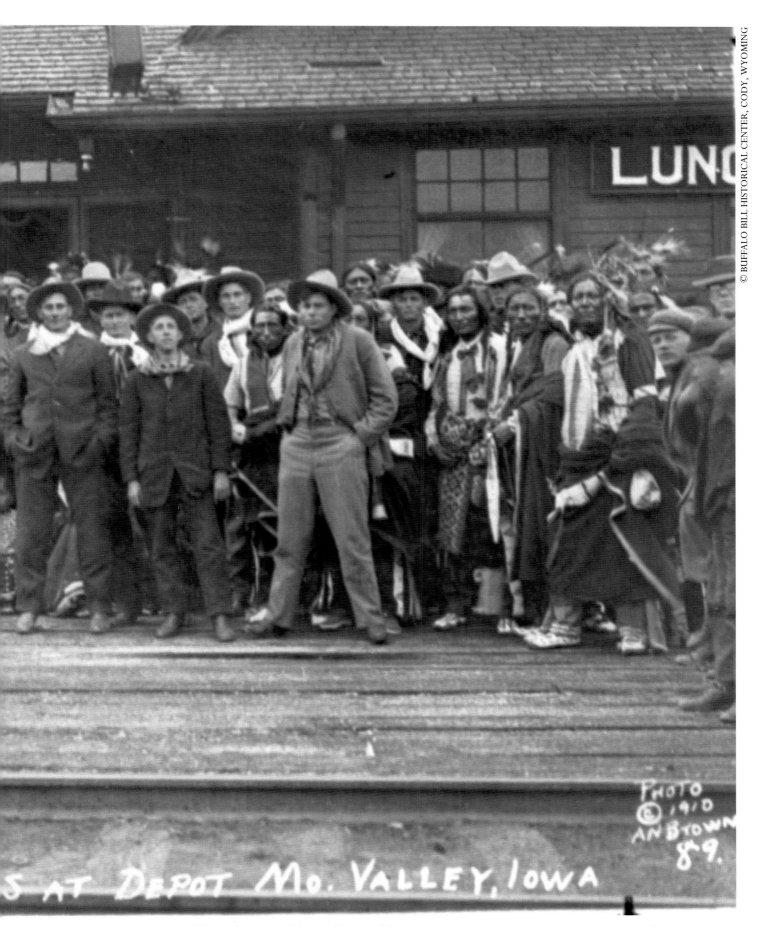

BEN BROWN (HALF LIT UP), WALT CAIN AND HARRY "DADDY" LEWIS IN HAT SHOWING ABOVE HEADS OF TWO INDIANS.
WE'RE ON OUR WAY TO JOIN THE BUFFALO BILL SHOW. THIS PHOTO WAS TAKEN AFTER BREAKFAST ON APRIL 15, 1910.

tan-bark and hit it running. I sure felt good.

Hearing a horse on my heels, I really speeded up. But instead of Blue Dog, it was Isham and the old Colonel who was jabbing the muzzle of his Winchester at my back. "Get a move on yuh, young gobbler!" he yelled. "Yuh move like a man seventy-five years old. Doggone your picture, you'll get the lead out of your britches if you expect to stay on this trick!"

Here I thought I'd performed a miracle and that old sonovabitch had to bawl me out. He hadn't even recognized me. To hell with him and his show. Talk about a Simon Legree!

I was still cussing when I saw Gaspipe mounting a bay called Dynamite. When assigning him, Cy had told Gaspipe to "glue down close because he's got a bag of tricks and just when you think you've got him in the sack, you're bucked off." Dynamite was just that. But Gaspipe seemed to be settin' him fine which made me glad, even if he hadn't spoken to me since I scared his girl away. Then I saw a tangle of chaps and cowboy go sailing through the air and land among a group of women occupying one of the boxes six feet above the arena floor.

The Colonel had dismounted to greet a beautiful redhead standing near his office and I heard his booming voice say, "Johnny, who's that man that just got bucked off?"

"George Mullison," Johnny Baker yelled back. "From around Cody, I think." Then I heard the Colonel bark, "Send him here," and I thought, oh-oh, here's where Gassy and I both get the gate!

The Colonel was standing with an arm flung around the redhead's shoulders when Gaspipe reached the bunting barrier. "Well, Mullison," he said in the foghorn voice he used to impress people, "let's hear your alibi."

"Alibi, hell!" Gaspipe said, all flustered. "That bastard simply throwed me so high the bluebirds could o' built a nest in my behind [he used the abbreviation for "behind"] before I come back down. That's…"

But the Colonel wasn't waiting to hear more and as he ushered his charge in his office, the fringe on the shoulders of his buckskin coat was doing a dance from the Colonel's suppressed mirth. We were to see that cutie many times at the Colonel's silver-serviced table during the season.

The show cars (fifty-three cars, pulled in two sections) had been left across the Hudson River and orders had been posted at the entrance to the Garden's dining hall that twenty cents a day ferry fare would be allowed us. Those who chose to remain in New York would have to pay their own room rent. What the others did, I don't know, but we cowhands weren't about to make that ferry trip every night and morning so we rented rooms a couple of blocks from the Garden. Four of us got a nice room, two beds, for three dollars a week for the room.

The landlady was a motherly soul and looked after us like a hen with chickens. Only trouble was, Smoky Warner nor I could sleep with the bright gas jet burning all night. We put up with it a week, then I said to the landlady, "Mother, is there any way you can fix that light? It's hard to sleep with it shining in our faces."

"Good heavens, yes," she said. "Why didn't you turn it out?"

"Because," I said, "you've got that sign there, saying, 'Do not blow out the light.'" For a minute, she just looked at me, then she busted out laughing. "Oh, you poor dears," she said, "you poor darlings. I have those signs in every room. Last year a cowboy threw his boot at the light to extinguish it and we found him dead the next morning and the others almost dead. So don't ever blow out one of these gaslights. You turn them out."

"Now ain't that somethin'," Smoky said when she showed us how to turn off the jet and light it. I decided the trip East was worth a lot after all. We were learning things we never knew before.

For instance, I remarked to a man in a bar—it seemed every native wanted to spend money on us, treat us to drinks and feeds and whatnot—about the monster mugs of beer they served for a nickel. He said, "Listen, if you boys have time, I'll take you down to Sullivan's. He serves a beer that is beer. Isn't that right?" he said to the bartender. "Right!" that worthy said. Right then we didn't have time, but the next day John L. himself was up to visit the Colonel and the Colonel said, "John, these sagebrushers want to see what a real schooner of beer looks like, so take 'em down and educate them."

Mr. Sullivan was a portly, black-mustached man with big diamonds for shirt studs and over-awed us with his friendly way. When we reached his place, he looked up at the clock. "Lunch is just being set out," he said, "so you go right back in there and see how much you can eat and drink, on the house. Tim," he said to one of the bartenders, "wait on my friends, here." He told us, "Tim will take your beer to you."

Sullivan's Place catered mostly to the bricklaying, hod-carrying trade and they were pouring in like a trail-herd of thirst-crazy steers that smelled water.

That thirty-foot table of "lunch" flabbergasted us and as one of the cowhands said, "Those two-handled schooners must have originally been meant for horse-troughs." One of them and all the lunch you could

eat, for a nickel. But cow waddies for the most part being lean-bellied, found out one of those workmen could hold more beer than the nine of us.

Evelyn Nesbit Thaw was another real person we met. During the three weeks we were at the Garden, she was there every night riding in the stagecoach and if ever there was a living doll, she was it, and one we enjoyed "rescuing" when the Injuns were "tomahawking and scalping" the passengers. We couldn't blame her husband, Harry K. for gunning up on Stanford White over her.

It happened right over our heads, too. Up in the Roof Garden. Many times, after the night performance, Evelyn would take several of us cowboys to some nightspot or to her swank apartment for a one a.m. supper.

The noisiest and most colorful of all the numbers was the "Battle of Summit Springs." The Colonel had participated in the real battle as a scout so I guess that is why he chose its reenactment for one of the Indian scenes.

Dressed as cavalrymen, the cowboys, Windy Weediman and his soldier troupe, and Mexicans led by the scout, would

charge into the Indian encampment yelling and shooting. While the squaws tried to gather up their horses and papooses, the bucks would be pouring "lead" into us. Teepees would be knocked down, soldiers' horses dropping and Indians "biting the dust." It was a screaming, yelling bedlam.

But after the second day of yelling our lungs out, we all lost our voices and in the third day's battle our "yells" were weaker than a sick kitten's meow. One of the younger Mexicans who didn't know what it was all about anyway, was simply sitting on

AT THE BEGINNING OF EACH FLASHY, NOISY SHOW—THIS ONE IN LOS ANGELES IN 1910—THE INDIANS FOLLOW COLONEL CODY INTO THE ARENA, WITH COWBOYS FOLLOWING THE INDIANS. BUFFALO BILL IS RIDING HIS FAVORITE MOUNT ISHAM.

his horse. He couldn't yell and he'd shot all his shells. We saw scout Cody gallop over and ram his Winchester's muzzle in the Mexican's back and yell "Greeta, you brown rascal!" (Meaning to yell.) It scared the Mexican so bad he went right over his horse's head and lit running. Mexican Joe Berarri told us the young fellow thought the Indians had him.

Charlie Russell, the cowboy artist, was another celebrity who liked to hobnob with us. He had a batch of his paintings there during the International Art Exhibit and the Colonel supplied him with one of his silver-mounted saddles and a beautiful dappled-white mount so he could ride with us. He and one of the cowboys, Eddie Botsford, were the ones who had been looking after that Kansas City Company's cattle in the Judith Basin the terrible winter of '86, so they had a lot to talk about.

When the company could finally get word to Russell asking about their cattle, Charlie drew a picture on an Arbuckle coffee wrapper of a cow, her tail frozen off, every rib showing and a pack of wolves around her. He simply scrawled, "This is the last of your five thousand," and mailed it to his employers. That picture became famous, titled, "Waiting for a Chinook."

All the stock, horses, buffaloes, camels and elephants were stabled underneath the arena and after an afternoon performance one day we got a taste of the Colonel's temper. For his buffalo hunt act, a tub of water was sunk in the tan-bark in the middle of the arena to simulate a spring. When the herd of thirsty buffaloes were started up the ramp, they would head for the water and gather around drinking.

The Colonel would enter through a small tunnel under the seat section on the Madison Avenue end, ride in, stop and shield his eyes with his hand, ready his Winchester and dash among the buffaloes shooting right and left. The herd had been powder-burned so many times they would head pell-mell for the basement. With scenic mountains far off in the background it was a colorful act.

This particular day, however, things didn't go so well. It started off bad by a group of fellows who couldn't get seats (the show always had a larger audience than the Garden had seats for) and stood viewing the show from the tunnel. The Colonel couldn't get his horse past the watchers and "time

being of the essence" he was saying "Gangway, boys! Heads up!" When this had no effect, he spurred Isham among them.

"Look out, you old sonovabitch!" one smart aleck yelled. "You damn near run over me!" The words weren't out of his mouth when the old Colonel was off his horse and landed a haymaker on the fellow's nose. "I'll teach you some manners, you young whippersnapper!" he said, and pasted the blood all over his tormentor's face. Some of the group were voicing their accolades with, "Hurrah for you, Buffalo Bill! You get on through and we'll see that it's twenty-three for this shyster!" The saying "Skido-o-o! Twenty-three for you!" was sweeping the city at that time. But the Colonel hadn't seen anything yet.

Mad as a hornet, he was blazing away at his buffaloes when his horse stepped on a sixty-foot maguey rope trailing from a buffalo's hind leg and went tail over head. One of the Mexican fancy ropers had dabbed a loop on the buffalo's leg as they started up the ramp. But, unlike domestic cattle, a buffalo has a lot of fur clear to its hooves and the roper couldn't shake the rope loose so had given up and let the young cow drag it through the arena.

The tumble could have been a catastrophe but, fortunately, the Colonel was only badly shaken up. Gathering his Winchester out of the deep tan-bark and retrieving his big hat, he mounted to an applause that rocked the Garden. Nothing was said until after the closing act. Then Johnny Baker ordered all cowboys and Mexicans to the Colonel's quarters. Since both cowboys and Mexicans were waiting in the basement during the buffalo act, the roper could have been any one of us, as a few cowboys also had maguey ropes.

I never heard a more vitriolic dressing down without real cussing than we got. But we couldn't blame him. Most of us knew what it was like to be fogging a critter to turn it and have our horse "run a badger hole up its leg" and go turning houlihans, so we could sympathize with our sixty-four-year-old boss.

"Doggone your pictures," he said, shaking the rope at us. "If there's a real man among you, let him step up and claim this rope!"

No one stepped up, even if the rope was worth six dollars. "Alright," the Colonel finished, "the rope will be in my office whenev-

er its owner decides to claim it."

The "owner" knew a darn sight better than to claim the maguey or he'd have been on his way to Mexico. Even if he couldn't understand a word of English he could sure read signs.

I guess we had been in the Garden about a week when the Colonel noticed something was amiss in the rotation of the bronc riders. One big, loud-mouthed hand, Bud McDonald, who claimed he had won the diamond-studded bronc riding championship belt the year before at Cheyenne, hadn't been riding. He had been assigned Two-step (one of the worst buckers) twice and each time he had been "sick."

This third time, Cy was to hold for him and had Two-step in the arena but no Bud. The Colonel, who was always there on Isham watching, rode up. "Where's his rider?" he bellowed.

"Don't know," Cy replied. "He should be getting here."

"Well, by Godfrey," the Colonel said, "he's stalled for the last time! Out he goes!" All the other buckers had been ridden out and Two-step there without a rider was balling up the act. "Put someone else on him and get him out of here," the Colonel ordered.

Cy yelled, "Fetch your saddle, Webb, and hurry it up." At the last minute, Walt Cain had borrowed my saddle to ride an extra-bad horse and had left me his narrow-fork Garcia hull. When I screwed that dinky saddle down on the big, wild-eyed bay I knew I was in trouble. Double trouble. Two-step bucked different than any other horse and although I hadn't yet seen him do his stuff, Cy and a couple of the old hands had damn well schooled us newcomers. Two-step got his name from hitting the ground with his feet first out on one side then on the other, leaving the rider sitting on the stirrup-fenders more than in the saddle seat.

During that three-hundred-foot ride, I "rattled from his ears to his tail" but I at least was still on him when he hit the barrier and was snubbed by the pickup man. I not only got a good hand from the audience, but from Cy and the Colonel also. Cy later told me Two-step could make Harry Brennan (who had been with the show the year before and had twice won the championship belt at Cheyenne) bite the tan-bark any time he tried to ride him.

So Bud McDonald was out of a job and the Colonel said, "Anyone taking up a collection to get the four-flusher back to Colorado will be counting ties along with him."

There wasn't one of us who would have chipped in on a collection anyway, so Bud put on the crying act to Evelyn Thaw (who didn't know what was up) that his "mother" was on her death bed in Denver and he had no money to go to her. Evelyn had shelled out $250 and stained her pretty cheeks with a flood of tears as she hurried Bud on his way to his nonexistent mother.

One Sunday, Frank Winch, the show's publicity man and the manager of the Buick agency, came to the Garden and gathered up what cowboys and Indians they could locate for a tour of Coney Island, and presently twenty-three shiny Buicks, with Colonel Cody in one, were there to pick us up. The Buick man asked us to wear all our regalia but admonished us not to scratch up the cars. I don't believe there was a cowhand in the lot who had ever been in an automobile, so we jumped at the invitation.

Our hosts hadn't fared too well with the Indians. Sunday was always their day for a dog feast, so only about half the Indians were in the caravan. We had noticed their dogs had been diminishing but thought nothing of it until one Sunday Ben American Horse and Robert Little Dog invited us to join them in the feast. It so happened we managed to have "important business" elsewhere.

I had eaten dog stew with Old Yellow Calf and his young wife in 1906 at their teepee. Not knowing the ingredients at the time, I pronounced it a fine stew. The young squaw was so bashful she never once looked up as she squatted by the campfire, playing with her toes when she wasn't patting down the pancake-like pones on the ashy coals. They, too, were very tasty.

On the way to Coney Island, the car I was in caught fire in the middle of the Brooklyn Bridge and was abandoned. We were taken to a huge, circular, glass-walled restaurant for lunch and when a crowd gathered round with faces pressed against the glass, we cowboys decided to give them something to look at. We began eating like a sty of starved hogs, fighting over the food and hitting one another over the head with stalks of celery. Then Harry Lewis, a gangling, mean-looking hombre from Crazy

Woman Creek, Wyoming, and I unholstered our six-shooters. Some of the boys ducked under tables and the crowd outside fell over each other getting out of there.

That's when Buffalo Bill thought we were carrying our horseplay a bit too far. "Boys! Boys!" he called, hurrying over to us. "For God's sake, try to act like little gentlemen instead of a bunch of savages!"

THIS IS THE SADDLE AND SPURS THAT WENT WITH ME TO THE SHOW IN 1910. THE SADDLE IS STILL IN FINE SHAPE AFTER SIXTY YEARS OF HARD USE. IT WAS MADE FOR ME BY OTTO ERNEST IN SHERIDAN, WYOMING, IN MARCH 1910. I MADE THE SPURS FROM A FOUR-LINE MANURE FORK AT THE M BAR RANCH AND BRAZED THE SILVER ON THEM IN PHILADELPHIA IN 1914. NOTE THE EIGHTEEN-INCH SWELL FORK AND HIGH CANTLE.

Frank Winch hollered over and said, "This'll pack the house every show, Colonel. Best publicity we could get."

We were all mounted and lined up one evening for the Flags of All Nations entry when the Colonel came down to the base-

ment and said, "Cy, hold everything here!" We couldn't figure what was wrong and presently a prop man rushed down and stuck a white dove on the spike of Nobby Clark's British flag. As we made our entry to loud applause and finally stopped in a wide-spaced U, our horses facing the audience, the Colonel slowly entered and rode to the center of the arena. Taking off his hat, he announced in a loud, though solemn voice: "My friends, I know this will grieve you as it does me, but I have just received word that our beloved King of England is dead."

The stunned quietness seemed to pervade the Garden and instead of the lively martial music that always started us into an intricate, galloping spiral before exiting, the cowboy band improvised a soft dirge that accompanied our walked steeds through the back curtain. The gloom that handcuffed the audience rubbed off on us, for applause is the heart and soul of show business.

Our three weeks in the Garden had been a valuable "college of knowledge" to us cowhands. We had decided that old Buffalo Bill's bite wasn't half as bad as his growls. That contract, with its fear-inducing clauses, had become just so much hogwash to us. We were continually slaughtering every rule in it. We didn't ogle girls, we simply met oodles of nice ones (as well as many fine fellows) and when any of us wanted complimentary tickets for someone, usually girls though, we'd go to the Colonel's office. The pitch never varied: we always had run across a cousin or two, or an aunt or uncle.

"How many tickets did you say?" the Colonel would ask as he began initialing "comps." If everything had gone smoothly that day, we would up the number of "relatives." He never refused us, but once when I hit him up for some comps, he wagged his head as he signed the ducats. "It sure beats hell," he chuckled as he handed me four tickets, "how danged many relatives you cowboys manage to scare up back here."

The last day we were to be in the Garden, I had gotten a comp for a particular girl who I wanted to come see me ride that night. Furthermore, I had asked Cy to give me Two-step, as I had never ridden him but that one time. I felt I would have no trouble this time, as I'd have my own wide-fork saddle.

Cy held for me as before and I wasted no time on preliminaries. Reaching for the reins (which were always tucked under the headstall below a bucker's left ear) I said "Cut 'im loose!"

Two-step's first leap was always head towards the sky and this time, when his head came down under his brisket, it pulled me down with it. Someone had substituted the bucking-mule's short-reigned bridle for the regular long-reined one.

At the first jump, my chaps belt hooked over the saddle horn and I was riding on my belly. I couldn't get bucked off and I couldn't stay on. Then, near the barrier, the chap lace broke and I hit the tan-bark on my stomach, sliding feet first. My shirt was shoved up over my head, my chaps hobbled me, both wrists were sprained and my eyes were blinded from being full of tan-bark. Not having a guide dog, I had to be led out of the arena. It was a very ignominious ride, although ultimately that girl became my wife until death did us part.

Later, my ex-friend Gaspipe came up and said, "Now, you smart bastard, maybe you won't try chasing any more girls away, if I ever find another!" I then "saw the light." We were even-steven and good friends again. What with both wrists swollen and hurting so bad I could scarcely hold the weight of my bridle reins, my eyes still streaming water and being sure I was ruptured from that saddle horn, I decided the old Colonel had told the truth at our first meeting about his show broncs being tough. Well, he'd had his bad tumble and didn't bellyache none, so I guessed I could take it.

That night as we were ferried across the Hudson I got the scare of my life. Mexican Joe Berarri, Smoky Warner and I were in the forward end of the ferry to guard against the buffaloes jumping overboard as there was nothing but a big chain across the bow. At the first blast of the foghorn, the buffaloes made a run at us, crowding our horses tight against the chain. But that wasn't half of it! Over 100,000 pounds of frightened, trumpeting elephants were squashing the camel herd and their tender against the buffaloes, which nearly mashed our horses. That black water was the most ominous sight I ever want to see.

After a week on the road, we began to realize the enormous expense attached to a show. The average cost of moving the two sections was around $5,000. Three thousand meals a day at twenty-one cents a meal. Mountains of hay, straw, oats and bran would be stacked on the lot when our second section composed of Pullman and stock cars (the latter only for arena stock and buffaloes) would pull in.

The first section preceded the second by many hours, so the "razorbacks," canvas men and cook-tent crews, could be on the lot when we arrived. The twelve-ton range wagons and those with the huge steam cookers were always the first loaded so they would be the first ones off the long string of flat cars. The ranges would be fired up and the steam boilers steaming even before they reached the lot.

The first weeks on the road in the spring are often the bad ones. Rain, mud and sometimes snow are not conducive to big crowds and we often heard bitter arguments between Colonel Cody and his "silent" partner, Gordon W. Lillie (Pawnee Bill). One day a big one erupted and could be heard all over the lot. Pawnee Bill, either on his ranch or with his own show before teaming up with Buffalo Bill, had been a stickler for low wages. (He also owned a bank, so perhaps that was the economic reason.)

"I can get all the cowboys we need for $30 a month," we heard him say. "So why throw dollars away?"

The Colonel's booming response should have shredded the walls of his private tent. "I'll tell you why!" he said. "In my book you get just what you pay for! We've got three of your pet Oklahoma Sooners here now and they're not worth their oatmeal. One more peep about my boys' wages and we'll split the blankets and split 'em quick!" From then on, if Pawnee Bill voiced a peep, he did it in the solitude of the pay wagon.

There were very few days during the entire season that the redhead was not at the Colonel's table, but in Auburn, New York, we missed her— missed her because she was so friendly, down to earth. We soon discovered the reason for her absence was that Mrs. Lulu Cody had arrived on the scene. And after being around her for a week we cowhands hoped the redhead would soon be on deck again. Mrs. Cody only stayed a few days, then returned to her Scout's Rest Ranch at North Platte, Nebraska. The Colonel had tried for many years to divorce her but couldn't make the grade. He said she had gotten everything he possessed and hounded him for more. She was no sooner gone than our redhead showed up.

We had Sundayed in Auburn and the Colonel decided to give a show for the fourteen-hundred inmates of the prison. That was a day to leave an indelible mark on our memory. The entire show, prairie schooner and stagecoach was inspected at the big gate and four overhead guards counted everyone, on horseback or on foot. When we were ready to start the show in the many-acred yard, the prisoners—all except those awaiting the electric chair—were brought out.

In addressing them, the Colonel used his usual greeting to audiences, except that he now omitted "La-a-dies and…" He now said, "Gent-le-men, you don't know how glad I am to see so many of you here today. I…" He got no further. Hundreds of stools (they

BORN IN OHIO, ANNIE OAKLEY WAS ADOPTED INTO THE SIOUX TRIBE BY CHIEF SITTING BULL, WHO NAMED HER LITTLE SURE SHOT. SHE APPEARED IN BUFFALO BILL'S WILD WEST SHOW FROM 1885 TO 1901. HARRY MET HER IN 1910 AND AGAIN IN 1913, "SHE WAS A WONDERFUL PERSON AND WE HAD MANY PLEASANT VISITS."

were also the prisoners' toilets) were tossed in the air and roars of laughter lasted a full minute. Whether the Colonel had made the blunder through repetition, or did it on purpose, it gave the felons the heartiest laugh of their lives.

The Colonel (to the discomfiture of Pawnee Bill) was always giving blocks of tickets to police, firemen and children's institutions; in fact, just about every organization. In one city, he arranged for dozens of blind children to be brought in so they could meet and touch the clowns and enjoy the laughter. We often wondered how the show made any money. At the entrance, where Major Burke sat taking tickets, there were two containers and it seemed there were as many comps as there were paid admissions. Owners of every store and building where the big lithographs were displayed got free tickets.

Furthermore, we learned that in 1906 when the show was abroad, even though foul weather was plaguing him, he had sent $6,000 in checks to the Mount Vesuvius homeless and San Francisco earthquake victims.

Business had been great all through the Mideast, but when we hit central Illinois we ran into a drought-stricken land that cut down attendance until we were showing to more comp holders than we were those with money. This put a mantle of gloom not only on the Colonel, but on the performers also. Then we were in a Wisconsin city where the Colonel said, "By golly, Johnny, we'll make up for all the money we've lost these past weeks."

The show lot was on a big flat and the Colonel had one hundred feet of extra canopy and seats installed on each bleacher section because at least twenty thousand patrons were expected. But that's where old Jupiter Pluvious got in the act. An all-night, all-day deluge put a foot of water between the street cars and the show lot four-hundred feet away.

With rain still pouring down, we put on two full shows to about fifty people in the afternoon and exactly nine that night. Needless to say, all except one held free tickets. We performers, especially the bronc riders, were furious and said so, but the Colonel said, "Those people are just as entitled to see a full show as if we had a full house."

It took ten teams and two pusher-

elephants to get some of the wagons to the paved street. Rosie and Queen, with heavy pads on their foreheads, literally lifted the rear end of wagons out of the mud. Their tremendous power caved in the doors on one commissary wagon and while they were helping, they also ate a forty-pound sack of oatmeal and a crate of crackers that had been crushed when the doors caved in.

Of course, the drought and then this flood didn't put the Colonel in what might be termed a "joyous mood" and the next day two of the top bronc riders got fired. Drunk as hoot owls, Buffalo Vernon and Ben Brown had wrecked a saloon and whipped a bevy of police. The Colonel did get them out of jail though, before giving them their walking papers.

But sunshine and enormous crowds soon had the Colonel in fine fettle and it was a good thing he was. Gaspipe had come staggering in just before an afternoon show as we were all sitting around a few feet from the Colonel's tent, and said to Cy, "'Spose th' old Tiger'll give me a couple o' comps?"

Gaspipe was lit up half the time but it didn't affect his riding. "Sure he will," Cy said. Some of the cowgirls egged him on, as he was a barrel of fun and they all used him as a butt for their jokes. We could see the Colonel at his desk writing. Every free moment was spent writing. He wrote to hundreds of boy scouts and personally answered his fan mail. (He was one of the organizers of Boy Scouts of America, along the lines of the original organization in England.)

Gaspipe wended his way to the Colonel's tent and, gripping the pole with both hands, wobbled around. "Shay, Colonel," he said, all but pulling the tent down. "I've got a couple floozies out here an' won'ered if you'd give me shome comps."

As Gaspipe staggered back towards us with his comps, the Colonel watched him leave. Then, resuming his writing, we could see his shoulders shaking. Evidently, Gaspipe's frank speech had hit his funny-bone.

I believe as mean a trick as any played on Gaspipe was one executed to perfection by Goldie St. Clair, a bronc rider. During a three-day stand, Gaspipe had become interested in a very pretty girl and on our last afternoon, he was showing the girl and her mother about the grounds.

Furiously raking a hairbrush through her long, golden hair—Goldie shot out of the girls' dressing tent. "So, you're at it again, huh?" she all but screamed, brandishing the brush. "Well, you get in there and mind the baby you, you…" Crying as if her heart would break, she turned back to the dressing tent. Before Gaspipe could collect his wits, the woman and her daughter were gone. Later on Gaspipe said, "Goldie, I ought to yank that pretty head of yours off and throw it so damn far you'd never find it!"

Various writers have cast Buffalo Bill as a drunken braggart and a coward. Others have him a superman, a teetotaler and a great hero. He was none of these. As for his drinking, he drank alright. But it was in the form of heavily-spiked eggnogs. A tall glass of this potent drink was always on his desk. But working at the furious pace he maintained, he needed it. As to his being a braggart, I once asked him about that memorable knife fight with Yellow Hand and got a surprise.

"Bunk!" he snorted. "Just plain bunk. Ned Buntline concocted that story and as far as I know, Yellow Hand died of old age."

We often heard city folks complain about all shows gypping the public. That was one thing Buffalo Bill wouldn't stand for, but we saw instances where the show got gypped. Just before show time someone with the town marshal would come along and say, "You're on my land, here! Your lot is over there." It would be too late to tear down everything and move or investigate, so the Colonel twice handed out $500.

In one city they upped the fee for tapping a hydrant from $50 to $500, and water was one item we had to have. Not wanting to disappoint the children by moving on without giving a show, the Colonel paid the shake-down fee. Then, at the boundary line as we left Canada, the Red Coats wouldn't allow our section to leave until they recovered a bugle someone had taken from a small store's window.

For three hours, the police went through the train searching berths and valises, with the Colonel imploring the culprit (whoever he might be) to hand over the bugle. At last, the old beat-up five-dollar tooter was found under a soldier's bunk. That prank cost the Colonel a sizable amount for the extra train-hours and we came in too late to give an afternoon show.

Then, two days later, two of the range

wagon cars jumped the track in the mountains, and we not only lost another afternoon show but had the unique experience of eating three meals at one sitting. At the dining tent entrance, the caterer handed out the breakfast meal tickets at five p.m. and, just inside, the tickets were taken by a show official. Then while we were eating the caterer came along and placed dinner and supper tickets by all the plates, and in turn they were picked up. Looked goofy to us, but I guess there was a reason.

There were often damages to settle and lawsuits filed to put the Colonel in bad humor. In Sacramento, a mouse either ran up an elephant's trunk or perhaps simply scared it, and all hell broke loose. Yanking up the four-inch by three-foot picket pins, the herd went berserk. The show water wagon was bowled over and with trunks curled over their backs, they went trumpeting down streets, through yards, knocking everything in their way to bits. Their charge caused an ice-wagon team to run away, in turn breaking a fire hydrant. That no doubt cost the Colonel plenty, too. And we had just learned the Colonel had recently lost over $300,000 in an Arizona mining venture. No wonder he was sometimes moody.

In the mornings on reaching the lot, two cowboys would have to guard the buffaloes until their pen was set up and this often caused trouble; big trouble. Crowds were always on the show lot of a morning and just let the herders become more interested in girls than buffaloes and Old Barney or Bob (two monster bulls) would be tossing someone in the air as if they were a rag doll. This happened twice, and although we weren't called on the carpet we were steadily priming the Colonel for an explosion.

While driving the buffaloes to the show lot in Los Angeles, Old Barney and Bob suddenly turned aside and entered a big glass-roofed flower shop. When the attendants saw the shaggy monsters browsing on the plants and screamed, there was very little left of flowers or shop by the time we got the buffaloes out.

The show was nearing its closing date and everything that could aggravate the Colonel seemed to beset us. In El Paso, two sooty-faced young girls appeared before the Colonel with the complaint that they had spent the long night's run in the stagecoach with two "cowboys" who had promised them

jobs on the show.

This was serious business and when Johnny Baker ordered us to the Colonel's tent we demanded that the soldier string also be there. Soldiers, more than once, had put on old discarded hats and bandannas and pretended they were cowboys. Luckily for us, the girls put the finger on two soldiers. The soldiers were fired and the Colonel bought tickets and had an escort accompany the girls back home.

Shortly after this, Harry, the Colonel's valet, hadn't fixed the long white hairpiece right (the Colonel's own hair was pretty scraggly) and when the Colonel swept off his hat to salute an unusually large crowd, the wig came off with the hat. The crowd, as well as we performers, roared with laughter and Buffalo Bill made a hasty exit. When we got out of the arena, the Colonel was chasing Harry all over the place as he bellowed threats.

Then the next morning, one of the buffaloes badly mangled a man and woman and, as if that wasn't enough, the show lot was in a monstrous, worked-out rock quarry. It was a beautiful setting; horseshoe-shaped with trees bordering the hundred-foot-high cliffs. An enormous crowd was expected in that town and we weren't disappointed. Trouble was, with less than five hundred in the seats (probably, mostly comps) there were about fifteen thousand viewing the show from above. There had been skullduggery, somewhere.

Although this and the wig episode had nothing to do with our deportment, matters had progressed to the blow-up point and Johnny Baker notified all cowboys and girls and soldiers to be at the Colonel's tent immediately after supper.

We had expected a dressing down but nothing like what we got. The Colonel wasted no time on preamble. "I've called you rascals here," he began, "to tell you a few things, and doggone your pictures, you better take note! You've done just as you pleased all summer, but from here on out

you're going to dance to my music!"

Panting up and down before us, he raved on. "You've got so lazy and good for nothing that you've loused up and demoralized the entire show. But, by Godfrey, you're at the end of your rope! Not one red-penny of your holdback do you get! In my thirty years at this business, I've had a good many thousand boys and girls, but never a one as rotten as this whole group. And, Johnny, I want you to rehearse them until their legs fall off and if you don't you'll go down the road with them!"

Once out of earshot, Johnny said, "Whew!" and wiped his brow. It didn't worry him like us cowhands. Withholding our holdback spelled volumes. Wyoming was worlds away. Oh, Johnny made us rehearse a few numbers including the quadrille, which had been so bawled up a time or two by the girls that nobody could tell what we were trying to do.

Beautiful weather, short night jumps and packed houses put the Colonel in good humor, although we were taking no chance and trod the "straight and narrow." As the closing date neared, I was surprised one day when Pawnee Bill called me in the red pay-wagon to ask if I wanted to go to Maine with Joe Berarri to pick up a car of buffaloes he had bought for his big ranch at Pawnee,

THE WILD WEST SHOW DID NOT LACK FOR PERFORMERS. BUFFALO BILL IS SEATED ABOVE THE COWBOY BAND IN CENTER OF THE PHOTO AND TO THE RIGHT AND BELOW CHIEF IRONTAIL, WHO IS STANDING BY THE TEEPEE. PAWNEE BILL IS SECOND FROM BUFFALO BILL'S RIGHT.

Oklahoma. He said I could then help feed buffaloes and cattle until show time next spring. He was experimenting in crossing buffaloes and domestic cattle and already had quite a herd of them. They were called Cataloes. But when I learned I was to work for my board, I declined the offer.

The closing day in Texarkana was both joyous and sad. No longer would we have to wrestle broncs in mud up to our knees or in 110-degree heat, or have kneecaps and ankles dislocated by that five-foot football barreling at us with three tons of Injun horses behind it. This had happened to several of us who played this wild game against the Indians, and Gaspipe and I had had it!

Oh, there had been lots of fun and good times, too, and we were going to miss the Cowboy Band and Hyram and Symanthy Timothyseed (two of the funniest clowns in the business) and the jolly Cossacks. We wondered if we would ever see little Arlene Palmer again. Probably not. Nor Chief Iron Tail and all the friendly bucks and squaws, and especially Robert Little Dog. Robert had begged Gaspipe and me to go to the reservation with him for the winter. Then we would all join the show again in the

spring. A wonderful gesture but we had other plans.

Yes, this day would see the parting from many friends we would never again meet. Old Troupers told us, "Don't worry, when the old bugle blows in the Garden next year, you'll be there. It gets in your blood." We didn't know it then, but they were right.

The dining tent was festooned like a convention hall for our last show meal and the gold-embossed menus would add prestige to a Waldorf table. But unlike most of our meals, there was no horseplay or banter, as if all were bogged deep in the same thought—parting. Then Buffalo Bill was atop a table, voicing his farewell words.

Although his writing was a scrawl few could read and he knew little about spelling, he was one of the world's great orators. Few could equal him. But all that matters in his long speech is when he looked down at the cowboy and cowgirl table and addressed us. We were wondering if we would get our holdback pay. "We better," one cowhand whispered, "or there'll be a hell of a batch of cowboys ridin' th' rods home."

"In all my years running this show," the Colonel was saying, "I've employed thou-

sands of cowboys and cowgirls. Some bad, some good. But I want you to know, and I say it from the bottom of my heart, that you are the finest, the most congenial lot I've ever had. I can't recall a single complaint from you and I'm glad I've never had occasion to so much as raise my voice in an unkind word to any one of you.

"Most of the folks we have showed to this season we will not see again, as this and a couple more are my farewell tours. I know my years are closing in on me, but I hope the good Lord spares me for a while yet. At least until I see all your faces back for rehearsal next year. Charlie Meidus has your wages and holdback pay in envelopes waiting for you. Thank you all and goodbye."

Several of the cowgirls were weeping out loud and here and there cowhands' noses were being violently blown.

"Whatcha know about that?" Gaspipe said, once we were outside. "If them wasn't unkind words he flogged us with that time, by God, I'd hate like hell t'have him mad at me. I'll say this much though. He's all man!"

"Yeah," I said trying to clear a frog out of my throat, "the old booger's jake in my book, too." ∎

Cows and calves have been grazing the high country and it's time to bring them to lower ground before it snows. These cowboys are moving the remuda up to a line camp to use for the gather. Each has a string of six to ten horses and they will select their mounts depending on the day's work and the kind of country they will be working through.

"TRAILING TO THE HIGH COUNTRY" © J.N. SWANSON

The Day the Jarbidge Stage Was Late

It's still a mystery as to what happened during that storm of 1916.

Apprehension further corrugated the features of the half-dozen miners and freighters as they discussed the lateness of the Jarbidge stage.

"I still maintain," Bill Ball was saying, "somebody ought to take a horse an' head for the summit. That grade's slicker'n a peeled onion this time o' year an' I'm feared we'll find Fred an' his outfit hangin' in the pines a thousand feet down that mountainside."

Ball had hauled in a load of freight the day before from Rogerson, Idaho, and knew the danger that lurked along that grade in winter.

"Bill's right, fellows," one put in. "Yuh know how close the road hugs the canyon there for half a mile. Scared me just t'prod my jackass along that stretch o' the Crippen Grade."

"Well," offered another, "let's wait another hour and if Searcy ain't here we better start investigating. But the way I see it, if the stage did go over the rim, Fred would have jumped clear and could be walking in for help right now. He's young and I don't believe he'd stick with that stage if she slewed off into the canyon."

"Yeah," Jack McLaughlin put in as he stood in the door peering into the howling blackness, "but supposin' he was hittin' a pretty good clip an' shot off sudden like? You remember when Whistlin' Rufus' wagons slid off that Bullion Grade? Well, he jumped but hit the bank an' wound up under a wagon all smashed to hell."

So ran conjectures as anxious watchers took turns going to the door. Face-cutting snow and the eerie howl of wind screaming down Jarbidge's narrow street only added to their worry.

"I don't like the looks of this," Postmaster Scott Fleming said. "I'm like Jack, there. I'm afraid something drastic has happened. Searcy's a hell of a good teamster but that don't mean something can't happen on that grade and especially when it's icy."

He looked at a shelf clock. "Two hours late already. But it's a fearful night to go looking for anybody in a blizzard that cuts your eyeballs out. We should do something, though, besides stand around worrying."

But on this particular night of December 5, 1916, there was little anyone could do except worry. Suggestions of sending a rider to the grade came but as an early night had closed in they decided to wait a while longer.

Where the hell could he get to? Only a few hundred yards to go and four horses and a stagecoach disappear!

Jarbidge, Nevada, was a unique town in that it was located in a natural, monstrous amphitheater setting. According to one old inhabitant, some mighty upheaval had blowed one side of a crater out and slung gold from hell to breakfast. There had been gold everywhere, alright! Even as late as 1930, when the camp had passed its heyday and its most valuable asset being an ideal picnic and recreational spot, Oz Miller, a young Elko bank clerk, made a strike right beside a street that caused a resurgence of activity in the old camp.

While picnicking there, Oz had sat atop a huge boulder while his wife snapped a picture of him. He had handled plenty gold coins during his years with the bank and was qualified to know gold when he saw it, and he now saw it. That boulder enriched the fifteen-dollar-a-week bank teller by several thousand dollars.

Following that discovery, butchers, bakers and barbers rushed in and overturned every boulder and dug into every likely spot. But that one boulder had been it and the camp returned to a mecca for picnickers to play and rehash the events that had rocked this very spot in years gone by.

Those in the post office were still arguing plans pro and con regarding the next move when a roulette dealer came in, slammed the door against the gale, dug snow out of his overcoat collar and stood looking at the crowd. "What's the matter?" he asked. "You fellows all look like the mines had all gone bust!"

"Worse than that!" the postmaster replied. "No stage yet and we're worried."

"The hell?" said the newcomer. "Well, Newt Crumley will be a damn sight more worried if anything's happened to that stage. He sent me over to pick up a wad of cash he had coming on it to cash the miners' checks. Wonder what could have happened?"

"What we'd like to know," came the lament. "Fred's been late a couple times but never anything like this."

"You don't suppose...," began the Crumley employee, then halted.

"What was you about to suppose?" someone asked.

"Just wondering," came the thoughtful answer, "if the stage driver knew there was over $3,000 in the mail for Newt's saloon and decided to go west with it?"

This put a new angle on the missing stage but Postmaster Fleming discredited such a hairbrained theory with, "Searcy would never do a stunt like that and I'll bet my bottom dollar on it!"

"He's still human," Tuscarora Jack offered, "and subject to human impulses. If you happen to remember Joe what's his name who carried mail from Winnemucca to Denio on the Oregon line was also a fine fellow and look what happened there. Him and the mail sack disappeared when he got wise there was cash in that sack. Only $500, too, and here Searcy may have known there was several thousand in his sack."

"Still won't believe it of Fred," Fleming defended.

At that moment a new arrival had something to offer that not only shed light on the stage but deepened the mystery. "Now, that's damn funny," he said. "I happened to be talking with old lady Dexter and she mentioned seeing the stage go by her house just when the storm hit us and she says Searcy had a passenger beside him."

At this revelation, his audience could only look at one another in open-mouthed wonder. After much incredulous cussing, Bill Ball was dispatched with the news bearer to Mrs. Dexter's house at the far end of town. When they returned their puzzled faces and words electrified their listeners.

"Then where the hell could he get to?" several asked as questions tumbled over each other. "Only a few hundred yards to go and four horses and a stagecoach disappear! That Dexter woman must be seeing things that ain't."

However, this news set the town people running here and there like a hill of ants that had been poked apart by inquisitive boys. Even though they wouldn't go so far as to call Mrs. Dexter a liar, they had doubts about her vision or mind or both, and in minutes men with lanterns were scouring the snow-covered path the stage would have to travel that short distance to the post office.

"This whole thing is screwy," they decided and were on the point of heading for the Dexter home and "have it out with her," when a horse's sneeze off in the willows drew them hurrying in that direction. There they found the lead team tied to a willow clump and crumpled on the footboards in front of the seat was the body of driver Fred Searcy. A bullet had

THIS PHOTO WAS TAKEN OF A STAGECOACH AND TEAM ON THE SEARCHLIGHT, NEVADA, TO NIPTON, CALIFORNIA, ROAD IN THE LATE 1800S. IT WOULD HAVE BEEN A SIMILAR OUTFIT FOR THE JARBIDGE RUN.

entered the back of the skull and appeared to have emerged near the right eye and in the blood-soaked frozen snow on the dash they found a mushroomed bullet judged to be of 32-20 caliber. In moving the body a 32-20 Colt (a popular model of the day) was found shoved beside the left waistband of the driver's overalls. His heavy overcoat, with a wide belt around it for warmth, had prevented any defense of himself if there had been any suspicion in his mind of foul play.

It took but a glance for the awed and saddened men to piece together events. Somewhere along the willow-bordered stream the killer, probably known to Searcy, had hitched a ride. Either that or had taken advantage of the storm and boarded the stage from the rear unseen by the driver. So ran conjectures. Yet there was Mrs. Dexter's statement that two men were sitting on the seat when the stage had passed her house while it was still light and before spitting snowflakes had turned into a raging blizzard. No shot had been heard and why prop up a dead man and drive almost into the heart of town with the body?

"This whole thing is gettin' crazier by the second!" Bill Ball exclaimed.

In untying the team, large footprints were found where the willows had shed

the force of the drifting snow. Later, the slashed-open leather mail pouch was accidently kicked from under the snow near a small bridge that spanned the stream. It took no Sherlock to deduce that the murderer was headed for the opposite side of town from that of the stage, giving mute testimony that the killer was still in town. Frank Leonard took charge and gave orders.

"One of us must ride like hell to Rogerson or straight south for Elko and get word to Sheriff Harris. Some of us better stand guard at the stage and road. With only one way out of here it's a cinch we've got a murderer in camp!"

Bill Ball, having a fine saddle horse with his freight team, volunteered and in moments was crowding his mount through the night.

Sheriff Harris was a methodical man, loved by the general public and admired even by those he had arrested and brought to trial. His cosmopolitan nature allowed him to know practically everyone in his bailiwick and though he never jumped to conclusions, once he arrived in Jarbidge he listened to those who had already uncovered marks and objects that pointed a finger of suspicion at a man working in one of the mines. One thread of evidence lay in the track of a large dog beneath the stagecoach and near the bridge where the first-class mail pouch had been discovered.

Such a dog was known to the town folks as a hobo, belonging to no one yet a friend to everybody. Now folks recalled seeing the dog tagging along with a certain miner of late and this miner had an over-size foot such as the prints found by the tethered team. Aside from these damaging marks, the miner was in disfavor in camp over "jumping" a mining claim and cabin.

When the year's assessment work isn't done by midnight of December 31, it became open season for claim jumping seconds after the midnight deadline. This is the law in most mining districts. But the owner had been able to prove his assess-ment work had been more than met and the claim jumper had been fined heavily for his premature deed. Now it was known he needed money. So with several pieces of inanimate evidence, including a blood-smeared coat found in the suspect's cabin, Joe Harris met Ben Kuhl when he came off shift at the mine.

"Ben," he said, "I'm sorry, but from the looks of things you'll have to come to Elko with me so we can maybe get some certain matters cleared up."

That was Sheriff Harris' unostenta-tious way of saying "You're under arrest," and the reason half a lifetime was spent as Elko County's sheriff.

"Fine, Joe," Kuhl replied with almost a laugh. "Looks like you suspect me of doing in Fred Searcy. But Fred was my friend and besides I had nothing whatever to do with that dirty deal."

This writer happened to be in Elko the day Kuhl was brought in and heard on every hand the venomous statements and shouts of "That low-life bastard'll hang for this!"

Kuhl didn't hang. What had at first glance looked like an open and shut case turned into a mass of confusing evidence. There had been bloody handprints on the leather mail pouch and a 32-20 Frontier Colt, the exact model as that of Searcy's, found in Kuhl's cabin with one empty shell in the cylinder. As for this and the blood-caked coat found in his cabin, a

partner of Kuhl's swore that neither the gun nor the blood-smeared coat belonged to Kuhl. A couple other defense witnesses said Kuhl had been in Crumley's Saloon from the time he got off shift until the news of the murder broke. Pinned down on the time element they admitted it could have been the evening before.

But the one big drawback was the lack of expert ballistic and fingerprint testimo-

What had, at first glance, looked like an open and shut case turned into a mess of confusing evidence.

ny which is now so common and could have clinched the case. Defense lawyers lacking a spark of concrete evidence for rebuttal usually rely on confusing and dis-crediting witnesses, and so it was in the Kuhl case. A question by the defense sent a roar of levity through spectators and jury when Sheriff Harris was asked if he could "positively swear that Fred Searcy for unknown reasons had not shot himself?"

"I believe it safe to say," replied Harris, "that unless Searcy was a contortionist and had several lives, he could not have shot himself in the back of his skull and then placed his gun back in his holster, rifled the mail sacks and tied up his team."

Despite the fact that not a penny of the $3,000 consigned to Newt Crumley or another $1,000 the mail pouch held was found in or about Kuhl's cabin (and as far as anyone can say, never has been found), Kuhl was promptly convicted and sentenced to life imprisonment and served just under thirty years in the Car-son City prison.

But to some of the old-timers and to hordes of picnickers, that incident gave plenty of work. They upended every boul-der near the path the killer had taken between where the stage was found and Kuhl's cabin and to this day occasional neophyte "prospectors" have been seen going over that ground with Geiger coun-

ters and the latest metal detectors. Who can say, but perhaps someday a ready-made minted "mine" may be discovered in the old town by some member of that ilk whose faith never dies.

As for the few old-timers, they invari-ably used the Kuhl-Searcy incident as a calendar by which to reckon time. I was at Newt Crumley's Commercial Hotel bar in 1945 and overheard a dried-out, bony little individual arguing some point. It was Tuscarora Jack. (No doubt there were some who knew his name but if so they never bothered to use it.)

"No," Jack said, "you're wrong. We didn't find Searcy an' his stage the next day a-tall. It was that same night! It was just three or four days before that I'd made my first big strike an'…"

"Way off base, Jack," came his oppo-nent's positive statement. "It was the next day! Besides, I never knowed of any sec-ond strike by you."

"The hell I didn't!" Jack stoutly replied. "Made that one in Tuscarora an' ten years later hit 'er again at Lone Moun-tain! Made 'er slow but by God we sure cut Ol' Tige an' run the cats up the creek while she lasted! Ain't that right, Jim?" he asked the bartender. "I spent enough right over this bar to have owned the whole shebang here."

"You're right, Jack," the bartender agreed. "You sure slung the cash around while she lasted. Kept half the town drunk for two months and I don't mean maybe."

"You're damn tootin' I did!" Jack proudly admitted. "An' if my face is good for another round for me an' Hank I'll let yuh in on somethin'. I'm headin' for the hills tomorrow. Got my eye on a good outcropping up north o' here. An' for you," he said, turning his rheumy eyes on his free-drinking partner, "if anybody ever wants to know anything about the date that Jarbidge Stage was late you just send 'em t'ol' Tuscarora Jack." ■

Just Tell Me Where It Hurts

When Curley the barber turned chiropractor, he created more than a headache for Doc Irvine to fix.

 Our chiropractor in Elko was the most knowledgeable "bone crusher" I have known, and I have visited so many I might be called an authority on the art of "manipulation."

Dr. Irvine came to Elko in the early twenties and had his ad flashed on the theater screen at intervals, which really got him known in a hurry. His message, "Come in and let me cure your headache free," had sufferers flocking to his third-floor office.

One person who took advantage of the generous offer was our local barber Curley, a bull-necked fellow with Atlas muscles. As Doc Irvine related the experience to me, Curley came in complaining of an awful headache.

"Where is it, Curley, front or back?" he was asked.

"Hell, I don't know," Curley replied. "It's all over!"

"M-m-huh," grunted Doc, as he felt about the patient's neck and explained at great length the cause of most headaches. Then, catching Curley off guard, he snapped his chin over a shoulder, and after a vigorous massage Curley was asked about his headache.

"By God, Doc," Curley said, "she's gone!"

Now, barbers and bartenders being known as the most voluble of any human class, they are also credited with having a cure for most ailments. So it was with Curley. When Charley Sewell came in for a shave one morning, and Curley fished out a steaming beard-softener, Sewell said, "Wish you'd put one of them hot towels across my forehead, Curley. I got a

busting headache. I'd take Doc Irvine up on his free cure if I had time, but I've got to catch this train for Salt Lake."

"Well, we'll fix Mr. Headache in jig time," Curley promised as he returned the towel to the steam tank. "Sit up and tell me where it hurts the most."

"All I know," came the reply, "is that it feels like a man's in there running a jackhammer."

Curley ran his thumbs from skull bone to spine. "Yep. Just as I suspected. It's a slight case of occipitalis, which means a muscle spasm is pressing the occipital bone tight against one side of the transverse crest. But we'll…"

"Well, I'll be doggone, Curley," Sewell said in an amazed tone. "Where in Sam

Hill did you learn all that stuff?"

"Oh," Curley modestly admitted, "I just picked up a bit here and there on anatomy as I went along." Waggling Sewell's chin and skull in his ham-size hands, he gave a sudden snap that brought a yelp. "Whambo," Curley said, "that got 'er!"

Whether it got the headache or not is beside the point, but as Doc Irvine later explained it left him with the knottiest problem of his chiropractic career.

"I heard steps racing up the stair flights," he said, "and was thinking the building was on fire when in came Curley wild eyed and out of breath. 'Doc,' he wheezed, 'come quick. Think I broke Charley Sewell's neck!'

"When we got to his shop I was out of breath, too, but one glance at Charley and I was too scared to breathe anyway. There he lay with his eyes bugged out and his chin resting on his left shoulder. Hell, no, he couldn't talk. He couldn't do nothin'. We didn't dare try to get him to my office, so I went to work. Had to go easy or I'd finish what Curley had damn near already done, and by the time I got that occipital bone back in place half of Elko was crowding in the shop to see what had happened!

"But I'll bet a dollar against a hole in a donut ol' Curley will stick to barbering and let me do the manipulating around here. In fact he agreed that it was a little different than bulldogging a steer and he guessed it was a case of each man to his own trade." ■

Teenage Lion Hunters

Catching a mountain lion was no easy task for any rancher, so there was considerable excitement in Pine Valley when two brave girls bagged a too-bold cat.

Pioneer women were usually able to cope with any emergency, whether it was wielding a fifteen-pound rifle or expertly combating ailments that befell families. But those early-day females had nothing on two of

In 1916, the government had declared war on every breed of predatory animal, and in subsequent years employed hundreds of hunters and trappers. Sheepmen were annually losing ten to fifteen percent of their woollies—especially lambs—to

south for fifty miles, there were more of those killers of sheep, deer and horses than in any other area. Dan Rand, a Pine Valley rancher, and I got within a hundred yards of a pack of six lions while out hunting horses, but they all escaped into the timbered ledges nearby. Another time when we were following a band of mustangs along a mountain trail, we saw a lion leap on one and both go rolling down the hillside. Naturally, we couldn't stop to investigate the result.

But one particular lion in the area was not only a savage killer but also a loner and exceptionally bold. It also seemed to have a preference for horseflesh and particularly for those belonging to the Buckskin family.

Nooky and Maggie Buckskin had a small ranch near Mineral Hill with a few cows, a couple dozen good saddle and work horses, and so many children they were like the old woman who lived in the shoe. The two older boys were away fighting the Kaiser's armies, and an older sister, Hattie, was married. The youngest boy, Web, and four kid sisters—Emma, Florence, Mary and Nevada-Rose— remained at home.

There had been intermittent losses among the ranch horses for some time and the family believed that the deaths were due to the malady "brain fever," and that coyotes had been eating on them. Nooky set traps around the carcasses, and though many coyotes were caught, it was small compensation for what he supposed was this brain disease.

Then one day, out in the big juniper-speckled pasture, he found a horse carcass covered over with sticks, tree limbs and raked-up dirt. According to legend, this was a sure sign of a lion kill and that Mr.

TWO CUTE LION KILLERS, FLORENCE AND EMMA BUCKSKIN.

my Pine Valley neighbors. The girls in this little drama were of Shoshone blood, and as for bravery and versatility, Emalene and Florence Buckskin could put the old-timers in the back seat.

coyotes and bobcats. But the most cunning of all killers of grown stock was the mountain lion.

Along the rugged range beginning at my Pine Mountain ranch and extending

Lion had covered the horse for future use. But after Nooky set traps around the carcass, the lion never came back. Even with Nooky's traditional cunning, the big cat was a problem beyond his know-how. Lion hunters were known to have little success unless the lion had been treed or run to cover by experienced lion dogs, and the Buckskins had but one small ranch dog.

To outwit the lion, or lions, Nooky took to keeping his horses in the stockade corral, but this was a nuisance and used up winter hay. After there had been no loss for a week, the family decided their horse killers had moved away to satisfy their appetites on deer and sheep. Bands of sheep were then trailing south to winter range around Tonopah, so there was no lack of lion food.

One November morning before sunrise, Nooky went out to the corral to let the horses out in the big pasture. On reaching the gate he noticed that the horses were moving nervously about. Suddenly a big lion leapt off an old shed roof onto a horse's neck, and the horse dropped as if felled by a sledgehammer.

With a yell, Nooky ran for his rifle, but on his return the lion was headed across the meadow with the little dog yipping in pursuit. The commotion brought the family running to the corral where the horse lay thrashing about.

"It's Brownie!" little Nevada-Rose screamed. "He's killed Brownie! Oh, Daddy, do something, don't let him die!" Brownie was the girl's pet horse, and she was inconsolable.

Just then a neighbor rode up. He and Nooky had planned on going to a silver prospect but the bedlam of crying girls changed that plan in a hurry. The two men tried to get the horse on its feet, but it was beyond help. After all ministrations failed, the bullet that had been meant for the lion ended Brownie's suffering.

Exasperated, Nooky sent word to the chief of the Biological Survey in Reno to send up a government trapper with lion dogs. But since no such hunter was available, it was up to the Buckskin family to make out the best it could.

By December, no more horses had been molested and the family believed that the little dog's chase had scared the

lion away for keeps. But they continued corraling the horses every night.

One Sunday, Nooky, Maggie and Web went to do some work on the silver vein, leaving the four girls at the ranch. Emma, sixteen, and Florence, fifteen, were to keep watch over the pastured horses while their younger sisters, Mary and Nevada-Rose, were left to their own devices.

At noon, Emma and Florence galloped home for a hurried bite to eat. On returning to the pasture, they saw where a horse had slid down a steep hillside in the light snow. They could tell from the first scattered marks that a lion had leapt from a juniper tree onto one of the horses. Still mounted, they were staring in wonderment when some magpies flew up from the sagebrush in the draw below. There the girls saw the lion tearing at the neck of the dead horse, so they cautiously retreated out of the animal's sight to form plans.

"Emma," Florence chattered, "you hurry back and get Daddy's gun! Hurry fast, and bring the .22 rifle, too. I'll stay and watch and if it leaves I'll try and scare him up a tree." It took but a few minutes for Emma to race the half-mile home, grab Nooky's 25-35 carbine and the .22 pump-action Winchester.

The lion was still eating when Emma returned. Sneaking through the junipers, the girls selected a good spot and opened fire, dropping the beast in his tracks. On circling the carcass, guns ready, the girls could see that Emma's 25-35 bullet had torn half the animal's skull away and Florence's .22 had entered its ribs. But in their excitement they put several more slugs in him for good measure. As Nooky said later, "That lion skin looked like the girls had been practicing on it all day with shotguns!"

The girls had a hard time at first getting a horse near the lion. Then, tying

Emma's horse to a nearby juniper tree, they blindfolded him with her coat and hobbled him with a bridle rein. Then they dragged the lion over to the horse. Amazingly, they were able to lift the heavy, blood-soaked beast into the saddle. They later explained, "It was because we were so excited and determined to accomplish everything ourselves that it lent us a strength we never knew we possessed."

There was a lot of rejoicing in the Buckskin home that night when their parents returned. And if it had been a hippopotamus or Bengal tiger the girls had slain, it couldn't have caused more exclamations as the news spread over our fifty-mile punkin-line telephone.

But just killing the lion and ending their horse losses wasn't quite enough.

THE PROBLEM LION, AFTER THE BUCKSKIN SISTERS DID SOME VERY CREATIVE TAXIDERMY.

Emma and Florence decided to make a trophy. After the lion was weighed, tipping the steelyards at 135 pounds and measuring just over nine feet, the girls carefully skinned it. Then they spread a paste of cooked oatmeal and saltpeter over the flesh side for tanning.

When the skin was tanned and pliable, they sewed it back to shape. Then, with the help of little Nevada-Rose, who was a natural-born sculptress and designer, they stuffed the lion skin with straw and paper. And all of us who viewed the somewhat shortened form, caused by tanning, pronounced it an excellent job of taxidermy. ■

Old Spook

Around Cortez Valley, this wild horse was a legend.

 My friend Al Hernig insisted that I could catch that uncatchable wild horse. Most mustangers referred to him as The Walker Black. Indian Dicey called him Old Spook. I called him, at one time or another, everything in a mule skinner's vocabulary.

I refer to him as a mustang, but he was no more mustang than a thousand others around him. He was a little of everything from the early Spanish pony to our modern Morgans, some Hackney, a bit of Arabian. But regardless of size and ancestry, if they were wild, to us they were mustangs.

This story had its inception, I suppose, when I emerged from the Hay Ranch barn cussing like a bogged-down freighter and shaking my rawhide riata which had suddenly acquired as many ends as a centipede has legs. A blankety-blank pack rat had chewed it to pieces as it hung from my saddle astride a manger. To further compound the loss, it was the only rope on the ranch. It was then I noticed our weekly stage halted in the road and the driver, Charley Walker, was hunched forward on the seat arguing with my friend Al Hernig.

"Hell's fire, man," I heard Charley say, "might as well send a blind man out to catch bullet-hawks with a dip-net!"

Charley was an old mustanger of few words but when he did speak you could bet your boots it was gospel.

"Harry'll get him," came Al's voice. Such definiteness made Charley sit bolt upright.

"The hell he will!"

"The hell he won't!" returned Al with finality.

Reckon I'd best introduce Al so you'll know what I'm talking about. He was one of the Philadelphia Hernigs of dairy fame, and like many city fellows was nuts over horses, saddles and such doodads. Also, when he took a notion for something he got it; there was a heap of mule in Al. If he called a Clydesdale an Arabian, by gum it was an Arabian. Also, or worse, he had a hero-worship complex and I was it.

I had met Al when I was east with Buffalo Bill's Wild West Show and he thought I could do anything the book called for. For instance, I was hardly back on Nevada soil where I was working for the Hat outfit, when he wrote asking me to get some elk tushes as he'd joined the Elks Lodge. For a while this had me stumped. There weren't any such critters in the whole state and here I'm supposed to shoot him a couple right now. Only things in my neck of the desert were Indians, mustangs and whirlwinds. But, as always, I was Johnny-at-the-rathole and through a Jackson Hole friend Al had his molars in jig time.

Anyway, another year had rolled around and here he was on a look-see around the West. He'd expected to have to fight Indians every step to the ranch but he figured it was worth it for the three-day stopover. And having everything else—including a Tennessee walker—he'd taken a notion for a mustang to ship home; hence his pestering the stage driver to sell him one.

Charley had an overabundance of them. To him they were just so many junipers. Buy one and he'd throw in two, all for ten dollars. Providing, that is, you caught them. But being a mustanger, and square, he didn't want to unload one on Al. He'd never take advantage of a tenderfoot. Oh, wouldn't he?

"Harry'll get him," persisted Al. "Just because you guys can't catch him doesn't mean he can't." Al was getting himself, and me, too, more disliked by the minute. Charley was shouting something about the so-and-so dudes as he wrapped the lines around the brake staff. I meandered over.

"What's th' rumpus?" I asked.

"None-a-tall," said Charley, stuffing something in his pocket. "I've just sold this [Charley described him] the Owyhee Injun Reservation, is all!"

"What's the deal, anyway?" I asked Al when Charley was out of earshot.

"I just bought a horse," he said, hopping about. "I offered him a hundred dollars," he all but whispered, as if it was a downright steal, "and he finally took it."

"Any particular one?"

"Old Spook," he said triumphantly. "The one…"

"Well the jumped up…!" I began, then thought better of it. "Al," I said, "you don't know a mustang from a load of hay or you wouldn't give a plugged nickel for one. At least, not that one! Now who in hell's gon'ta catch him?"

Old Spook wasn't exactly a pinto. Outside of a white head and white stockings to his knees and hocks he was jet black. Instead of being chalk-eyed like most "paints" his right eye was black as coal. That is, until he got mad. Then it glowed like a big ruby. Indian Dicey had given me Old Spook's pedigree and the amazing story of his early life. It was unbelievable, yet one confirmed by other mustangers.

Old Spook was the foal of an ordinary "broom-tail" and sired by a hot-blooded stallion that had escaped the Dean Ranch to mingle with the Cortez Valley mustangs two years before he had been recaptured. Charley Walker and some Indian mustangers had corralled the pinto's band and for the promise of a pint of whisky, Dicey had volunteered to ride the queer-marked stallion that had been the object of many a long, hard chase. Forefooted and saddled while he was down, Dicey had stepped aboard.

With murder in his ruby eye and dynamite in his feet this bellering critter had gone "higher'n the moon and swapped ends faster and wickeder" than anything his small audience had ever witnessed. Finally the latigo broke and Dicey and saddle came down on top of the stockade corral. Someone forefooted and "busted" the raging animal and in a few minutes he was wearing Charley's Bar H brand and minus his reproductive glands. The instant his feet were free he leapt up, landed on the seven-foot fence, hung there a moment before tumbling out and streaking for the hills.

That was in 1906. The black's bridle teeth showed him to be over five years old at the time. Although he was seen at intervals and chased aplenty he escaped being corralled again until July 1910 when, by a lucky break, Dicey, Shelton Raine and Joe Walker, brother of Charley, slapped the gate shut on him at the Tom Jewell ranch in Pine Valley.

Once again the suggestion was made, augmented by a jug of spirits, that someone "scratch out" the so-and-so right then and there. The lot fell to Shelton and in a matter of minutes the pinto was forefooted and saddled, and with Shelton all set the fireworks began.

But the glossy ten-year-old had profited by his years, and before many jumps Shelton dropped his shot-loaded quirt and went for leather. Then came a terrific crash as the gate flew to splinters, and with his rider left among the wreckage the black was out and away once more.

This time, however, he didn't get far. Hitting a barbed wire fence he slid along the top strand until a post sheared off and he fell squealing and kicking in the tangle of sawing wires. By the time Jewell and Dicey got to him, his pumping life stream had already run twenty feet down the adobe slope.

Jumping on his gory, flailing head Dicey at last got him by the under jaw and nose, but his bull-dogging was wasted energy; the cyclone of a moment before was fast sinking into helplessness from loss of the hissing blood. From his right breast to the top of his neck was a gash you could lay your arm in and unable to stomach the sight, Jewell held a wobbly 32-20 Colt and sent a bullet through the black's neck right behind the ears. The saddle off, they returned to the corral and bolstered themselves with generous swigs from the gallon jug.

"Now," someone said, cussing, "we'll have to wrangle a team in the morning and drag his carcass away!"

When morning came, Jewell stood on the porch in his drawers gazing about. Then he let out a startled yell that aroused the others. Unbelieving, they hurried partly clad to investigate. Even though they'd consumed a lot of whisky there sure wasn't any mistake about this. There were the weaving splotches of blood leading up a sandy wash to prove it hadn't been a dream. Numerous wallowed places showed where the animal had fallen, lain and risen to stagger on. Making no effort to overtake him, the three hastened back to finish the jug. Well, one good thing, they wouldn't have

to wrangle that team!

Months later, the black was jumped out of a gulch on Stafford Mountain, bordering Cortez Valley. But this time there wasn't that seal-sleekness to the coat nor the beautiful arched neck that had caused mustangers to halt their mounts and gaze in open-mouth admiration. He was now bony and shaggy. It no longer mattered, though. All who knew of his deep scars, and few didn't, were no longer interested. The only interest was the wonderment as to how he could possibly have survived not only the tremendous loss of blood but Jewell's bullet also. His survival became legend.

As the months passed, he was unmolested in so far as mustangers were concerned. Nor were they interested in the chunky roan always seen trailing close upon the black's heels. Sometimes they would be flushed out of some coulee but more often the two would be sighted atop some peak, as if alert for their enemy on horseback. Let a rider a mile off turn in their direction and they'd be gone.

This uncanny wariness came near being their undoing, though. Mustangers and cowhands who thought they had a fast mount took to giving them a whirl just for the fun of it, then finally in dead earnest. The two inseparable geldings had become a cactus in every mustanger's boot. If it wasn't a single foe disrupting their browsing it was finding themselves fogged to hell and back by whole relays of determined riders. These were the tough customers to elude, but Old Spook, as Dicey now called him, had become a pastmaster at dodging and sneaking.

One March day when mustang vitality is at low ebb, half a dozen riders were scattered at strategic points, with Willow Corral Pass the stakeout for the remuda. That day, their grain-fed mounts had forced the two weary-legged fugitives to near run their hearts out before night ended the chase. At least seventy-five muddy, slushy miles had been put behind them and if there is any such thing as a "horse laugh" those mustangers must have received it that night.

Had Old Spook but known it, though, his escape was by the mere skin of his teeth. Two riders, who had lately turned to killing mustangs for their hides, yanked

THE WALKER BLACK, BETTER KNOWN AS OLD SPOOK. THIS PHOTO WAS TAKEN IN 1916, ONE YEAR AFTER I CAPTURED HIM. IN THE TEN YEARS I TRAPPED FOR THE GOVERNMENT, OLD SPOOK CARRIED ME OVER THIRTY-THOUSAND MILES.

carbines from their scabbards just as the staggery victors topped a ridge but a few yards away. But a third man, with a six-shooter in his fist and a sense of fair play in his gizzard, slid his mount to a halt and hit the ground.

"I'll kill the first sonovabitch that plugs one o' them horses!" he yelled. So the steaming renegades were spared to put the shelter of a hill behind them and drop down into the night.

Summers and winters passed with other pitfalls aplenty to guard against; the most subtle of all being the secret corral that, overnight, sprung up in some canyon, its flaring wings hidden in the hillside bushes. But Old Spook outsmarted this by leading his roan partner along high divides and never running in gulches or canyons when crowded by his enemies. He also learned to forsake water for days on end when water holes were flagged by mustangers. But now, on this August day in 1915, let us return to my friend Al.

All afternoon and well into the new day I argued with him that I couldn't catch the black, even if I had the best mount in the country let alone the worst. The only horse on the ranch where I was stationed that could be called a mount was a blue roan I used to chore around on as I watched over a field full of broodmares and their colts.

Blue was a ridgeling and was mine to worry over for the simple reason no one on the home ranch would have him around. For the edification of those not familiar with these half-eunuchs of horse-dom, let me say that they are the pure essence of worthlessness. They'll haze every mare to a whisper and chew the backs off any gelding they can outrun. And that not being fault enough, he was ringtail. Before a ringtail horse can be jumped out to head a critter he must first wind up his tail before his brain seems to grasp the idea that he also has legs.

Anyway, here I was with old Blue for a mount, a hunk of rat-eaten rawhide for a

lariat and I'm to jog twenty miles or so to find and catch an uncatchable mustang. Might as well try holding back the dawn, though, as to argue with Al, so to keep the peace and convince him I had at least tried, I'd go off somewhere and lay in the shade of a cut-bank 'til evening then come in with a big "No luck" tale.

It now being two a.m., I decided I might as well feed Blue some rolled barley, drink some java and with a biscuit in my pocket get going. Nothing like an early start. It would also look pretty much legitimate to Al.

A smoky moon was sliding behind the high Cortez Range to my west when a sudden desire gripped me to cross over and take a look-see down in the valley, but long before we had gained the summit the east was already a blaze of fire. Going to be hotter'n hell with all the blowers going, I told myself. Ten o'clock found us on the shimmering Cortez Valley floor with Blue panting like a lizard and me asking myself what I'm supposed to do now. Hunt some shade, I reckoned. Then Al's unshakable faith in me began taking effect and I found my eyes scanning distant horizons. Then I thought of my mount and the absurdity of the whole business. What a joke!

Suddenly my gaze was riveted on a tiny speck that had topped a rise a mile across the valley—mustangs. I started to move on. Then the huddled, drab picture changed color. Just how was not perceptible. Yet something had changed it from just mustangs. It looked like—by the powers of Mount Kelly, it was! No mistaking that blaze of white! My heart raced as I bent low over Blue's motionless neck. Then I had to laugh. Times on end I had come in close contact with this wily critter when I had a top mustang-horse between my knees instead of a mount that would be as useless as a plow mule.

The little group would mill around, pause, then come forward a few yards. That was Old Spook's method of looking things over. What puzzled me was the fact

that he had taken up with any bunch. They came forward slowly, warily. A good thing they were looking into the sun. Growing bolder they began playing and scampering like kids as they galloped somewhat towards me on a trail that led to a mud spring near some dilapidated buildings.

When a depression hid them from view I lost no time in getting behind a small knoll where sly peeks told me of their progress until they were abreast of me but a few yards away. But, I had been mistaken. Old Spook was the only wild one in the bunch. All the rest were gentle Morgan mares and a few colts belonging to Ed Thomas, the former owner of the tumbledown premises a short distance away. With his glossy mane waving out from the high arched neck he was more regal than ever I had seen him. They passed so close I could see the white splotch on his neck, a reminder of where the 32-20 slug had passed through. I wondered about his roan partner; probably dropped by some hide-hunter's rifle.

Old Spook was plenty pinched in the flanks yet he showed no signs of sweat and this revealed a story as if I had witnessed it. Indians, preparing to catch mustangs, had flagged all the water holes around Stafford Mountain, Willow Corral and Scotch Gulch. For lack of other material they do this flagging by uprooting large sagebrush and standing them, roots up, about the water holes. Mustangs give these terrifying objects a wide berth. After a few days Mr. Injun slips out, removes the brush and is ready to rope any mustang that's fool enough to tank up.

The sight of those Morgan mares made me want to shout in glee. They'd been corralled, pampered and petted by their owner until you could almost walk up to them on the open range. Oh, for a decent mount! Such a chance came but once in a lifetime and this was it. The horses were nearing the abandoned homestead so, being no cover between us, I might as well show myself. I recalled having seen a small sheep corral near the spring and I began laying plans. The mares were on home ground now and should be easy to corral in any sort of pen.

Mounting, I came from behind the knoll. Just as I expected! Old Spook had me spotted instantly. He whirled, circled,

Spur, whip, shout and turn, with the dust so thick I collided with a cow as she dashed out of the water hole. I wondered if Old Spook was still with us.

came back a few jumps then tore through the mildly interested mares as if he had to be in Texas by sundown. I moved closer. The corral was still there and the mares headed for it as if they were used to being there. Old Spook dashed back into the bunch and I whipped up. Never let a mustang slow up. That's when their noggin starts working. Before I realized it we were abreast of the open-end corral and on past it. I whipped and spurred, and the mares turned easily, only to dodge past the opening going the other way.

It was whip, cuss and gee-haw Blue around until horses were going in every direction, with Old Spook running rings around the whole layout. Oh God, if I could just scatter out! Two sixteen-foot panels had been removed from the corral but the mares simply wouldn't pause long enough to see the hole. And still, for some reason, Old Spook stayed with them. It was uncanny. I firmly believed it was ordained that I was to capture him.

Spur, whip, shout and turn, with the dust so thick I collided with a cow as she dashed out of the water hole. Dust so dense I wondered if Old Spook was still with us. He was! I cussed, cajoled and pleaded. Poor old Blue was so winded, so slow in turning that I came near jumping off and going it afoot. Then, without making sense, Old Spook streaked through the opening with the mares hot on his heels and Blue right among them. Tired as he was, this blasted ridgeling was running true to form and letting sex crowd all else out of his head. Seconds later, what with fighting Blue to keep him away from the mares, I had us fenced in. So far, so good!

I unbuckled my riata. Damnation! Never expecting to have any need of it I had brought along this twenty-foot piece of the honda end. As I tied the end fast to the saddle fork I cussed every pack rat ever to be born. I'd have to work fast before Old Spook got his bearings.

Trouble soon commenced, though. The instant I eased Blue toward the crowding mares he threw his mouth wide open and lunged for Old Spook who knocked down a couple of colts and cleared the fence. But he stopped just as suddenly as he had

departed, so jerking back a panel I was soon whipping at an angle around him. Hearing a commotion I turned to see the mares coming hell-bent right in my dust. By now Blue was so addled he could only ring his tail and trot, but I somehow got the band back in the corral. How? It was one of the world's mysteries. This time Blue went "cold-jawed" and plowed in among the squealing, kicking mass and had his forelegs over a mare's ridgepole when my kneecap stopped a pair of hind feet. Then, when I was bent double from pain, another old biddy almost kicked my face off. I'll never know how I got there but I found myself on the ground far outside the corral with the mares and my quarry still inside.

Eventually, and swinging Blue around like one would a saw log in a pond, I spurred back and got the panels wired up.

Every time I started toward Old Spook he would tear through the bunch and threaten to hop the fence. How in Sam Hill was I to get close enough to snare him with a twenty-foot rope?

But every time I started toward Old Spook he would tear through the bunch and threaten to hop the fence. How in Sam Hill was I to get close enough to snare him with a twenty-foot rope? That was the problem. With the tiny loop ready to be tossed I eased ahead and when Old Spook's eye told me I had reached the limit of sneaking I socked in the spurs and threw. But instead of the one quick jump needed to shorten the distance, Blue only went "oomph" and rung his tail. Old Spook did a lot of milling around but didn't jump the fence so I dabbed another loop that bounced off his ears. If he just had horns, I told myself after a dozen throws, I'd have had him easy! There simply wasn't enough loop left to go over his head.

Then it happened. A loop no larger than a dinner plate went smack over his nose and up over his ears. I had him! Hooray for me! Just then about half the mares in the corral got their bellies over the rope and were taking Blue, Spook and

most of the corral with them. When the air cleared, he was still tearing around on the end of the rope and the next oversized problem was to build a hackamore on him that would stay put.

With a decent mount under me I could have "busted" him in short order, but after trying out every trick I knew luck favored me and he got tangled up and went down. At last a makeshift hackamore was on him and I stood back and took happy stock of conditions. By now my knee was as big as a county fair pumpkin, my clothes were like a hula dancer's skirt, and my busted lips stuck out like the bloody snout of a razorback hog. But, man, was I happy!

Now it was poor old Blue's job to drag him home and for the next five miles we played leapfrog with each other. If he wasn't up in the saddle with me he was heaving back and leading about as easy as a plow under a foot of sod. Well, if Blue could hold out and lug him up the mountain we'd be hunky-dory once we got to the top. We'd have a downhill pull from there, plumb to the ranch. But the steady drag was starting to cause trouble. The half hitches were cutting into Old Spook's nose, shutting off his wind. Wasn't much I could do, though, but keep going.

Blue was staggery tired as we neared the Cortez summit. It took frequent rests for him to navigate at all, and when I'd urge him on his tail would go round like a windmill. I'd been guarding against this but it happened! His tail got over the rope and was clamped down on it. Now if there's one thing that will rejuvenate a fagged-out cayuse this is it. Like an explosion, Blue's nose went between his hind legs and with Old Spook snorting and kicking we took back down the mountain in twenty-foot leaps. Between the bucking and the rope sawing into my thigh I could neither stay on nor get off, but the problem solved itself. We all got tangled up and went rolling over and over.

The next thing I knew the rope was parted at the saddle fork and Old Spook, now spooked aplenty, was tearing down the mountain. At sight of this my heart sank so low I never even thought of giving chase. It wasn't any use. He was a goner this time! But it just goes to show you what luck can do. No sooner had he hit the flat than he went end over end and began cutting all sorts of didoes. Hopping on my one good leg to where Blue had quit rolling, I crawled on and wasn't long in getting to where Old Spook was turning back flip-flops. It was plain he'd be strangled in the next few seconds for the loops around his nose had cut off his breathing.

In roping wild horses on the range we become hardened to the sickening sound and sight of a strangling horse, but to see this beautiful animal swaying and gasping for just one tiny bit of precious air was too much for me. We had all cursed, threatened and admired him at one time or another but the memory of all his cunning, his stamina, his continuous struggle for survival, now brought forth an overwhelming surge of pity. Disregarding the flailing feet that tried to batter in my skull, my fingers fought to loosen the nose hitch before he pitched forward. I would gladly have cut the rope and let go but even my knife had disappeared. Gradually the rope began giving and with a final heave it came free just as a tremor ran through him and he lurched forward, his head and me under him.

Perhaps it was sheer imagination but I could have sworn there was a light of gratitude in his puffed, bloodshot eyes as air and life rushed back into him and he just laid there, legs twitching, sides heaving. It was then I noticed Blue had near been scalped in his roll down the mountain and, even though he had done everything wrong and wasn't worth the lead it would take to kill him, I hurriedly anchored the riata once again around the pommel then put my arms around Blue's neck and hugged it to my throbbing face. There's something about a horse that makes a feller do those things.

Travel was slow on the homeward journey with me groaning every step and fearful that at any moment Blue's tail might get us kettled off again. But I can say this for Old Spook, he never once let the lead rope so much as tighten.

A bright, midnight moon found us back at the ranch, the corral gate wide open as if there was no doubt that I'd bring home the bacon. Well, I'd sure

delivered the goods and expected an effusion of praise and backslapping. None came. Only: "God what a beauty!" Al kept saying as if reciting a litany. Finally: "Have any trouble getting him, Harry?" My mind was murdering him but I mumbled a nonchalant, "Not a bit; easy as pie."

"I knew you wouldn't," he agreed. "Now tomorrow I'll break him gentle and ship him home when I go." Oh, what fools we mortals be, I thought.

Al didn't break Old Spook "tomorrow." He didn't get any closer than the tip of the bronc reins, much less mount him. But Spook didn't mind it a bit when I petted and handled him. He even seemed to like me as I hobbled about and led him around.

I again handed Al the reins, but Old Spook jumped past him and kicked him in the stomach. I'd have to ear him down that was certain, even though I hated to disillusion Al. He maintained the horse wouldn't buck if he could just get on him. Getting a mouthful of ear I pulled Spook's head down while Al worked his shoe in the stirrup and got aboard. When I let go, Old Spook let out a squall like a butchered pig and his belly went higher than my head. As I have said, Al was stubborn. But after four bad falls, the last time landing on his back on the snubbing post, he called it quits and I fell heir to Old Spook. Al was mighty glad to be rid of him at a loss of a hundred dollars and a lot of skin.

Perhaps this narrative should have its ending here, for to give Old Spook his dues would fill a book. But he deserves a bit of eulogy.

He was easily broken and in two months was running mustangs alongside the finest mounts in the country. Many a fine mustang fell victim to my loop, but Spook was so fearless on the steep downgrades that it would make your hair curl to let him have his head.

During the many years I rode him, he never got over his aversion to upside-down sagebrush. Mere sight of one and he'd swap directions like a rubber ball thrown against a rock wall. Being thick through the chest gave him a strong heart, and although you could see the big artery pulsating in that deep neck gash, he was tireless and indestructible. In the ten years I trapped for the government, he carried

me over thirty thousand recorded miles. His lot was hard. Yet, in the middle 1930s he still looked and acted like a six-year-old. To be sure, his eyes weren't what they used to be; he now saw upended sage where none existed and his moods were unpredictable. As Charley Russell once said, he'd "kick your head off one minute and help you look for it the next."

In 1938, I was joking with Charles B. Sexton, general manager of the Eureka-Nevada Railway, that I'd bet him twenty bucks Old Spook could outrun his train to Eureka. The train (termed the Slim Princess by the natives) and roadbed had fallen into such disrepair that the schedule had long been nine hours between Palisade and Eureka, its terminus a distance of eighty-one miles.

Perhaps I would have lost my bet but I still think not. However, before we were to compete, fate suddenly stepped in, in two forms. The railway—locomotives, roundhouse and track, in fact every piece of metal—was sold to the Japanese for scrap. Then, as the wreckers were pulling up the last joint of rail on the Palisade end, Old Spook also was no more.

With six fine saddle horses in the field I took Old Spook—he being the handiest—to run in some work stock from the range. The job wasn't as easy as expected and before the bunch was corralled my mount had to get down to some real mustanging. It was in the corral I noticed Old Spook was a mass of lather and staggered as he walked.

Tossing my saddle on the ground, I watched him dropping down and getting up, all symptoms of colic, and when the usual remedy failed to help I headed for a vet friend in Elko, fifty miles distant.

Doc Henderson guessed it to be a ruptured blood vessel, probably in the stomach, as this was quite common among old horses, and while he offered no hope he urged full speed on the return. Doc owned and loved horses, but we were too late. His diagnosis had been correct.

As I knelt beside that old, scarred head I looked up through the swimming haze to ask Doc something. But he had turned his back and was fumbling for his handkerchief. ∎

"Time to Think" © J.N. Swanson

A ROUND JUNIPER-POLE CORRAL IS MADE LIKE A STOCKADE AND USED
TO TRAIN A GREEN HORSE, WITH POSTS HIGH ENOUGH SO THE HORSE
CAN'T GET DISTRACTED. HE WEARS HOBBLES MADE FROM GUNNYSACKS
AND HAS A HIND LEG TIED TO A ROPE AROUND HIS NECK WITH AN EASY-
RELEASE SLIPKNOT. THERE IS A HUNK OF CANVAS TIED ON THE BACK OF
THE SADDLE WHICH FLAPS AS HE TROTS. HE'LL KICK IT UNTIL HE GETS
TIRED OF THAT AND THEN THE COWBOY WILL GET IN THE SADDLE. THE
LEATHER BAND ON THE HACKAMORE CAN FLIP DOWN OVER HIS EYES TO
TEMPORARILY BLIND HIM AND KEEP HIM QUIET WHILE GETTING ON.
RIGHT NOW HORSE AND RIDER ARE THINKING AND THE COWBOY TAKES
TIME IN THE SHADE FOR A SMOKE.

The Last Shoot-out in Palisade

The young schoolteacher and the two old-timers named Bert were cozy as hens on a roost, until that explosive winter night in '32 when everyone jumped for cover.

 Palisade, Nevada, hadn't had a shooting for two whole months, which wasn't a bad average for a town of sixty residents. That is, the population might be called "fluid," like when the Southern Pacific was blowing a thousand-foot nubbin off the sheer "palisades" in order to take a kink out of its line.

As we have said, shootings were rare unless Old Judge Van Laningham came down from his monarchy at Buckhorn. "Judge Van," being marshal, deputy sheriff and Buckhorn's J.P., could always be counted on for double trouble in any town he visited until the night a .45 slug through his neck put him out of business for a couple of weeks. But since everyone said, "The old booger had it coming," no charges were pressed against Van's assailant.

The old judge had unlimbered his .45 and shot up Palisade's main saloon. Then he took potshots at those escaping from doors and windows, until a hunk of lead laid him low.

Yes, our town was ordinarily a peaceful spot. Moderns would term it a "togetherness town." A bit too togetherness it appeared after a cute Little Miss by the name of Margaret Watson took on the problem of teaching youngsters from six to eighteen years of age their three R's. Teachers in these small Nevada towns usually came from eastern cities as it gave them opportunity to absorb western lore as well as a fine chance to latch onto a husband.

Miss Watson may have been one who wasn't interested in a husband, because at the time of which we write, she was on her second term in Palisade and still

unmarried, although there were no lack of suitors from the nearby ranches.

Perhaps in time some cowhand might have gotten her in double harness had it not been for the most unorthodox triangle any town had experienced since the Klondike Gold Rush, when Rex Beach's two chief old characters quarreled over a chit of a girl, sawed their boat in two and dissolved their partnership.

Come summer on her second year back in Palisade and it looked like the town would have Miss Margaret Watson as a permanent teacher. For $75 she had purchased two small houses and a huge ex-ice house thrown in for good measure. One of these cabins, with the help of neighbor Bert Gilman, was turned into a dollhouse for herself and she rented the other to another Bert by the name of Bruffey.

The sheer-walled palisades formed a funnel for storms and blizzards to sweep through and the school house being a quarter-mile from Miss Watson's house, it behooved the two sixty-five-year-old Berts to look to her welfare especially so in winter.

Bruffey and Gilman were both good cooks so each morning Gilman would fetch over a fine breakfast of hotcakes, bacon and eggs and steaming coffee. Then in the evening Bruffey would have Margaret's house warm and a fine supper cooking for the brain-weary girl. There was little doubt but that Miss Watson appreciated this on a par with the two Berts' love of catering to her. And with a salary of sixty dollars a month and no food to buy, the town folks said, "Margaret sure has it made."

The winter of '32 was a bad one and

with Bert Bruffey's odd hours of wading through belly-deep snow to the Western Pacific line during nights put him in the Elko Hospital with double pneumonia. For weeks the prognosis was all bad and the general conversation among his Palisade friends amounted to "Looks like old Bert's a goner, wouldn't you say?" And Gilman was always the loudest worrier over Bruffey's probable demise though many detected a nuance of joy with his lament.

In Miss Watson, Bruffey had a loyal supporter and each Saturday found her by his bedside, something Gilman disapproved of, at least to those around Martinelli's Saloon. "Don't see what the hell good she thinks she's doing him," he would grumble. "Ol' Bert needs rest!"

One night, when several of us were present, Myra Hawkins asked Miss Watson if the two men, despite all their kindness, weren't often sort of nuisances when she preferred to be alone. "No," Margaret said, "those two old dears treat me as if I were a hotel guest. Naturally, there are times when just getting myself a snack would be a grand treat but I can't hurt their feelings. But just to let the poor dears know that being a teacher doesn't render one a total loss around the kitchen I often cook dinner on Sundays and have them over. No, there isn't the slightest problem."

Miss Watson might know the secret feelings of her pupils, but she was certainly blind to those of her two old benefactors. Bert Bruffey, assisted by Margaret Watson, stepped off "Number Two" of a late Saturday evening to find her house cozy with warmth from the kitchen stove. Gilman had known she would be on that train, as Number Two was the only westbound train, excepting an early morning train that stopped in Palisade. Apparently, he had no inkling Bruffey would be coming home.

There's an old saying about "No fury like that of a woman scorned," but whoever the author of those words was should have been around Bert Gilman when he glanced out his door that bitter cold night and through Miss Watson's window observed her with an arm around "Uncle Bert's" shoulders as he sipped something from a cup. His two months bout with pneumonia had robbed him of half his weight and nine-tenths of his strength.

When a terrific explosion blew half the window out and shattered Miss Watson's Coleman lamp, the ailing Bruffey was rejuvenated enough to drag Margaret to the floor with him just as another shot finished the window.

Then came several blasts and shotgun pellets demolished the bedroom window and splintered chunks from the thin Celotex partition between bedroom and kitchen fell on the huddled pair. "My God," Miss Watson gasped, "he'll kill us!"

"Prob'ly," Bruffey calmly replied. "That is if he don't run outa ca'tridges first."

But Gilman wasn't running out and as he yelled and circled the house he pumped shots through window holes and door. A twelve-gauge shotgun blast can make plenty noise at best but by the time several explosions echoed and reechoed off the palisades, folks later said they thought the S.P. powder house up by the ballast quarry had blown up.

"Why, oh why doesn't Nat show up to stop him," the terrified Miss Watson cried, "before he comes in and murders us?"

"With all this racket," Bruffey strove to assure her, "he oughta be showin' up pretty soon. That is if he don't hunt a hole like it seems everybody else in town has. Wish I was at myself," he added. "I'd go out an' bust that gun over the old fool's head."

Then he birthed an idea. "Maybe when he gets shootin' through the back window again you can slip out the door an' make a run for it." Folks always said if

you poured coal oil on Bruffey and set him afire it wouldn't excite him. Like when the narrow-gauge depot was enveloped in flames and the superintendent C.B. Sexton ran up to Bruffey in the act of eating a bag of apples. "What can we do, Bert," he moaned, wringing his hands. "What can we do?"

Bert studied the fire a moment. "Watch her burn, I reckon," he finally drawled through a mouthful of apple. Palisade had no firefighting equipment so there was logic in his answer.

The opportunity came, and Miss Watson was running as fast as her young legs

could propel her through a foot of snow, screaming, "Nat! Somebody find Nat!"

When a cry like this went up it meant real trouble, and be it a kid had fallen in the river or someone had cut a hand off on a buzz saw everyone looked to Nat Hawkins to remedy the situation. Nat was the town marshal and deputy sheriff.

Right then Nat was in Eureka, eighty miles distant, but that didn't mean the town was without law. The marshal and deputy sheriff job only fetched in fifty dollars a month so Nat often went on the narrow-gauge run to Eureka if the fireman, conductor or even the engineer

happened to be sick. At such times he handed his badge over to saloonkeeper Frank Martinelli.

Martinelli, like everyone else, had been alerted by Gilman's berserk shotgunning. Trouble was, Martinelli had put the gold and silver badge in the safe and in the excitement couldn't manipulate the combination and wasn't about to face maniac Gilman without plenty visible authority.

By the time the badge was finally pinned on, the Watson house had been riddled by upwards of twenty shots and Gilman was still shooting. The writer's

son and Nat's son Myron, and several other know-nothing kids who didn't know danger when they saw it, were first on the scene imploring the shotgun wielder to quit shooting.

Gilman had run in his house but came out shoving shells in his pump gun just as Martinelli and other grown-ups arrived.

"Bert," Martinelli ordered, "you're under arrest! Toss that gun down!"

"Like hell I'm under arrest!" Gilman bellowed. "I ain't throwin' no gun down, either, an' I'll kill any sonovabitch that tries to take it!"

It was a touchy situation and no fool-

BERT BRUFFEY, STROKING MISS WATSON'S CAT. AFTER THE SHOOTING, THE CAT LEFT THE HOUSE AS FAST AS ITS OWNER, BUT IT NEVER CAME BACK.

ing. Then someone remembered Miss Watson and not knowing Bert Bruffey had returned supposed Gilman had for some reason vented his wrath on her.

"If you've hurt that girl," Justice of the Peace "Pope" Lucey shouted, "we won't bother with the law! We'll hang you from the nearest telegraph pole!"

"Miss Watson's up to our house," Myron Hawkins piped up. "She's okay. He only scared the pants off her." That was good news all around.

"Well," the J.P. shouted, "he needs hanging anyway."

"You dry up, Pope," Gilman yelled back, "or I'll blow that big paunch o' yourn off!"

With that he swung the muzzle from Martinelli to the J.P. and pulled the trigger but Pope had already leapt behind the house. Everyone had too much respect for a shotgun to crowd him so remained at a safe distance, trying to shout him into dropping the gun and going along with Martinelli peacefully.

It was during this state of affairs that Bert Bruffey came weaving his way around the Watson cabin. "Hell, Bert," he said as he drew closer, "have you gone plumb crazy? You keep on an' you'll kill half the town! Give me that damn gun an' stop all this foolishness."

Bruffey was known to be a bit slow, both in head and action, but whether he was exceptionally brave or a twenty-four-carat zombie it made little difference to the awed crowd.

"Come a step farther," Gilman yelled, "and I'll blow your head off!"

To everyone's surprise the wobbly, stumbling Bruffey came a step farther and grabbed the gun barrel.

"Damn you!" Gilman yelled, as they wrestled for the gun, and blew a hole in the snow. Due to his weakness, Bruffey fell, pulling Gilman down with him.

"Somebody better get this old fool," Bruffey panted, as he hung onto the gun barrel, "before he hurts somebody."

Everyone immediately became a hero and Gilman was being held by a dozen hands and soon being pushed, led and dragged to the little jail up on the hill. He was known to be a cyclone when drunk but during the two seasons he and Bruffey had elected themselves a committee of two in watching over Miss Watson's welfare he hadn't been known to take a drink. Now it was evident the sight of Miss Watson administering to Bruffey had been the final straw.

Pope Lucey felt the circumstance far too serious a matter for him to handle legally, so Judge Edgar Eather was brought down from Eureka, the county seat, for a consultation. There was no doubt in Judge Eather's mind as to the seriousness of the incident. Even in Nevada, shooting at someone was a crime to be dealt with severely.

Testimony and the judge's on-the-spot investigation showed all windows shot out, door ruined, while every dress and unmentionable in a closet looked like all the moths in Nevada had concentrated on Miss Watson's finery. Also her dishes, porcelain ware and skillets "wouldn't even hold hay, now," as old John Craig observed.

Then there were curtains and little irreplaceable whatnots and jewelry to be considered as well as Margaret's mental anguish, to say nothing of attempted murder. A whopper of charges faced Gilman. Yet, there was the unquestionable friendship that not only the three principals had enjoyed, but the entire town as well.

"This is a case," Eather allowed in his summation, "that would have made old Solomon scratch his head twice before handing down a verdict."

Everyone excepting Miss Watson was in agreement. "What about my house?" she wanted to know. "And my dresses— everything?"

"That," the judge ruled, "would be a civil case. And it would be foolish to sue someone for damages when that someone has nothing."

The judge was reluctant to send Gilman to the Carson City prison, yet he needed to be punished for his night's foray, so he sentenced Gilman to the Eureka jail for eleven months for "disturbing the peace."

Bruffey and a few young and old admirers of Palisade's pretty teacher repaired her cabin the best that was possible but when that school term ended Miss Watson sold her three buildings for seventy dollars and vowed never to return.

Evidently she had absorbed all the "western lore" she cared for. ∎

Fightin' Larson

That woman would fight a buzz saw and give it a five-minute start.

 When Mary Larson died at age 87 we simply couldn't believe it. Although Mary barely waggled the scales at the hundred mark and was wrinkled as a prune, she was rated a well-preserved woman. Folks said, "Why wouldn't she be well preserved? She's stayed pickled all her life!"

Mary was a kindly soul, but cross her and you had a fight on your hands. As an old ex-sailor said, "Rile Mary and it's a case of batten down the hatches and abandon ship! That woman would fight a buzz saw and give it a five-minute start!"

Mary had a miraculous capacity for whiskey and her chief claim to glory was, "When Bing Crosby was Elko's honorary mayor I drank him under the table four times!" Many citizens discounted this by fifty percent.

However, Mary's yen for liquor never seemed to curtail her ability to acquire property. Aside from her ranch down the river she had lots scattered all over town, although until recent years lots in Elko were on a par with a row of post holes in Siberia.

The last time I saw Mary she had just had a veritable axe fight with a rancher by the name of Manuel Machado. It was something over a cow. Mary was working Manuel over with an axe handle and Manuel, taking umbrage at this, had dropped her with a saucer-size rock. She was on the highway walking toward Elko to have him arrested when I came along.

"I'd've shotgunned that Portuguese sonovabitch," she panted, "if I'd had 'ary a shell on the ranch!"

By the time we reached town she had had a change of heart. "Reckon I shouldn't o' fit with him, though, 'cause it was my fault." Instead of getting a warrant she got drunk.

One of the classic stories folks like to tell about Mary was an occurrence years before. Seems she had bought an old house on the south skirts of town and after fixing it up in apple-pie order, she decided she didn't like the location. She owned a lot a couple blocks away, and decided to have the house moved on it.

A freighter friend by the name of Reed happened by with his six-mule team and Mary wanted him to hitch on her house and haul it to the new location. Now when Mary wanted something done she wanted it done immediately if not sooner. But Reed had another hauling job that day and said, "I'll move it first thing tomorrow, Mary."

Mary had been hitting the jug and being in no mood for delay she gave him

> ## 'When Bing Crosby was Elko's honorary mayor I drank him under the table four times!' Many citizens discounted this by fifty percent.

"a piece of her mind" that equaled a bogged-down mule skinner's cussing.

When Reed got back to her house later that day, he found she'd gone on a binge and had passed out on a horsehair couch. When he couldn't wake her up, no matter how he tried, he jacked the house on his skids and hitched on. Thinking all the racket should have fetched her alive he went in for a final try, but no luck. Mary was still dead to the world. Not wanting the stovepipes on the kitchen and heater stoves to fall down while moving and ruin everything with soot, he took them down. He carried them out and shook the soot out of them and laid them on the little porch by his house jacks.

At the new location he had the house jacked up, the skids pulled away and was letting the house down on its wooden templates when the door flew open and Mary came tumbling out yelling at the top of her lusty lungs, "Fire! Fire! Where the hell am I? How'd I get here? Fire-e-e!"

There was a fire alright. Smoke was pouring out of every place there was a crack. To add to the bedlam, the six-mule team stampeded through town for home with the skids wrecking everything in their path. Elko's Volunteer Fire Department consisted of businessmen and a hose cart, but the clang of the fire bell gathered them on the run. By the time they reached the scene, flames were belching through the roof. In seconds, the hose was making the cart-reel hum as men ran looking for a hydrant. Then it was discovered the nearest fireplug was a full block away and there was but a hundred feet of hose.

Mary was cussing everybody as she staggered around asking, "Who the hell set my house afire?" But other questions were in order and, as the house burned, between her and Mr. Reed the firemen eventually deduced what had happened.

Mary had woken up and, thinking it was morning, decided to cook breakfast. As unstable as she was, she hadn't noticed the missing stovepipe but had managed to get wood from the box by the kitchen stove. After stuffing the firebox full, she had emptied a gallon of coal oil on the wood for a quick fire and lit it. There being no stovepipe, the enormous flame had shot up through the hole where the pipe had been, setting the ceiling and attic ablaze.

The aftermath of the situation came the next day when Mary was sober and friends were advising her to sue Reed for the loss. "No," Mary said, "I can't do that. It wasn't his fault. It was the fault of that damn whiskey I must have drank a wee too much of."

"Well, Mary," the minister warned, "let that be a lesson to you. Never let a drop of that devil's brew pass your lips again."

"Yes, Reverend, you're right," Mary admitted. "But a little nip now and then is the only thing that keeps me healthy." ∎

Memoirs of a Government Trapper

It was a dangerous business alright, and not just for the critters.

 Uncle Sam is always instituting some sort of a "crash" program but one I look back on was of especial urgency. That was when, in 1916, a couple of rabid coyotes had been killed near Bruneau, Idaho, and before the fearful disease was conquered—or had run its course of its own accord—it had reached epidemic proportions, not only in Idaho but it had spilled over into Elko, Eureka and Humboldt counties in Nevada.

The first mention of rabies to reach us in Nevada was of little concern other than being amusing. The story was that an Idaho rancher, thinking to rid his vicinity of coyotes that were decimating his lamb crop, had trapped a coyote and had a veterinary friend shoot a Simon pure shot of rabies' germs into it before turning it loose; the theory being that it would bite others of its breed and soon—no more coyotes.

But, like the farmer who set the rat on fire so as to scare all the rats away, his theory backfired on him. The blazing rat ran from building to building thus setting them afire until every structure on the farm was ashes and the inoculated coyote set off a chain reaction that soon had predators of every description going rabid. Not only the predators were to become a nightmare, but a Frankenstein had been created that had ranchers, sheepherders, cowboys, and ranch wives looking four ways before venturing out of a house or tent.

We hadn't thought too much about this death-dealing monster until Miles McKinnon went rabid in our little town of Palisade—twelve miles from my ranch—and scared the daylights out of his longtime friends by hurrying among them, bidding them farewell hours and minutes before his horrible death.

Lizzie Walker and her husband ran the general store in Palisade. She told me: "I was frightened to death when poor Miles put his arms around me and tried to say something I found out was a last goodbye."

Rabid coyotes had just begun working that far south of the Idaho line but Miles had not been bitten by a coyote but a friend's pet bulldog while visiting the dog's owner. Still, this being an isolated case, those of us in Elko County weren't alarmed until a Basque rancher had a bobcat leap on his back while going to his barn in midday, biting and clawing him about the neck and face. Several days elapsed before he was persuaded to undergo the Pasteur treatment in Reno with the result that the inoculation only hastened his agonizing death.

This was followed by sheepherders being attacked in their beds by coyotes, bobcats, or even their own dogs. A person could no longer trust any pet. One trapper, Harry Ivester, swore he saw a rabid rooster at a ranch. Anyway, we all knew that when a predator came near a human or let said human get close to it, it was either rabid or had to be in a trap or dead from a bullet. Once the people realized the horrors of a rabies' death they became afraid of their own shadow.

By then it was apparent that Idaho and especially Nevada were up against something far more sinister than a blackleg or hoof-and-mouth epidemic among the cattle or the "sleeping sickness" that struck among our horses with the result that even saddle horses had simply lain down under their riders and stayed in a coma until dead.

This time we were up against a foe there seemed no escape from. Furthermore, we in Elko and Eureka counties bore the brunt of the rabies invasion for the simple reason of being the largest cattle and sheep counties in the state and having more coyotes and other predators than all the other counties combined.

Ranchers were losing range stock of all kinds that had been bitten by either a coyote or bobcat or perhaps a rabid dog. A nip on the heels was all that was needed. An example of this was witnessed by two ranchers moving a small bunch of cattle from one ranch to another. A coyote suddenly showed up among the herd biting right and left and in less than three weeks six of the herd had become ferocious attackers before death quieted them. The number of days for the rabies bud to incubate can be any time after eleven days, but it could lie dormant for exceptionally long periods.

So, with scores of letters pouring into Senator Pittman's office in Washington by laymen and heads of cattlemen's and woolgrowers' groups, Uncle Sam hopped in with both feet and began a crash program of kill and destroy. E.R. Sans of Reno was appointed Chief of Biological Survey for Nevada and California and he in turn began advertising for and appointing "hunters," as the trappers were designated.

Many trappers were soon in the field at seventy-five dollars per month so this lucrative job attracted many who didn't know a Newhouse trap from a monkey wrench. Three dozen #3 Newhouse traps were supplied each trapper and more later on if he wanted them. One trapper, Ed Thomas, trapped from May 1 to August 1 with a total catch of one badger. In disgust he had long wanted to quit but "Old E.R."—as Mr. Sans was referred to—prevailed on Ed to keep trying. On August 1, Ed gave up and never bothered to go pull up his traps.

These government hunters were welcome to make any ranch their headquarters as, by July, ranchers, their workers and even ranch wives had experiences with rabid critters and were glad to have the hunters around. One trapper staying at C.H. Rand's ranch in Pine Valley, ten miles from my place, was almost in Ed Thomas' category when it came to outwitting a coyote.

After three months and a catch of only seven coyotes and a few badgers he reported that he had caught all the predators in our district and asked E.R. to transfer him "to California to poison squirrels," which was done. The truth was, with coyotes thicker than sagebrush all about the ranch, Mrs. Rand, after having to race a rabid coyote from the barn to her kitchen, simply told the trapper to vacate. That's when yours truly became a government hunter.

Without consulting me, two ranchers had written in asking Mr. Sans to appoint me, and, without asking whether or not I'd consider the job, E.R. took it for granted I would. On August 2, 1916, one of the freighters hauling ore by my ranch from the mines in Bullion dumped off three boxes of traps, a letter and bulky envelope of "Field Diarys," pelt tags, and monthly report forms.

"Hot Dog!" I said to Jay Ball, the freighter. "This letter says my pay will be $75 starting on the first day's work shown on my monthly report. So here's where I begun work yesterday morning!"

Thus began eight years of pleasant association with Mr. Sans. Not only that, I gained more knowledge of rabies, its early symptoms, its two entirely separate forms and their terminals than a few doctors or even our government bulletins expressed, besides witnessing a score of tragic incidents—incidents that were tragedy mingled with comedy.

I had trapped a few "loafer" wolves in Wyoming and had profited by knowing one of the best trappers in that state, Jack Ketchum, and had long learned that a coyote can be foxier than a fox. I also knew that many of the early crop of government trappers relied on some sort of "bait" rather than scent for their sets. That was why so many couldn't catch a single coyote if they had him in a barrel.

I was fortunate in having some sweet anise and oil of rhodium for a starter until I could get some fish oil for a base. So, with this meager scent, twenty sets were made the first day and the balance on the second, all within five miles of my ranch. On the third day I was on the trapline and after finding the first three sets sprung by cattle, but with plenty coyote tracks in the dust, it was with a heap of misgiving about my "scent." That oil of rhodium attracted cattle like flies to sugar! And I had wanted so badly to show Mr. Sans what a real trapper could do.

However, cows couldn't be in every place and at the next set a big bobcat hit

THIS IS NEVADA AS I LIKE TO REMEMBER IT. OLD SPOOK THE MUSTANG WAS SO SMART HE BECAME A LEGEND AMONG MUSTANGERS FOR SEVERAL YEARS. SPOOK'S WITH DIXIE, MY TRAIL DOG, AND JIMMY, THE BEST CAMP BURRO IN ANY MAN'S LAND. THIS WAS ABOUT 1935 ON A SNOWY DAY. THAT'S THE WAY A HORSE SHOULD BE BROKEN, TO STAY PUT. [HARRY GAVE SPOOK'S LADY'S-LEG BIT, REINS AND ROMAL TO PUBLISHER C.J. HADLEY.]

the end of the chain with a menacing snarl. I carried a prospector's pick for trap setting and heaving it as a knife artist throws his knives a whack on the cat's snoot laid him low. Resetting the trap, I turned to skin my first catch and my heart went to my boots on seeing him weaving drunkenly away.

Having no gun with me and throwing rabies caution to the wind, I grabbed the pick, ran and jumped astraddle of him. He

Resetting the trap, I turned to skin my first catch and my heart went to my boots on seeing him weaving drunkenly away.

was regaining his normal senses and I was tattered and clawed up aplenty before my pick silenced him for keeps.

When the last trap was reached, four coyote and two cat hides were tied on my saddle and from then on I made damn sure any bobcat was dead before I reset the trap.

That month I turned in sixty-two coy-

ote and cat pelts and a few days later a letter came announcing that I had led the list of thirty-seven hunters by forty-nine pelts and henceforth my salary would be $100.

I didn't know at the time what a jolly joker Mr. Sans was and he had added a postscript that burned me up by saying: "I'm puzzled as to how you trap and shoot so many predators in your district where our former man reported them all trapped off. You wouldn't by any chance be buying pelts, would you?"

"Send me three dozen more traps," I wrote back, "and I'll puzzle you more than ever." In the meantime I picked up several #3 Victor traps at the Rand ranch and it wasn't a week until I wished to hell I'd never seen a Victor trap. We all knew they were far inferior to a Newhouse but I needed traps, and pronto.

I was riding this new line and had taken five coyotes and a bobcat, with one more set to visit. I was sure I would have a bobcat there as the trap was in a small patch of catnip with lots of cat sign. Coming to a knoll overlooking this patch I saw a big animal raise up and begin lunging about, then race away towards the nearby timbered crags.

On reaching the set I was so mad I stood cussing the nitwit who ever invented the Victor trap. The animal had been (from his tracks) a huge *lion*. Pieces of that trap were scattered thirty feet along his trail, a jaw here, a spring there and other components farther on. The jaws of a Newhouse trap are riveted in, whereas in a Victor the ends are simply held in holes by their tension and a strong pull could yank the jaws free.

The next month I was again high man on the Honor Roll (to be on the Honor Roll the minimum catch was twelve animals) which E.R. had established, and was notified my salary would henceforth be $125. From then on I usually topped the list until Ed Olds, one of the department's best trappers, began using a car on his traplines that covered several hundred miles in both Nevada and Idaho. Ed often turned in as many as two hundred pelts each month.

More and more skilled trappers joined the force until we numbered between fifty and sixty-five in the field. And with coyote pelts bringing as high as thirty-five dollars each and bobcats around sixteen at the St. Louis fur sales (due to no furs coming from Russia on account of the war), we were quite an "asset" for Uncle Sam.

It seemed, though, we were trying to bail the ocean dry so far as any visible inroad on the so-called predicators. And, likewise, with each passing month and year, more and more rabid coyotes, bobcats and other furbearers showed up to say nothing of sheepdogs, ranch dogs and domestic critters of every kind.

My first encounter with a rabid animal was when I rode into the Hat Ranch one day and found two of the cowhands, George Mullison and Pete Arrascada, perched on the high standards of a wagon gear yelling bloody murder as a big boar chomped his slavering tusks and tried to reach them. On spying me, the boar took after my horse and gave the fellows a chance to make a run for the corral fifty yards away. But the boar had left me and was at their heels when they hit the top pole. I had missed two running shots, what with my horse turning wrong side out, but at the corral my .38 Special dropped Mr. Boar.

It was on that same ranch one winter day, where I had stopped for dinner, that my own dog went berserk while I was eat-ing. A group of cowboys were there and one, Pete Hawkins, came tearing in and said, "That damn dog of yours is rabby [most cowboys pronounced it that way] as hell and near got me! Look here!" The right leg of his Levi's was ripped open.

I couldn't believe my gentle dog, knowing Pete well, would attack him, but he sure had. Other cowhands were perched on the high woodpile unable to reach the bunkhouse where their six-shooters were. "Where is he now?" I asked, looking about. Just then my dog spied me from around the bunkhouse and as he headed for me I jerked my .38 from the spring holster under my armpit. My overshoe soles were worn smooth and the ice in the roadway was like glass and as I put a bullet in his chest I slipped and went

Be they your gentle horse, milk cow, range critters, coyotes or whatever, they attack anything that moves.

down with the dog on me. But he only succeeded in getting a mouthful of hair from my angora chaps.

I knew he had never been bitten by any rabid animal but I thought I knew how he had been infected. He had a wire cut on his front leg, from running a rabbit through a fence, and in traveling along a trail the cut had come in contact with saliva dropped on a sagebrush by a rabid cow or perhaps coyote. Several times I had observed a cowbrute going along a trail or standing tearing a bush or willow to shreds with its horns as it bellowed its fury and drooled thick saliva by the pint.

Any animal acting in this manner, brother, you better stay clear and not run on one while afoot, for they are in the throes of "violent" rabies. Be they your gentle horse, milk cow, range critters, coyotes or whatever, they attack anything that moves. Drooling heavy, their heads, and often their bodies, are palsied.

Those with the "dumb" rabies act just the opposite. I have often seen a coyote trotting towards me on a meadow where it had an unobstructed view for hundreds of yards yet showing no sign of seeing me. It took but a glance for us who were familiar with the disease to know whether it was violent or dumb. I have walked out in front of these coyotes on meadows, sat down and waited until they were within twenty feet of me before pressing a trigger. Naturally, we never skinned them, but took the scalp and reported them "Rabid."

After my second year, I was furnished all the ammunition I wanted and I used plenty. E.R. said from the reports he had he knew I didn't use the ammunition for target practice as he had found many of the trappers did. I often shot as many coyotes as I trapped. Few cats were shot as they were usually through hunting by daylight unless they were rabid. One morning at the George Goodfellow ranch we spied two groups of coyotes on or around the haystacks and my 25-35 carbine accounted for six of them before they got off the meadow.

It was on this same ranch that Ross Plummer (one of Goodfellow's cowboys) and I were routed out of bed one bright, moonlit night by the yelling of Ye Gun, the Chinese cook. Ye Gun stuck to his honorable ancestors' sleeping habits and preferred a wide, sloping plank with a blanket on it, and the notched, wooden block for a pillow, to our "Melican beds."

Any unusual commotion around a home or ranch spelled but one thing, rabid critter! Grabbing my six-gun and Ross picking up a piece of stove wood as we raced through the kitchen, we ran to where all the ki-yiing was coming from. It was a hot July night and Ye had left the door of his outside room open. Stopping in the doorway we could see Ye clinging to a side windowsill by his fingers and toes, jackknifing his body so that his rear end hung but a foot from the floor. In the middle of the floor sat a big bobcat oblivious to Ye's awful yowls. After shooting the cat we had to pry Old Ye Gun's fingers loose to get him down. "Damn lucky for Old Ye," Ross said, "that this cat had the dumb rabies instead of the whoop'em kind!"

One evening a few weeks later while I was at Goodfellow's ranch, three cowboys—Ross Plummer, Jack McLeod and Frank Hale—and I were bounced from the supper table by the barking of Mrs. Goodfellow's pet spaniel and a commotion across the wide porch. Everyone had long ago learned to keep a gun or club handy and Frank grabbed his Winchester pump shotgun.

Just as we reached the porch, the frightened dog came around the corner followed by a big coyote. As they raced across the porch Frank pulled the trigger. No shell in the chamber. It was lucky he fast pumped up a shell as the coyote had swapped ends and leaped at Frank, receiving the charge in its chest.

When I returned to the ranch one afternoon two weeks later, the spaniel was missing. "Been gone since yesterday," George Goodfellow said. As we stood talking about the possibility of the dog being rabid (although all of us were sure the coyote hadn't even caught up with the scared pooch) we saw the dog trotting across the meadow, its nose pointed on one side. As it neared the house I called its name and its master patted his thigh and whistled, but we may as well have been thin air. The spaniel trotted by us not six feet away. Although it showed a terrific weariness it never broke its trot and went on its brain-dulled way.

"Rabid," I said. "But at least he hasn't bitten anyone or anything because he's got the dumb type."

"Dumb or otherwise," George said, "grab a horse and go kill him!" Which I did. I believe I and the Goodfellow cowboys killed at least ten rabid coyotes right on the ranch. One experience Goodfellow had was funny. For us I mean. A rabid coyote had kept him prisoner in the privy for three hours one afternoon until Jack McLeod and I came in from working some cattle and rescued him.

I had a little experience of my own one hot August afternoon at my ranch. I had come in from a trapline, eaten a bite and stretched out on the floor for a spell before riding a trapline near home. I was lying on my back between open outside doors where it was the coolest. I must have dozed off because I found myself looking up at what I first thought was my dog's nose a few inches from my face. Didn't take long, though, for my wits to tell me it was no dog. As the animal's head turned to where my wife lay on a couch, I slowly slipped my Colt from under my armpit. The blast of that .38 bounced the Missus a foot high and left a bloody mess to clean up. How that coyote walked in without my dogs detecting him is still a mystery—unless they were snoozing down by the corral.

Of course the coyote had been rabid and while the odds were against it biting me, the drooling saliva could be almost as dangerous, as proven by my dog that had attacked Pete Hawkins and then me. So a thorough disinfection was in order.

I was bitten by a big fat coyote one day as I went to stun him with my pick. The pick missed and as the coyote lunged at me the trap chain broke and Mr. Coyote sunk a tusk through a Levi jacket and two heavy shirtsleeves deep into the palm side of my wrist. The wound spurted blood a foot, but before the coyote got twenty feet away I downed him with my Colt.

That afternoon on reaching home, I learned what not to do in administering a homegrown antirabies shot. I had a small rubber syringe in the barn for use on stock, and filling this with a strong solution of creolin I poked the nozzle deep in the tooth wound and pressed the plunger. The instant I pressed that plunger I went out like a light and had heart pains for a month. Long afterwards, a doctor couldn't believe I was still alive. He said the creolin had been forced directly into a vein and I was lucky there hadn't been an air bubble in the tip of the syringe or there would be a mound of dirt over me now.

As the years went on, despite the thousands of coyotes and cats we trappers had eliminated, the crop of predators appeared to increase. In fact we found the embryo count greatly increased over previous years. No logical reason for this phenomenon unless old Mother Nature was determined to lick us.

To worsen matters, coyotes especially had handed down to their offspring a cunning that had us at wits' end. Not all, but many were so smart and tricky we had to admire them. I have gone along two miles of trapline and found every trap exposed. One particular booger I termed "The Professor" not only scratched until locating the chain, as some often did to expose the trap, but went them one better by lifting up the traps and turning them face down.

Not only were many of these customers hard to deal with but scent that was once an irresistible lure now became a joke. After a skiff of snow, we would see tracks leading to traps along a trail only to detour each trap as they came to it. Just as an example of how one particularly obnoxious coyote figuratively thumbed his nose at me and added insult to injury, listen to this:

After having a line of traps dug up and no coyotes, I pulled up every trap on that line and piled them alongside the trail. I planned on bringing a packhorse the next day and moving them beyond the Bullion range where I wasn't having such smart

alecks to deal with. I had ridden up on a knoll the following day to pull up a trap there when I spied a big black-maned coyote trotting along the trail about a hundred yards below me. Something about the looks of his head puzzled me.

Stepping back to where my saddle and packhorse were I got my carbine, took a knee rest and let him have it. On going down to get him I couldn't believe my eyes and had to sit down laughing. Lo and behold, one of the traps I had piled up was still gripped in his mouth. Where the old booger planned on taking it I had no idea. I only know I felt a twinge of remorse over killing him.

I didn't bother to load up that batch of traps from where The Professor had snitched it. Instead, I reset the whole line and hauled in coyotes as easy as shooting fish in a rain barrel.

From early May to September, the department no longer required us to turn in the pelts, as such furs were unsalable, so we only tagged the scalps. These tags were lines for various data such as the following example: Coyote (or whatever). Male. #325. S.C. (stomach contents) rabbit, mice, cow meat, sheep (or whatever traces of fur or hair indicated) or perhaps, "Empty." Where and how taken—Pine Valley. Trapped. Shot. We were also to note the embryo count in our monthly report.

Leave it to the "white collar" boys (who wouldn't know a coyote from a police dog) to think up chores for the lowly trapper. Not only were we expected to be a crack shot and fine outdoorsman but a biologist, an obstetrician and an autopsy specialist all rolled up in one skin. For instance, they had us clean all flesh and brain matter out of all badger skulls and send them in for examination.

No doubt a commission had been created to study these skulls to determine if environment changes the shape of a badger's dome. You can bet we didn't report many badgers taken, although they were the bane of every trapper. A trapped badger could pile up more dirt in an hour than a modern skip loader and ruin that spot for a set.

Harry Ivester, a top trapper, and I

A NO-GOOD VICTOR TRAP I BROUGHT TO LOS ANGELES WITH ME AS A SOUVENIR. I CAUGHT A LION IN ONE LIKE IT BUT FOUND PIECES OF THE TRAP STRUNG ALONG FOR FIFTY FEET. HAD IT BEEN ONE OF MY NEWHOUSE TRAPS, I'D HAVE HAD ME A LION.

turned in more shot animals than all the rest of the force. Ivester was not only a crack shot, but a "crackpot" as well. While visiting E.R.'s office in Reno after being called in for a "consultation" (due to Ivester getting mixed up with a bootlegger), he said, "Hell's fire, E.R., you know damn well that if it wasn't for me an' Harry Webb the whole country'd be so goddam overrun with coyotes they'd even tie up traffic between here and Salt Lake. Fire all the rest but me an' him if you want to fire somebody, because me an' him can lay in bed an' shoot more coyotes than all the rest of your pinheads can trap!" E.R. didn't fire him and that classical outburst was told and retold all over the state and E.R. had it typed for his own amusement and that of "inspectors" from Washington, D.C.

An episode happened to me one day that put my name on tongues wherever "hydrophobia" was mentioned. I was coming from Handley Brothers sheep ranch near Eureka late one afternoon in my battered Model T and was hurrying against time as I had put a pair of fifty-candle-power bulbs in and found that every time I switched on the lights these high-power bulbs took all the juice from the magneto and killed the motor.

As much in a frantic hurry as I was to get over the Union Summit and to the Goodfellow ranch before it was dark, it seemed every little way I would spot a coyote. Stomping on the pedal I'd yank the neutral lever, put a 25-35 slug through Mr. Coyote, run, drag him to the car and toss him in. No time for skinning coyotes! Knocking over coyotes kept me busy until the backseat compartment was full to the top of the doors with coyote tails hanging over them.

Hurriedly pulling into the Sadler Ranch beside the road to water the leaky radiator, I was working the pump handle at a well in the yard when pretty Mrs. Sadler came out. "Good heavens, where did you get all those coyote skins?" she asked, going over to the car.

"Shot 'em," I wheezed, pumping and lapping up water because I was dryer'n a powder horn. "But they ain't skins, they're coyotes I don't have time to skin. Got no lights." She stood by the car admiring the lot and remarked about one having a beautiful white tail.

"Yeah," I told her, "he's a beauty. Got him a couple minutes ago. There's seventeen of 'em there. Missed once so it took eighteen shots." I was pouring water in the radiator when Mrs. Sadler fell back screaming and took for the house. I was looking at her, wondering what had kettled her off, when a big coyote plopped to the ground and was taking off when I grabbed its tail and began wrestling it. Mrs. Sadler was screaming for me to be careful, that "it might have hydrophobia!" But aside from sinking its teeth through the instep of my boot he did me no damage and I soon had the life tromped out of him. The bullet had just creased his skull between his ears and the way he had dropped I supposed I had centered him.

Cranking up, I was on my way, but I couldn't keep from glancing back, hoping I wouldn't see a coyote standing back there on the hill looking me in the eye. With all that delay I barely made it to Goodfellow's by dark. The next morning I was about a mile on the road home when seven coyotes ran across the road and up a chalk-butte hill and in a jiffy I had the brake lever yanked and hit the ground blasting coyotes.

Running up the hill for shots at those

that had disappeared I got one more as he went up a rise and on dragging him back to the top of the butte I discovered my car several hundred yards from where I had left it and still moving down the deep-rutted road. I'm betting that was the fastest and longest race any trapper ever ran.

I had sent $500 worth of Liberty Bonds to a friend in Rhode Island by the name of Bill Jacks as I wanted a Model T to use on distant traplines, as Ed Olds was doing. Bill said he could get me a good one for that figure and he would drive it out as he and his wife Vera wanted to come West. Trouble was, I had to wire $200 to get him out of Denver. "Broke down again," he said.

When he arrived at my ranch that $700 heap looked like he had retrieved it out of some dump in Providence. I'm still sure he had. Steam and oil smoke rose out of that old car until I could scarcely see the driver and the folded down top trailed streamers of cloth.

Well, I was stuck with it and spent several hundred dollars on it before I dared venture anyplace. This eighty-mile trip to Handley's was the first and last time I tried trapping with anything but my horses, although I had to admit I'd sure hauled in the coyotes on the trip.

The switch box on the dash was broken and the switch was always on. To stop the motor, I had to pull a choke wire that Bill or some previous owner had run through the radiator cores. Out of breath, I overtook the slow-moving car and running around in front, trying to get hold of the choke wire, I fell and the car ran over me. Fortunately, my body wedged in front of a hind wheel and the one horsepower it still retained quit of its own accord.

While clawing and digging to free myself, I discovered why the brake hadn't held. Both motor supports were broken and the neutral cam had no effect on account of the motor bellying down, letting the pan slide along the high road center. Using a pair of skid chains to support the motor I finally was back in business.

After retrieving my rifle and four coyotes, I was so fed up with making money for Uncle Sam that I vowed to quit when and if I got home, as my ranch was being neglected through this everyday grind.

By trapping for myself only when the furs were prime, I could make as much in a month as I now was making a year. I summed up my two days killing. Over $3,000 worth at the present market price. "Fooey on Uncle Sam!" I said. "Dammit, it's too bad I didn't quit three days ago and not have to turn in all these fine pelts."

I don't believe my experience while employed by Uncle Sam would be complete without telling of Harry Ivester's

By trapping for myself only when the furs were prime, I could make as much in a month as I now was making in a year.

predicament when he decided to quit the government service and trap for himself as Ed Olds was doing.

Ivester had a beautiful team of bays (both top saddle animals) and a good light Studebaker wagon. He used these, camping wherever he pleased, and he moved from one trapping district to another. Once camped, he would load a batch of traps on one horse and riding the other set out fairly long traplines.

But after a talk with Ed Olds, Ivester saw how Ed was getting rich by car-trapping, and decided that was the ticket for him.

"Saves bothering about carrying hay or hunting grass for your horses," Ed told him. "Just set your traps along county and by-roads like I do. Run a string of traps from Winnemucca east to Battle Mountain, Austin, Cortez, and Grass Valley to Ely, then north through Wells into Idaho and swing back through Oregon to Winnemucca, Nevada. I'll guarantee you'll pick up two hundred pelts a week. Get yourself a car and you've got 'er made!"

That did it. Ivester managed to swap his team and wagon for an old Model T pickup. Loading his camp gear, a couple hundred traps, plenty of grub, ammunition and two cases of gasoline he was off for "the pot of gold at the end of the rainbow," he told friends as he cranked up. He had never driven a car—but anybody

could drive a Model T he was told. That is, anyone with two hands, two feet and a heap of patience.

Weaving in and out and around, he began stringing traps and shooting coyotes along the way. At the Dugout Summit before dropping over into Grass Valley to the south, he ran into trouble. The old car failed to pull the short but steep summit, and the more he tried, the hotter the motor got until it had no power. He would get back where it was flat, pull the gas lever to the bottom for the quadrant and take a run at it, only to stall ten feet from the top.

Pete Damele, a rancher on Robert's Creek, told me the finale of Ivester's big trapping expedition. "Dick McGee and I had about reached the summit as we came from Grass Valley and all at once we saw a billow of smoke boiling into the sky.

"'Grass fire!' Dick yelled, and we raced over the summit and down the north side. But it wasn't a grass fire, it was Harry Ivester's car. How'd she catch fire, I asked, wondering why he hadn't shoveled dirt on the motor before the whole works got burning like it was. Flames and smoke were going a mile high and shells exploding like firecrackers.

"'Emptied a case of gas on the sonovabitch,' he told us, 'and tossed a match on 'er! She wouldn't pull this hill.'"

That cleaned Ivester out—everything he owned in the world. I met him several weeks afterward but he was so queer I didn't relish talking with him. A few days later he stood in the street in Battle Mountain and hollered to Fred Hurd standing on the balcony of a hotel. For no reason he put a bullet through Fred's heart and four more from his .45 automatic through his chest before Hurd had time to fall. Getting off scot-free, it was but a short time later when he riddled a sheepherder at the Winzell ranch and again escaped conviction.

He then began working for a Cortez mining company and somehow had fourteen tons of gold ore concentrate from one of the company's dump trucks dumped on his head in Beowawe while down in a chute repairing a loading gate. Harry Ivester had found his "pot of gold at the end of the rainbow" but not quite the way he had planned. ■

A Part of Will James' Life Few Knew

He did a lot of drinking and talking, but he was one heck of a cowboy.

 Without doubt, the name Will James has been on more tongues than that of any other cowboy, as his books and western stories were of worldwide fame. From the ground up, every inch of the six-foot writer was cowboy. His background was cattle and mustang country, and in later years his books and paintings had the tang of branding hair and the squeal of fighting broncs in every work, for he wrote exactly what he had lived. He was rough and tough, yet kind and considerate. But there were facets in his life that heretofore have remained hidden from the public.

My first knowledge of Will James came in May 1915, when I came to Nevada to break broncs for the Hat outfit and became acquainted with Al Thatcher, a rancher on Pole Creek where James and one Tom Hall stayed while running mustangs. But it appears these two were not of the same ilk. While James practiced "turning the other cheek" on some wrong done him, Hall believed in "an eye for an eye."

James, Hall and Thatcher had run a band of mustangs for hours and when the bunch split up, Hall and Thatcher followed one band and James the other, as there was a beautiful black stallion in that bunch which Will James vowed to get if he had to "stick with 'em 'til hell froze over."

Thatcher and Hall finally succeeded in capturing their bunch in a blind corral in Thatcher's canyon and were working out a few branded horses when James pulled in.

"I got that stud," he enthused, "and is he a beauty!"

"Well, where is he?" Thatcher asked. "Lose him or find out he was branded and turned him loose?"

"Neither," Will said. "Drug him 'til my horse couldn't haul him any farther, so I tied him to a chokecherry tree and come in for help." Near dark an hour later, the three had returned on fresh mounts only to find the stallion gone.

"Christ, Will," Hall said. "You never should have left him! He's busted your riata and hightailed it."

"Wait a minute," James said, "this rope's been cut! I knew damn well a thousand-pound horse couldn't break it!" On examining the area, they found tracks showing where two riders had been skidding and hazing the stallion along.

"We can't do nothin' tonight," Hall said, "but come mornin' we'll track 'em to hell an' back if necessary an' get your horse or somebody's scalp."

Following the tracks to the Raines Hay Ranch, the three saw the stallion in the round corral with a fresh Hat brand on him. As they sat their horses, Jim Raines and two of his sons came out of the house and hurried to the corral.

"Listen, you guys!" Hall demanded. "Get in that corral and vent that brand you stuck on our horse an' be damn quick about it!"

"What you mean, your horse?" one of the Raines said. "We came along and that horse broke loose and after chasing him a mile we managed to rope him. He was a gone goslin as far as you're concerned. And since we roped him, he's ours."

"Like hell, he broke loose!" Hall shouted. "Look at that fellow's riata there. A city dude could see that's the work of a knife!"

"Well," Jim Raines said, "the boys say they roped him and that's good enough for me. So what you go'nta do about it?"

"I'll show you what I'll do about it," Hall said, unholstering his Colt. "You're venting that iron or you'll never live to get any use out of that horse!"

"Oh, to hell with 'em, Tom," James said, as he grabbed Hall's arm. "Let 'em have the damned horse. We don't want a killing over a mustang! These lousy thieves are welcome to him as far as I'm concerned."

"It's your horse, Will," Hall said, calming down. Addressing the senior Raines, he shouted, "Alright Jim, you birds can have the horse, but I'll make him the most expensive goddamned mustang you ever latched onto!"

Back at Thatcher's, James laughed off the episode. "I don't care so much about the horse, but the lousy bums ruined my sixty-foot riata. Now as soon as I can get a fresh cowhide, I'll have to make me another."

"You'll have one tomorrow, Will," Hall told him. "I got to butcher one to take to George Snyder at Buckhorn."

Hall had almost a dozen head of steers in Thatcher's field but the queer part was, although he butchered two a week for the mining camps his own little herd remained the same.

The next afternoon when Thatcher and James came back from the mustang corral where they had been roping the catch and tying bolts and burrs in their foretops (so they couldn't do more than walk slow or they'd get their skulls whacked), a fresh hide was draped over a pole and Hall was gone with the buckboard.

"Well, Will," Thatcher said, "looks like you can start round and round that hide with your jackknife! Let's see whose critter it is this time. Uh huh, just what I suspected. Tom's been working on Dean Ranch stuff, but it now looks like Jim Raines is due for some losses before Tom gets his money's worth for that black stud."

"Gosh all hemlock!" James snorted. "Is Tom trying to break into the penitentiary?"

"Tom don't give a hoot about the law," Thatcher replied. "If someone does him dirt they're go'nta get paid in kind. Old Joe Dean beat him out of a month's wages when he was breaking broncs there, so Tom's been peddlin' J.D. beef to the boardinghouses in Blackburn and Union ever since. He never bothers any little rancher's stuff, though."

"Well, I've run across fools," James said, as his knife circled the hide, cutting a single inch-wide-long strand, "but he's the dumbest yet and I wish he wouldn't be so generous with other people's stock! But this is the only pelt I've seen since I came here and still he's butcherin' every few days."

"Enough hides buried around here to fertilize the whole meadow!" Thatcher admitted.

"Well," came James' edict with finality, "as soon as I get me a riata braided, I'm vacating! If you fellows will give me ten dollars for chow money, you can have my share of the mustangs and I'm vamoosing while the gettin's good. Maybe get on riding for the McGill outfit down near Ely."

Thatcher related these events to me and praised James for showing good sense and said he was also glad Hall had departed before he got them all in the hoosegow.

I had found the Raines people a very nice outfit to work for and Jim Raines laughingly corroborated Thatcher's story regarding the black mustang. Old Jim liked to tell tales, even on himself. Jim had one glass eye and told us about two big Indians, Booney and Boo-hoo, who were cleaning out a mile of ditch on the ranch but weren't making much headway. Jim said one day he walked up the ditch and found the Indians lying in the willow shade, so—taking out his glass eye—he put it on a post and told them he was leaving one of his eyes to watch them and see that they worked hard, or the eye would tell him and he'd fire them.

"Those redskins shoveled more ditch that afternoon," he related, "than they had in two weeks."

One story Raines never told was probably because he never knew he was but thirty feet from death one day. Tom Jewell, a rancher near the Raines' home ranch, supplied this story.

One afternoon, Tom Hall had stopped at the Jewell ranch with his buckboard and after dinner he said, "Tommy, I'm going down the fence here a piece and butcher a beef. I see a lot of fat ones layin' around there and I got to take one in to Bill Ebberts. So I want you to lay jigger for me and if anyone comes this way you fire your six-shooter so I can duck back in the bushes."

Jewell said he was in the yard keeping an eagle eye out when he heard Hall's six-shooter and knew he had a beef down. But a few minutes later Jim Raines rode up. Seeing Tommy with the six-shooter, he said, "Was that you who just fired a shot?"

"Yeah," Tommy replied. "Shootin' at a chicken hawk."

Tommy told me he was shaking like a leaf and tried to get Raines to get down and come in the house but no luck, as Raines said he wanted to ride down the fence and see how his cattle were doing.

"I started to fire a shot," Jewell related, "and found there wasn't a damn shell in the cylinder. I was scared stiff as I knew Jim would come up on Hall skinning a Hat beef but all I could do was wait. In about an hour, Hall came back for his buckboard and I says, 'Christ, Tom, how come Jim Raines didn't see you beefin' down there? There wasn't any shells in my gun so I couldn't warn you.'"

"The ol' booger saw me, alright," Hall told me and laughed over it. "But when he got close, he rode by lookin' off toward the crick. I was layin' down with the barrel of my ol' Hogs-leg restin' acrost the half-skinned beef just waitin'. If he'd dared look my way I'd have blowed that other eye out of him just as sure as God made little apples!"

"Well," I said, "we've got to admire Hall's nerve, even if we do have to damn

ROUGH AND TOUGH BUT KIND AND CONSIDERATE, WILL JAMES BELIEVED IN "TURNING THE OTHER CHEEK," NOT "AN EYE FOR AN EYE" LIKE TOM HALL.

71

his judgment. I've heard a lot about him and it's a wonder he wasn't slapped in jail long ago. Raines isn't one to take such open-handed butchering and do nothing about it."

"Scairt, that's why!" Jewell said. "Same as ol' Joe Dean was when Tom was butchering J.D. stuff. But Hall's probably in jail somewheres 'cause I read in the paper where they finally got his partner up for cattle stealin' down…"

"Who's this partner you just mentioned?" I cut in.

"Feller by the name o' Will James," Jewell supplied. "Him an' Tom was mustangin' up around Pole Creek. But I see in the *Eureka Sentinel* they got James an' some other feller for stealin' cattle by the carload."

To me, this was bad news. Although I didn't know Will James from Adams' off ox, I had a deep admiration for him just from what Thatcher had told me. I especially recalled Thatcher saying, "Funny thing about that James. He always had a notebook and pencil wherever he was and was always jotting down things. Maybe it'd be some remark by a miner or a cowpuncher or the Chinese cook over at the Dean ranch. Made no difference, down it'd go in that book."

Now as we look back to the Will James' classics, we can see that while he was running mustangs, he was laying the foundation for a writing career. Perhaps "Smoky" was beginning to jell right there at Al Thatcher's. I asked Al if he had heard the news about Will James, as related by Jewell.

"Bunk!" Al said. "I don't believe a damn word of it! He was one of the finest, straight-from-the-shoulder boys I ever met and I won't believe it until I get one of old Skillman's *Sentinels* and read it. Won't, by God, believe it then!"

At that time, Will James was just another name to us Pine Valley folks and although he had run afoul of the law, several such cases were then being disposed of in various courts, so the incident was quickly forgotten.

Some years later, I began reading stories by a Will James, a Montana writer, and wondered if there could be any connection between this author and Will James, the Pole Creek mustanger.

It wasn't until 1949 that I learned these two were one and the same. A lovely young woman, Bea Masters (who later became my stepdaughter), gave me an insight of Will James, which, though covering but a short span of this Montana cowboy's life, was the kind we like to hear.

Bea was one of the secretaries working for Ruth Duignan, chief of the secretarial division at Paramount Studios. She had been told by Miss Duignan that Mr. Will James had phoned in to have a "typist sent over as soon as possible." James, Bea understood, had been writing for the studio at a salary of $100,000 a year and she supposed he had an office, but on reaching the address, found she was to do the typing in the writer's apartment.

"Being alone with this six-foot, bleary-eyed person had me so frightened," Bea

'I'm a sagebrush cowboy who likes to string words together and sell them.'

related, "I could scarcely talk. I could smell whiskey on his breath. When he said, 'Please sit down, Miss Masters,' I didn't know whether to sit down or run out. There was no typewriter, no Dictaphone, no nothing on his desk except a telephone and as I was looking about, his voice made me jump."

"You're frightened stiff, aren't you, Miss Masters?" he said. Bea managed to tell him she was, as she thought all the Paramount writers had offices right in the studio's buildings.

"I did at first," he told Bea, "but my bosses are a pack of nuts and if I had to work where they could run in on me every few minutes with some crackpot idea they wanted incorporated in a story, I'd be as locoed as they are. No, I have to be alone in order to think. I've turned in two fine stories but when they got through injecting their Hollywood ideas it wasn't my story at all. So I'm giving them one more chance and, unless they keep their noses out of it, I'm heading back to the sagebrush."

Bea said she suggested they get to

work to see if he was satisfied with her and asked about a typewriter. "Oh," he said, "you want a typewriter, eh?" Bea said she had to laugh and told him she usually used one when she typed.

"Okay, we'll get a typewriter. What kind you want?" Bea asked for Royal and he picked up the phone and ordered one. "And send up the best you have and don't be all day about it! Now that we have that settled, may I call you Bea? Because first we got t'get acquainted."

Bea told him it was alright, as Bea sounded better than Miss Masters.

"Fine, Bea. Now you try and relax and we'll talk. We'll skip work talk and just talk about ourselves. I'm no high-toned writer, Bea, though lots of folks seem to think so. No, I'm just a sagebrush cowhand who likes to string words together and sell them. But I see you're still nervous, so calm down, girl. Relax! Cowboys don't bite pretty girls and you're certainly a beautiful girl, Bea. But that's beside our point. Now…"

"I had just begun to feel at ease," Bea related, "when he poured half a water glass of whiskey and downed it. That did frighten me, but a moment later he said something that eased my fear of this spike-heel-booted man."

"Bea," he said, "I hope you'll excuse me for not offering you a drink, but I hate to see a girl drink liquor."

"I told him I didn't drink anything stronger than Adam's Ale and he laughed until he choked."

"Atta girl," he said, "stick to Adam's Ale. You know, Bea, that's real cowhand talk and I see we're going to turn some stories once we get 'em. You're the inspiration I need."

Bea said after he had downed a second drink he started griping about his bosses. "They'd drive a saint to boozing until he saw pink elephants and zebra snakes! Another little nip and I want to tell you about a cowpuncher who ran all around our hotel room one time fighting imaginary one-eyed snakes with a pillow."

"Try as I might," Bea said, "I couldn't get him to get down to work. Several times the phone would ring and he wouldn't even go near it and each time it rang, he would yell 'I told you no—and that settles it!' Then he would say, 'That was RKO Pictures trying to get me to write for them. They want to buy my contract.' That always disturbed him and called for a bigger drink as he apologized for shouting.

"He had an old actor who was out of work staying with him and sometimes he would have to go out in the yard to find him. 'Here, Weasel Face,' he would say, 'take this ten spot and go get us a bite of lunch.'

"Lunch!" Bea said. "Those lunches were banquets and after eating it was more talk, as he pointed out and described dozens of wonderful paintings of his. But with all his drinking he never showed signs of being drunk. His diction was perfect and words flowed out of him like so much honey and I thought, if he would just talk his stories that way, it would be easy to type for him.

"He said he couldn't use a Dictaphone because it reminded him of a drunken cowpuncher he once saw arguing with a cigar store Indian in Billings, Montana. I believe he told me the names of half the cowboys in Montana and Nevada and had some funny story to tell on every one of them.

"He talked of cows and wild horses and campfires and the smell of burning sage until I felt it was hanging out my ears, yet I knew he was telling me all this because he was a lonely person. He was out of his element in Hollywood and had to get it out of his

HARRY AND BEA, 1975.

system by talking and drinking a quart of whiskey every day.

"Ordinarily, it would have been nice listening to him but, dear God, enough was too much and besides, I had a living to make and wondered if he figured just talking and listening was all the pay I needed. Every evening when I would leave, he would say, 'Now, Bea, you be here by nine in the morning because we

have a lot to talk about you know.' When I was leaving for home on Friday evening, I told him I had been there a week now and wondered if he intended to pay me anything for it. 'Oh, Bea,' he said, 'I plumb forgot!' Then he wrote out a check for a hundred dollars.

"As I stood looking at the check and about to tell him that was much more

He happened to have been caught in a net of circumstances where even the prosecutor asked for leniency.

than I had expected, he surprised me more than ever. 'Oh, that's just a starter, Bea,' he said, as he poured a drink. 'When we get down to work next week—or maybe the next after the next—you'll be paid better, so be sure and be back Monday.'

"I promised him I'd be back," Bea told me, "but if he paid me a thousand dollars a week, I don't believe I could have stood all that drinking and incessant talk. I phoned Ruth Duignan and told her Mr. James was the finest gentleman I had ever met, but if I had to go back there, I would be climbing the walls with the heebie-geebies!

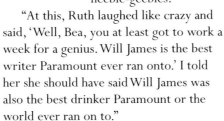

"At this, Ruth laughed like crazy and said, 'Well, Bea, you at least got to work a week for a genius. Will James is the best writer Paramount ever ran onto.' I told her she should have said Will James was also the best drinker Paramount or the world ever ran on to."

Luckily, Paul Sloane was writing "Geronimo" and through Miss Duignan, Bea worked for him all through the writ-

ing and filming of the story, which he also directed. As for Will James, Bea said she guessed he must have written the great story he had planned while she was with him, because the news broke that he had become so incensed over the scriptwriters emasculating a fine story on him he had flattened a few noses, told the producers what they could do with his contract, and headed back to the tall grass country he loved so well.

In telling this story, it is not the writer's intention to show Will James as a lawless character and a drunkard. Far from it. It is too easy for those who may have heard of his incarceration and, not knowing all the facts, to label him a "jail-bird." In truth, he happened to have been caught in the net of circumstances where even the prosecutor asked for leniency in his particular case.

Also, we have endeavored to follow Bea's account of her experience with that master-craftsman, Will James, and when she read these pages she said, "Yes, he was a horrible drinker, but he was driven to it. I worked for three other studio writers and they all had the same complaints as Will James. And looking back, I now realize what a fine person he really was at heart. He was a gentleman—first, last and always—and never once swore before me or even told an off-color joke."

I then handed her some documented pages concerning Will James' arrest and tenancy in the Nevada State Prison (which, incidentally, just recently came into my hands). As Bea finished reading them she said, "I don't care what it says, I still won't believe it. It must have been another Will James."

When she was handling his letters to the Parole Board, she only glanced at them and burst out crying.

"Would you say that was his handwriting, Bea?" I asked.

She was too dazed to speak and only nodded. ∎

A Cowboy Thanksgiving

We should have stayed in camp.

It sounded like just what the doctor ordered when my brother Charley suddenly said, "Dammit, I've half a notion to go to Lander for Thanksgiving! I'm fed up on Soapy's cooking!" Pulling the saddle off the bronc he'd been riding he vented his yen for a fling in town by landing a boot toe in the bronc's belly.

I had to admit Soapy couldn't boil slop for a hog much less cook for humans. His specialty was sour milk biscuits, which would have been alright only that he tossed Arm and Hammer soda in the mixture as if he was throwing wheat to the chickens, causing the dough gods to look like they were made of mustard.

"I second your motion and add the other half," I said, yanking my own saddle to the ground, "and I'll go along." I better explain that our M Bar boss George Pennoyer had loaned us to Charlie Blonde (pronounced Blon-dee), owner of the Anchor Ranch, to break a couple dozen broncs at seven-fifty-a-head and we each had sixty-five-dollar checks that were burning holes in our pockets. I had been wanting to get a pair of black and white batwing angora chaps, a fancy bridle bit and also some winter duds.

"You're sticking right here," Charley near shouted, "and keep working these broncs we've got goin' good! Give 'em a couple days rest and they'll be worse than when we started 'em."

I knew what he was leading up to but it made no difference. My mind was set. "You just put your John Hancock on your check and I'll fetch what junk yuh want," he added as though the matter was closed.

I didn't tell him I wouldn't trust him with my check any further than I would trust it in Soapy's red-hot stove on bread-baking day but I thought it. I had celebrated my eighteenth birthday a couple weeks before my being bucked off in a bed of rose

cactus and sent rolling until my hands, face, back and rear end resembled a porcupine. And with money to spend I thought I deserved a good restaurant turkey dinner as much as Charley did.

But I knew it wasn't just a restaurant meal he hankered for. I'd noticed the groundwork he'd been laying for a sashay to Lander to see Lorraine Wagner. He wasn't fooling me. He had sent to Bon I. Look & Co. in Denver for a "Special in men's outfits." For twenty-two dollars and fifty cents he had gotten rigged out in a nice black suit, black shoes and sox to match, white shirt, striped tie and a celluloid collar that was so high it gouged his chin.

I'd seen him secretly admiring himself in a cracked mirror in Blonde's room, so I put two and two together. My twenty-one-year-old brother was a handsome booger at worst and decked out in this store special he really looked scrumptious.

Blonde had had a bronc kick him in the right leg just as he had a foot in the stirrup, breaking the leg until the bone stuck out through the side of the calf, so whenever rheumatiz set in real bad in that leg he would head for the big hot springs down in Thermopolis. That's where he was when Charley decided all of a sudden to go to Lander for a Thanksgiving dinner.

As the crow flies, Lander was seventy miles south of Blonde's Anchor Ranch on the South Fork of Owl Creek in the Big Horn Basin, but to a lovesick swain the distance was a mere nothing. Charley had said with an early start we could be in Lander by sundown. I'd said I was going, too, so that was settled.

"What are we riding that can travel like that?" I wanted to know.

"I'm ridin' Snorter," he replied, "and by God he'll put me there or I'll chop his damned legs off when we get back! As for

you, since you're bound to tag along, you better ride that gray that piled yuh in the cactus. Be a good workout for him."

Blonde had told us when we took the job, "I want those horses broken so a man can do some work on them and not have a bucking contest and knock down a few cottonwoods with his kneecaps. So I want these broke. And any that you can't break like I want 'em, we'll shoot 'em!"

So that had been our agreement and the only one so far that showed he'd rather buck than eat was the chunky gray.

"Alright," I told Charley, "the gray it is, but I'll probably break his heart before he can make it to Lander in one day."

Charley's horse was a big sorrel and the meanest animal God ever put legs on, but once he got the kinks out he was a go-getter for distance. He snorted at every move and I often wondered why Charley didn't break him of his worst habit—and he was full of them—or sell him. Every time Charley mounted him it was like trying to mount a grizzly. Snorter would plant a hoof in your thigh or groin every now and then while tearing around in a circle.

Charley had packed his new store duds carefully in a timothy-seed sack and at day-break—with the sack atop the corral posts—we were ready. Charley said after he'd got mounted he would carry the bundle until Snorter cooled down, then tie it behind the cantle.

"Be a hell of a wrinkled mess won't it?" I asked. "And why cart all that stuff along anyway?"

"That's my business!" he snarled as he and Snorter went into their act of horse trying to kill a man. That's when a slight delay hit us. As Charley was being skidded around the yard, Soapy tossed out a dishpan of water resulting in Charley getting a leg kicked from under him, losing his hold on the bridle-cheek and Snorter taking to the far side of a meadow.

Unsaddling my gray I grabbed an old sheep-kneed wrangle horse, but trying to get a bunch of spooked broncs and Snorter corralled was like trying to corral a band of antelope. I'd get the bunch close and Snorter would dodge me and be gone again while my brother stood screaming like a maniac over the delay.

When I finally had the bunch nearing the corral I spied Charley hid in a ditch with his six-shooter in both hands, but, as if Snorter knew he was about to be a dead horse, he went through the gate. "I'd have killed that bastard," Charley panted, "just as sure as God made little apples!"

This time Snorter got mounted in the corral and by ten o'clock we had only reached the summit of the Owl Creek Mountains two miles above the ranch. So instead of being in Lander by sundown we were but a bit over halfway and spent the night at a ranch on the north side of the Big Wind River.

That's when we ran into another delay in the form of Ed Sopher, who Charley happened to know. Sopher was an insurance salesman and he had been peddling insurance all around the ranches. If folks hadn't the cash he would take a cow or horse or most any negotiable thing in payment. At the moment he was riding a roan mare and McClellan Army saddle which he had taken in on a $5,000 policy. And against his wishes, Charley persuaded him to go on to Lander with us although he said he wanted to work on down the river to Shoshoni and north to Thermopolis and Basin.

The next morning, we found the Big Wind running slush-ice and the banks framed in skim-ice a few feet out, so Sopher's mare wouldn't go near it. This kept

us fiddling around until the day warmed up. Then when Charley could no longer stand the delay we got our horses behind the roan and bunted her into the river, near drowning Sopher when the mare landed on her side.

I had always been subject to leg cramps and as we reached the middle of the river where the water was breast deep, I stuck my heels up near the saddle skirts and threw a knot the size of a baseball in each thigh muscle. Groaning and yowling with pain, my

spur must have gigged the gray near a hip bone and he went high, wide and crooked right there in the river. With those knots in my legs I was fairly riding him on my knees

and all but pulled the horn out by the roots trying to stay on. With cramps pulling my heels against my neck I'd have been a goner if I got bucked off.

I was still whining with pain when Charley halted in front of the Chinese laundry shack at the north end of Lander's main street. "Hang on to Snorter," he said to Sopher, "while I go get these Chinamen to press my suit." It was near sundown and Sopher's duds were pretty well dried out by then, although Charley said, "If you're taking in the dance tonight, Ed, you'd better get that coat pressed."

"Never mind the coat," Sopher replied, "all I want is to get some victuals inside me."

I supposed we would leave our horses in Welsh's livery stable as Charley and I knew all the Welsh family, but Sopher suggested, "Let's go to one by the river," so we put our horses in Ed Farlow's livery barn. That was when we learned why Sopher chose some place besides Welsh's. He had unloaded some insurance on them and failed to file it with the company he represented. One of his habits was to get the money and keep it for himself, so practically half his customers were buncoed.

We all cashed our checks (Sopher had two from customers, and Charley had the same amount as mine) at Bill Lannigan's Saloon. Charley and Sopher decided they'd have a drink or two while I went to the Fremont Hotel and got a room for us.

"And hurry back," Charley said, "because my belly thinks my throat's cut."

Eating had been on my mind all day as we hadn't had a bite since early morning. "Let's eat, then get the room," I argued.

"Get goin', dammit!" Charley flung at me as they headed for the bar. He always did boss me around so I got goin'. I got a nice room with two beds and an electric light hanging down on a long cord, all for a dollar and a half. Then I hurried back only to find them in a poker game with Bill Lannigan's brother Hoe and another man.

"Let's go eat," I said, but I may as well have talked to a stump. That Sopher was as rabid a gambler as my brother.

"Soon's we play a couple more hands," Charley said, "and don't be hangin' over my shoulder. You'll change my luck. Scram!"

"Call you and raise you five," he said to somebody. I could see he had several stacks of chips so I scrammed.

While waiting for them to play a "couple more hands" I wandered up the street to John Buckley's Saddle Shop to see about chaps. "Doggone it, kid," Buckley said, "I just sold the very kind you're looking for, white angora with black inlays all down the legs. But I can make you up a pair in about a week as soon as some chap leather comes in."

"Naw," I said. "I don't want to wait that long. You ain't got nothin' like I want?"

"Nary a thing," he said, getting ready to lock up, "except this white pair. That's the longest and silkiest mohair I ever got hold of. Look at the marcel in it. Besides, for range work these will outwear three pair of the inlaid ones and cost half as much. The inlaid kind are pretty but a skin has to be cut and the inlay patches sewed in, so no matter how well they're made they often just go to pieces."

I could see where he was right as for wearing quality, but my heart had been set on a pinto pair. These were beautiful chaps though, so I went back to Lannigan's with the $28.75 chaps, a double bozal for my hackamore and a lady's-leg bridle bit.

"Thought you wanted an inlaid pair," Charley grumbled. "Never mind the eats for awhile," he added, "Ed an' I've got to get back some of our money before we take time out for supper, so you go ahead and put on the nose bag. And don't be pestering us. We'll be along directly."

I saw the bartender fetch a round of whiskeys. "On the house," he said.

I dreaded going in a restaurant alone so took a walk to the hotel and after admiring my purchases I lay down on the bed. My legs still hurt from those charley horses and it felt good to lie flat. I guess I wouldn't have woke up 'til morning if it hadn't been for the light coming on and someone feeling in my pockets.

"Why the hell don't you get your duds off," Charley thickly mumbled, "when yuh go

t'bed?"

"I musta fell asleep," I told him. "What time is it?"

"Only a little after two. How much money you got?"

"Thirty dollars and…and a quarter," I stammered. "Why?"

"I'll take the thirty," he said, "before you go blow it on some more trinkets. How was the supper?"

"Never had any. I was waiting for you."

"You're the biggest damn fool of a kid I ever saw," he scolded. "I ought t'disown you."

Not knowing what else to say I asked if he got his suit from the Chinamen and if he took his girl to the dance. He and Sopher had talked about this Thanksgiving Eve dance all the way to Lander.

"Now don't go givin' me no third degree," he said, "because that's none o' your damn business!" When I started whimpering he softened. "There, there, now. You take that quarter an' go downstairs an' get yourself a good bite to eat an' I'll see you in the mornin'. Ed and I are goin' t'hit 'em for all they got before daylight. I've got a lucky hunch."

With that he left. Getting undressed, I turned out the light and cried until I fell asleep. I worshipped my brother and his mania for gambling tore at my heart.

The sun was peeking in my window when Charley barged in bleary-eyed and asking if I had any more money. Before I could answer he began going through my pockets until he found my lone quarter. "If you hadn't got on that spending spree," he grumbled, "you'd o' had some money! Now, by God, I'll have t'sell my six-shooter!" With that, he stomped out.

For a while I lay there wondering what now? What about our Thanksgiving dinner—a lot of things? When I entered Lannigan's, three new players had replaced Joe Lannigan, another man and Sopher, who were all standing glumly by the bar. But what made my eyes bug out was stacks of chips before Charley and he was raking in another pile.

Pulling at his shirt I tried to get him to cash in his chips, knowing that from their color he had over fifty dollars before him. "Get t'hell away from me," he snapped. "I've got 'em on the run!"

Back at the bar I found Sopher was cleaned out and trying, without success, to sell the bartender a two-thousand-dollar,

double-indemnity policy. With one ear I heard Charley say, "I'm seeing what yuh got for the pile," so I went close. The fellow squinted at his cards a long time then evened up the stacks against Charley's. "Try and top these!" Charley said, laughing as he spread out four kings.

"Four bullets," the man said, and hauled in the stacks.

"Well the jumped up petrified Moses!" Charley cursed, as he pushed back his chair and kicked it over. "How about one for a starter," he said to the bartender, "and a bottle for the trail?"

"Sure, Charley, and better luck next time." I saw Charley was minus his gun and holster.

"Now," Charley said once we were on the rickety board sidewalk, "what about our horses?"

"Yeh," I said, all but crying. "What about 'em? If we had left them at Welsh's, Mr. Welsh would let us send him the money, but…"

"Old Farlow will too," Charley said, "so you go down an' talk like a Dutch uncle to him. Put on a crying act if you have to." I didn't have to put on a crying act. It was for real, and Mr. Farlow said we could send him the money for the feed bill.

"If this isn't a hell of a note," he said as we saddled up. "Three goddamn four-flushers and can't pay me two dollars and a quarter to get their cayuses out of hock!" But he was laughing.

We were past the Chinamen's laundry when his head got working. "Oh," I said, "what about your suit?"

"Yeh!" Charley said, setting Snorter up. "Go back and put on your bellerin' act, and don't come back without that suit or I'll bat your ears down!"

"Not me!" I told him. "Them Chinamen would kill me!" I explained how Lon Welsh and I had thrown a batch of mud in the door on a pile of white stiff-bosom shirts one time when I first hit Lander. Those Chinamen had grabbed butcher knives and chased us down the street yelling, "Dammie Amelican bloy me killie you!" I could see their long pigtails flying yet, so I wasn't taking a chance on going back.

"Come along and hold my horse, Ed," Charley blustered, starting back. When they came back Charley was orie-eyed. "Those slant-eyed pups looked meaner 'n a wasp with its ears laid back!" he said in answer to my questions. "But if I'd had my old hog-leg I'd o' got my suit or there'd o' been some dead pigtails! Let's git goin'."

"If this isn't one hell of a Thanksgiving day," Sopher grumbled, "I never saw one!" Then he pulled the old mare to a stop. "Say! Why not send the kid back to that saddle shop and get the money back on some of this junk he bought? Then we could eat. I'm famished."

"Damn good idea," Charley said.

Not for me, it wasn't. "I'm not turning anything back," I told them. "You guys made your beds so you can lay in 'em 'til hell freezes over for all I care!" I jumped the gray into a lope north.

Later when they caught up with me, Charley said, "We'll hit an Injun camp on the reservation and git somethin' that'll take the slack out of our guts."

"Maybe," I replied, "if you can go dog stew."

"I could eat their dogs raw right now," Charley said, cussing me for "blowing in" all my money. I had been empty so long now I had gotten over being hungry. I was downright happy just listening to them gripe about being starved every time they took a swig from Charley's bottle.

At the Little Wind below Fort Washakie we ran into a likely looking Indian camp and an old fellow and his squaw appeared happy to feed us. Yellow Calf was his name. I'll say one thing, nothing ever tasted as good as that Thanksgiving pot of meat and onion stew. We were all sure it was beef but Yellow Calf said, "Cow no good. Him dog meat."

We were through eating when Charley near got himself killed by pulling a smart-aleck stunt. He was rolling a smoke and Snorter was snorting and jumping around, maybe scared of the teepee or just didn't like Indian smell, so Charley had tied the hackamore rope to the shank of his heavy cross-ell spur. "Go ahead and snort!" he yelled and hit the ground with his big floppy Stetson.

Swapping ends, Snorter got the rope between his legs and stampeded. Charley's foot was even with the horse's left leg and as Snorter tore off among Injun canvas, upsetting everything in his path, he was kicking Charley every place but his face. That boot came off after a hundred yards or so or I'd have had a dead brother and no fooling.

When Snorter went out the opposite side

of the river, Sopher and I could see the boot flailing first on one side of the horse then the other. By the time I had mounted and given chase, Snorter was out of sight over the sagebrush-covered hill.

I had covered half a mile or so when I saw the badly spooked horse circling back toward the river and managed to corner him in the cottonwoods where a rimrock jutted out. But no boot or spur. A hoof probably had cut the small hair rope or the boot had hung up on a sagebrush.

The three of us backtracked the dug-in

hoof marks and searched the sage each side for two hours but it was a cinch Charley had added a boot and spur to his losses. "Ed," he said to Sopher, "by God I think you're bad luck! So the quicker I'm shed of you the better I'll like it." Charley could be downright blunt when he was half shot.

"Well," Sopher retorted, "the feeling is mutual and I'm shedding your company right here and now!"

The last we saw of him, he was headed downriver towards the Arapaho Agency.

We planned on making it clear to Blonde's even if it took all night. Fortunately we ran onto the Padlock roundup wagon at a little ranch on the Muddy which was owned by a bachelor name of Metzler. Folks said he peddled whiskey to the Indians. Maybe so, as there was plenty in sight. Several cowhands

were there including reps from various outfits who were out branding any big calves that had been missed during the summer roundup. Naturally, Charley was in for a lot of ribbing in the Metzler shake that night as we were all well acquainted.

"By God," Eddie Ilg roared, "I've met a lot of shoe and sox waddies in my time, but old Charley's the first one-booted hand I've ever run across!" Eddie had repped for the Bay State pool with the M Bar wagon that summer and I'd had my eye on the beautiful black and orange batwing chaps he wore and

SNORTER UPSET EVERYTHING
IN HIS PATH AND WAS KICKING CHARLEY
EVERY PLACE BUT HIS FACE. THAT BOOT
CAME OFF AFTER A HUNDRED YARDS OR
SO OR I'D HAVE HAD A DEAD BROTHER
AND NO FOOLING.

had tried several times to buy or swap him out of them. He had always complained about them being too long for him, but still he wouldn't part with them. I had noticed them flung across a saddle at the corral and hungered for them more than ever.

"Eddie," I said, "I just bought these fine chaps yesterday but they're way too short for me. How about a swap for yours?"

"Eddie won't part with 'em," Lash Hinton said. "I've tried to get 'em for myself."

"Well," Eddie said, "I dunno. I never liked a shotgun-leg chap. Always went in for the batwings. But I'm either gettin' shorter legged all the time or them damn chaps are gettin' longer and I don't know which. Lemmie try yourn on."

I kicked off my white angoras, thinking I'd offer Eddie ten dollars to boot, when I got some money from Blonde, if he insisted.

"By cripes these are prezactly my length," he beamed. "How come a shipoke legged critter like you got 'em so short?"

"The only ones Buckley had in his shop. But just look at the length of that mohair," I said, "and the marcel in it. Buckley said it was the finest skin he'd ever got hold of." Eddie's fingers kept playing with the long waves and I knew I had him hooked. "Well, what yuh say?" I asked, trying hard not to sound too anxious.

"Oh, what the hell," he finally gave in. "Let the tail go with the hide! The pocket is sort of wore out from packing my six-gun in it, but if you don't mind that you've got a deal."

"I don't care about the pocket," I said. "I'll sew it up. So it's a trade, even-steven?"

Going out to his saddle, I buckled on the chaps and fastened the snaps in the leg rings. All puffed up over my luck I ran my hand down the pocket to see if I could sew it up, but to my surprise my hand went right out through the angora. Feeling down the wide batwing I found I could run my hand through wherever an orange inlay had been sewed in. The other wing was rotted out even worse!

Buckley had said in time these inlays usually started coming apart but I never expected to see a chap disintegrate like these had. This made me sick all over, but I couldn't blame Eddie. He may not have known how bad they were. But I knew one thing—the chaps weren't worth the matches it would take to set 'em on fire!

When I got back inside I found I had sparked a trading business. Those cowboys were passing a gallon jug around and swaps were taking place right and left. John Sales had traded his plain, C.H. Hyer boots for George Brown's "alligator" boots, not knowing they were imitation and wouldn't last a month. Sam Kramer, an M Bar hand, then traded his buckskin pants for Ed Payne's angora chaps and Emil "Red Dog" Rothwell—whose dad owned the Padlock outfit—was saying, "Sam, you'll be in a hell of a fix if the seat of your drawers wears out and a blizzard hits us!"

Charley was dickering with Lash Hinton for Lash's six-shooter and outfit. "What yuh got t'swap me for it?" Lash asked.

"Not a damn thing," Charley answered,

"but one boot for the off foot and a cross-ell spur. But let me have the gun and outfit and I'll send you twenty dollars as soon as my boss gets back from Thermopolis. I feel plumb naked without a gun." Charley wasn't mentioning that a poker game had cost him a new .45 and outfit.

"Twenty dollars is just what I don't need," Lash said, "and as long as I've got two feet, one boot ain't no good."

"Better take my advice, Lash," Sales said, "and swap him. You ain't shot that ol' cannon in five years and you could sell the boot and

This made me sick all over, but I couldn't blame Eddie. He may not have known how bad they were. But I knew one thing—the chaps weren't worth the matches it would take to set 'em on fire!

spur to that one-legged bronc stomper over at the Double Circle. He only needs a right boot."

"Tell yuh what I'll do, Charley," Lash offered. "If yuh can swing a deal with his Nibs there for them batwings, I'll give a trade my careful, unbiased consideration."

Lash didn't know it, but right then I would have swapped those chaps for one of Yellow Calf's skinny dogs. I was sick of our whole Thanksgiving trip. Sick of everything. I just wanted to be back at the ranch, so I spoke up. "If Charley will give me the twenty dollars he offered for your outfit, shells and all, I'll part with the chaps." Of course I knew I'd never get a cent from Charley.

"Here's where I put some fittin' clothes on your big brother!" Lash said, unbuckling the cartridge belt. "I can't see him goin' around feelin' naked as a moultin' jay bird."

Charley was hugging me and pounding me on the back until I could barely get the chaps unsnapped. "Now here's a brother worth havin'!" he said to Lash.

It wasn't until we were loping along the

next morning that I told him about the chaps not being worth a plugged nickel. Yanking Snorter to a walk he looked like he was about to throw an epileptic fit. He just sat there giving me the dog eye.

"Of all the low-down, contemptible, Injun tricks," he finally said, "that's the lowest of 'em all! Well, I'm makin' it right with Lash, and by God it'll come outa your money, Bub!" He was boiling mad.

"Who'll make it right with me?" I asked. "What about my brand new chaps Eddie Ilg gypped me out of?"

"Shouldn't o' bought 'em in the first place!" he near shouted. In four hours and miles (until we topped the Owl Creek Mountains at the peak of the long dug-way, looking down on the Blonde ranch), that was the last word he spoke to me. Hadn't even answered me when I said, "Well, if it wasn't for them chaps you wouldn't have that nice gun outfit."

"Whoa!" he suddenly said. Getting off he handed me Snorter's reins and said, "Here's where I make me a batch of bounty money." I thought he'd gone daffy until I saw several wolves trot away from a cow carcass a few yards away and stop. Charley was sitting down holding the .45 in both hands with the long barrel resting over his propped knees when he pulled the trigger. The explosion was so terrific it sounded like several explosions, which it was, and through the smoke cloud I saw Charley rolling around moaning. While I got our spooked horses settled down Charley was crawling to where the gun lay. After looking at it he flung it down the mountain.

"Wha-what happened?" I managed to ask.

"Damn chambers-was-rusted-through-I-guess," he said jerkily. "Blew-up-ever-shell. Help me on—I think both my kneecaps-are-busted-an'-an'-maybe-a-wrist."

Nothing had been "busted" except the gun, but it was a miracle. It was more of a miracle that Snorter for once let me help Charley in the saddle without a horse and man fight. Doubled over the saddle horn he pushed plenty venom in his words when he groaned, "You wait 'til I see that son-of-a-bitchin' Lash Kinton! You just wait!"

I didn't say it but I thought it. Yeh, and while I'm waiting, Lash will probably be on a huntin' trip for us. ∎

"Making a Cowhorse" © J.N. Swanson

Mothers with young calves don't like to be messed with and they try to escape from the cowboys during a gather. This cowboy is riding a green colt in a hackamore, and they are trying to guide the renegades back to the herd. The cowboy on the right is ready to help if necessary.

Lame Charlie Speaks

A mammoth cross in the desert at the Maidens Grave led me on a thirteen-year search for the identity of a woman "with hair like ripened grass."

 It was while running mustangs in May 1915 that I first saw the massive, incongruous cross rearing its broad arms high above a small butte on the flat Nevada wastelands. Halting my horse, I studied the black inscription readable a mile distant, and pondered the why of its existence.

"Maidens Grave." In those bold letters was an indisputable tang of mystery. As I circled the hill, I could see a name ten feet wide: "Lucinda Duncan." Now who was Lucinda Duncan to rate such an impressive monument?

Obsessed with delving the past, I started on the backtrack of time. Questions among young and old brought but one answer—beyond this, none could go: a workman's shovel had unearthed the remains down near the Humboldt River.

I learned that when the Central Pacific was straightening a curve in its tracks, the mortal remains of a blonde female, presumably young, had been exposed. The Chinese grade builders had moved the bones and tangle of hair to the top of the nearby butte. Later, a section worker had found a weathered, termite-eaten board near the site of the old grave. Apparently a name had been carved in the board. This rotted remnant of a wagon end-gate had prompted the company to erect the cross and, as they deciphered it, inscribe a name.

But who was she? How did she die?

Years of inquiry led me from one old-timer to another until I was somewhat rewarded in the person of Charlie Kilpatrick. Charlie's name had been linked with incidents involving renegade Indians along the lower Humboldt and freight roads to the south. I found Charlie at the

county poor farm at Elko, but like many of his ilk, he doled out information as if it were dollars.

After interminable wheezing and pipe stuffing and match searching he spoke of the death of his father, touched on the hardships that followed, and told of his family's excitement when news poured back East of the fabulous riches to be had for the shoveling in the California streams. It had been a momentous decision when his mother scratched together her few coins so that Charlie might board a full-rigger which was loaded with mine and mill equipment bound for San Francisco.

"Figgered on gittin' a few pounds of gold an' sendin' back fer my folks, but she never turned out that way. Didn't find no gold so took a job swampin' fer a feller named Jack Guinert who was freightin' from Sacramento to Austin."

I led Charlie on, and he warmed up a bit. "Well, I hauled into Austin till Jack was kilt one night when some Indians run off our stock. I blowed one of them half in two with a .52 caliber Colt rifle I'd just bought. Next mornin' all I could find of him was a trail of blood and the marks where he'd drug hisself off. But yuh know what?" Charlie paused for a belly-shaking laugh. "Heard years later that blasted Injun lived to crawl way to hellengone to a medicine man. Not only that, but the varmint took to usin' my name."

"What about your folks?" I asked.

Events had been too swift moving and obstacles too numerous for Charlie to send for his mother and sister, and "a year or so later" a letter arrived from his sister. Their mother had passed away and, frantic and heartbroken, the fourteen-year-old girl was "talked into headin' fer Californy with some friends that was all het up with gold fever—but she never made it."

With that he lapsed into silence.

Some sixth sense whispered that through him I might yet be led down the years to some turbulent happening that would account for the little batch of bones brought to light by a workman's shovel.

"Indians?"

"No tellin'. Never could find out."

Did he know the party's name his sister was with? Charlie thought awhile on this. "Seems like it was Benson or somethin', but I don't rightly recollect."

From Fort Ruby near the headwaters of the Humboldt River, Charlie's family had received another letter dated September 5. This told of trouble aplenty. Mrs. Benson, a frail woman at best, lay buried near the Platte. Then, to worsen matters, the drover's eighteen-year-old son, Obediah, had "got an eye hooked out by some feller's ox." Drought had stalked the emigrant route until "some of the teams was next to buzzard bait, so her an' the others throwed in with another outfit whose

MAIDENS GRAVE.

TOP: SITE OF GRAVES AT GRAVELLY FORD, SCATTERED ALL AROUND FOR A MILE. ARROW MARKS JOHN SNYDER'S GRAVE. I ALSO FOUND FOUR MOUNDS OF DIRT AND ROCKS WHERE VICTIMS OF INDIANS WERE LATER BURIED BY OTHER WAGON-TRAIN PEOPLE ABOUT A QUARTER-MILE FROM THAT OF SNYDER'S. BOTTOM: LUCINDA'S MARKER. OPPOSITE: LAME CHARLIE AT HOME. [PHOTOS TAKEN BY HARRY WEBB IN 1916.]

stock was still pretty good."

"Was your sister's name Lucinda?" I asked abruptly.

Charlie's head snapped up. "Now how'd you know that?" he asked. I explained the name on the cross and that it might possibly be a clue to what became of his sister.

"Could be," he mused, "but girls with that name was thicker'n fiddlers in hell, so I never give it no thought."

After the letter from Fort Ruby all trace of his sister was lost, Charlie said. He had never been able to learn the identity of the new party Obediah and Lucinda had joined up with. They had vanished completely.

Charlie had given me nothing positive on which to hang any conclusions yet the trail had at least grown warm. For even though he had informed me that Lucinda was a common name in that era, the girl's last message, coupled with later Army investigations, seemed proof that she and her one-eyed companion had disappeared somewhere along that three hundred miles between Fort Ruby and Fort Churchill.

My trail, it seemed, had come to a dead end. Years were to elapse before it again grew warm. A Paiute Indian I knew told me of another of his clan: "Old, old man. Called Lame Charlie."

"Lame Charlie!" I couldn't hide my interest. Perhaps another link in a weak chain, but probably not. My informant, Boo-hoo, was at the time well saturated with toddle foot and talkative.

Lame Charlie's tribal name had been discarded somewhere in the past, but he had been the counterpart of Satan on horseback. Long ago Boo-hoo had heard stories he was not supposed to hear: of sorties by a renegade band of Paiutes who had plundered and killed all along the Humboldt River and particularly between Maggie Creek, where Carlin now stands, and Gravelly Ford near Beowawe.

Boo-hoo only shrugged when asked if Lame Charlie had a hand in any of these raids. "Maybe," said Boo-hoo. "Long time ago, pretty much coyote."

Did he know if Lame Charlie was crippled by a rifle ball a long time ago? "Heard he got shot," he conceded. But, according to Boo-hoo, no earthly power could persuade Old Charlie to speak of his past, especially the incident that left him crippled.

That evening I stopped at a little cow ranch a few miles from Charlie's domain and its owner, Al Thatcher, proved to be just the man I needed. Al claimed to be part Cherokee and not only could he "talk Paiute better than a Paiute can" but was on the friendliest of terms with Charlie. The old Indian owed him a sizable debt of gratitude for warding off actual starvation when his clan had left him without food for weeks on end.

Thatcher was dubious though about getting him to talk about the early massacres. Once, Al told me, when Charlie had discovered a pint of Boo-hoo's cached whiskey, he had whooped aplenty of his escapades, only to later grab a carbine and literally clean camp when questioned regarding these claims.

At Al's suggestion, we assembled some food parcels and a handful of small change, knowing Charlie would place a much higher value on several small packages than on a single large one. We also secured a box with an opening in each end on the left fender of my car and in it fastened my camera. This bit of trickery was devised so that I might possibly get a few pictures of the old fellow, who hated cameras.

Halting the car a few feet from Charlie's hut, I pretended to work on the car while Al reconnoitered. But Charlie was off in the brush. Al found him squatted by an ant hill appeasing his hunger, though the insects were growing scarce due to Charlie's voraciousness. After much argument, Al persuaded him to return to his e-no-vi where "much food" awaited him.

Al came over to the car and hauled forth our offerings. "I've told him," he said, "that you'd give him lots of spuds and bacon if he talked about Indians killing nin-nih along the Humboldt River. I told him the Great Spirit would be plenty mad if he didn't tell the secret he has in his heart."

Al went back and showed Charlie the contents of the bags. Charlie scowled and kept jabbing a finger in my direction and muttering a word I took to be "isham!"

I called to Al, "What's all the fuss about now?"

"He says you're a panther's liver and a liar." However, peace was made at last, and Al motioned for me to join them.

I gave Charlie the coins promised him, and with these tightly clutched in one fist he proceeded to gorge himself on our offerings, eating everything raw. A week's supply was devoured in a few minutes.

Al apprised him of his promise, getting a few halfhearted grunts in return. Al told me with a shrug, "Lame Charlie will speak when the sun dies."

As the golden tint was fading from the peaks far across Pine Valley, Al gave Charlie a few pokes in the ribs. Blinking dully, our host suddenly popped up like a jack-in-the-box. A few moments later came a string of deep-chested Paiute. "Lame Charlie speaks," Al said in a relieved voice.

Charlie cared not a whoop for my interest in individual spots or events. He was off on the history of his existence with each particular happening coming in its proper sequence. Nothing could change that. But in his deep-voiced Paiute, now and then interspersed with simple English, there was the spell of a polished orator as he wove fantastic tales of the origin of the Indian in Nevada, the land of storms. It was the story of the legendary lost Indian boy and girl being swallowed by a coyote who, himself then becoming lost, had strayed far to this land until "his children and his children's children" inhabited all this part of the world east of the "great mountains."

At long last, Charlie got down to the era when the gun-toting "nin-nih's wee-gans" (wagons) poured across his domain and the killings were on, though in the ghastliest of these he denied active part, explaining that he was already "pretty old man" when the whites forced the Indians to make war with them.

According to Charlie, many deeds were committed by a chosen band of roving renegades who traded the peace and starvation of the main tribes for the full-bellied, exciting plunder trail. Their atrocities were usually limited to two points, the Emigrant Trail along the Humboldt and the freight road to the south.

He touched but briefly on Nevada's winters for they were best forgotten. The renegades were then forced to mingle with the friendlies camped around the fortified express stations forty miles south of the Humboldt River. Stebbin's Post at Robert's Creek Mountain was a favorite

hangout. Here the stationmaster not only let the squaws screen the undigested grain from manure piles but doled out sacks of barley when the storms got too rough. At times, when the pine trees produced no nuts and the taboose roots failed to grow, this was their only sustenance.

Even when these crops were plentiful and stored for winter, the whites hunted out their caches. Such acts left the tribes further weakened and only served to add more lean-bellied recruits to the renegade band. Then, let summer roll around and these rabid cutthroats felt all the more reason to murder and plunder and, as our fire cast weird shadows, Charlie pulled a three-foot square of braided rabbit skin over his limbs and relived many of these red-blooded days.

He, then known as E-sha (Coyote), and several clansmen had been visiting peaceful members of the tribe who were camped along Maggie Creek at its confluence with the Humboldt, begging food from the wagon parties that all summer dotted the landscape. "One moon before the leaves fell," which would place the time at early September, they were basking in the afternoon sun, digesting the bread and beans given them by a young member of one wagon "with a rag around his head, and his squaw." It was to be their final feed from these wagons, which had fallen a day behind the others. Already the two families were readying their wagons and stock for the hard drag over ten miles of rocks to the summit.

A renegade leader Won-gata suddenly appeared. He had just ridden in from a hard day's jaunt, having visited a medicine man to have the evils of a rattlesnake beaten and sung out of his leg. Won-gata (The Striped One), arrogant and vengeful, had gained his name through his yen for painting bright stripes down his body from forehead to heels. Claiming the powers of Tu-ya-lu-ha Che-e-vo-gah-lu (One Who Speaks for Another), Won-gata had gone off on a mountaintop and held a two-sun communion with the Great Father Te-lu-gu-pu. That mighty protective Spirit had told Won-gata to make warbonnets of yellow-topped rabbitbrush and no white man's "shoot-stick" could harm them. From the moment these terrifying headgears were completed the band became eager to try out their charm.

At the moment of Won-gata's coming, every buck present was startled witless when "the young squaw with hair like ripened grass" unwound the bandage from the young drover's head.

"He looked from only one side of his face," Al told me, meaning the man had but one eye. This statement caused me to hang on Charlie's every utterance, as Al interpreted the matter-of-fact recital.

Won-gata declared that any paleface with such a jagged red hole in his head could be nothing short of a devil and "bad medicine." It took but a few moments of his exorcism to purge the men of the last morsel of food given them by the evil one. Vomiting until they could retch no more, the frightened braves pushed weak legs over their ponies' backs and slowly wended their way to the Indian village by the river.

Won-gata immediately assembled a pah-nu-e-tu-ve to discuss the destruction of the devil-possessed one. For unless he and those about him were killed, every Indian who had partaken of their food would wither and die. Against Won-gata's haranguing the peaceful members of the village, and especially one young squaw, held out against harming the white travelers. Won-gata, having revised his plans, now talked louder and faster. With the fervor of a born leader he harped on the loot—from flour to shoot-sticks and "boom-powder." Besides, did they all want to dry up like an old moccasin and die?

Before dawn, seven renegades mounted their ponies and galloped west. Two members carried rifles, the others hatchets and knives, and one a bow and arrows. Reaching the crest of the range at sunrise, they scanned the pass where the wagons should be. No wagons. Separating, they rode both canyon rims toward the river. Still there was no sign of life. The men were nonplussed over the distance their quarry had traveled during the night when a splotch of dust far down the canyon sent them galloping to head off the two wagons before they could reach the river.

Their planned ambush in the canyon failed. The wagons had already reached the flat when the Indians swept around the lead wagon with blood-curdling whoops, causing teams to jackknife and go tearing

out through the brush. Before the Indians had time to fire their rifles or loose an arrow, a volley from the rear wagon tumbled the two rifle-toters from their mounts.

The lead wagon hit a wash and rolled over, scattering occupants and their worldly goods every which way as the covered bed tore loose from the running gears. But two more smoking blasts came, and two more of Won-gata's braves were sent clawing the dirt.

But it had not been one-sided; hatchet and arrow had gotten in their work on

It now behooved the three disorganized renegades to get clear of the line of fire and hold council. Warily approaching from a blind quarter, they saw the girl and a buckskin-clad woman running toward the river. Exposing themselves to give chase would be foolhardy, so Won-gata crept close, bellied down and peeked over the bank. An explosion and eruption of black smoke attested to the evil one's presence as Won-gata's rabbitbrush charm was blown from his head along with half his face. The one-eyed devil was a tough one!

Another powwow brought new strate-

those of the wrecked wagon. As the Indians closed in on the second wagon, the team added to the bedlam by bolting. Won-gata tried to grab a leader's bridle but only succeeded in swerving the horses in a gravel-throwing circle until the wagon upset and was dragged on its side until the doubletree tore loose.

Their shelter gone, a man and the one-eyed youth were seen trying to reload their rifles while heading for a deep wash. The man was struck down immediately by a hatchet, but a bleeding-faced girl grabbed the fallen man's gun and joined the youth in the wash.

gy, and soon an armload of burning sage and grass was dumped down on the youth's head. As he leaped clear of the inferno, a heavy, well-aimed rock was heaved on his skull.

While they had won the skirmish and removed the curse of the evil one, it was a costly ending to what had promised to be a one-sided lark. Neither pausing to pilfer pockets nor to appropriate the two death-dealing rifles, the remaining Indians set fire to the overturned wagonbeds and tossed their anointed warbonnets, which had so utterly failed them, into the flame.

Galloping down the north bank, the

"Blind Mattie" in 1909. She gained nothing but a world of darkness for her heroic effort to save the emigrant party.

renegades soon spotted their quarry, though they could scarcely believe their eyes. One was a woman of their own race—the recalcitrant member who had argued against harming the whites the night before. They now knew why they had failed to waylay the wagons in the canyon. The young squaw had sneaked away and stumbled through the night until she overtook the party camped at the summit. Apprising them of the planned slaughter, she and the desperate group of whites fled down Stonewall Canyon. If they could reach Gravelly Ford the squaw was certain they would find many wagons camped. If not, there was a friendly Indian encampment a few miles farther down the river.

No such good fortune had awaited them at the ford, however, and now the Indian girl lay panting among the willows, her lungs near bursting from exhaustion. The men began a torture reserved for just such traitors. Her sight was destroyed with the points of blazing sticks. This finished, they left her to rue her perfidy—a huge mistake on their part. A party pulling into the ford on their way east found her sitting in the thick underbrush. The following day she was returned to her people on Maggie Creek. She named the raiders, and despite the horrible ordeal, lived to a very old age.

The Indians began a systematic search for the yellow-haired girl. While one beat the willow thickets, the other rode the high points north of the stream. From a big hill far down the river, the luckless girl was spied crouching in the sagebrush near the wagon trail. Soon mercy, in the form of death, came her way.

Three days later Charlie (E-sha) and two other henchmen who had arrived in the Maggie Creek camp from a foray to the south, accompanied the two raiders to the scene of the carnage in the hope of finding valuable booty. Their only reward was to see crows and magpies pecking at the swollen bodies of their fallen brothers and to view several fresh mounds where some of the victims had been found by other emigrants and buried where they fell.

The ferociousness of this raid climaxed this particular band's work for all time. Colonel Warren Wasson hastily dispatched Captain Everett Poole with cavalry from Fort Ruby to the Indian encampment. Here the peaceful members of the tribe, having already viewed the renegades' handiwork in the person of the blind, disfigured squaw, put the finger on the perpetrators. One chose to make a run for it and was riddled with Army lead. The other paid his debt as he strangled below a cottonwood beam at Fort Ruby.

With the Army now in constant patrol of the Humboldt and especially the Gravelly Ford sector, any Indian having a yen for pillage and murder had best try his luck in the remote regions farther south. And there is little doubt of it being down there that bullets brought about E-sha's less romantic title. Al put this question to him. A gleam of hate and suspicion burned in his eyes as he studied our faces, but instead of answering he suddenly pointed, as if alarmed at something momentous.

Far across the valley the glow of the rising sun was peeping over the mountain crest—apparently a signal to old Charlie that Te-lu-gu-pu's wrath had been appeased. He wasted no time in reminding us of our promise of meat, flour and tea.

So, out of Kilpatrick's meager knowledge, coupled with Lame Charlie's nightmarish tale, we can only try to piece together a misty tragedy that had its ending right where we had started—at a massive cross on a lonely butte. For there remains one irrefragable fact: although Lame Charlie had not revisited the scene of that bloody raid in upwards of half a century, he was able to give us the exact location of where the white people fell. And it was through the acuteness of his memory that we succeeded in finding three of the graves which he had seen when they were fresh mounds of dirt and stone.

I believe that the bones which now repose beneath the huge cross directly across the river from the "big hill" described by Charlie are those of Lucinda Kilpatrick, erroneously labeled Duncan. But how the names became garbled one can only surmise. ■

The Case of the Drunken Judge

It took a lot of "gargling" to get His Honor to the courtroom.

 When a lawsuit was filed in Elko, Nevada, against the Simcox Garage in the early '30s, it promised to be a hard-fought case.

A man who claimed to be a "businessman" from St. Louis had left a late-model Dodge in the Simcox Garage for some slight repair and said he would call for the car "in a couple days." The days lengthened into weeks, the weeks into months, until a year had elapsed, so Simcox sold the car to Sam Zunino for six hundred dollars. But Sam had no sooner driven the car home than the stranger showed up at the garage asking about his car.

"Sold it yesterday," he was told.

"Sold it!" the man yelped. "What the hell right did you or anyone else have to sell my car?"

"Needed the storage space," Simcox replied, "and it had set here ten months past the time limit. That sign there tells our customers any repair job left over sixty days will be sold. So, she's sold."

"I didn't see no damn sign," the man raved.

"You see it now," Simcox said by way of dismissal.

"By God, we'll see about this!" the man said and shortly thereafter Simcox and Zunino found themselves in litigation, not only for possession of the car, but there was a good-sized amount tacked on for "punitive damages." According to the complaint, the owner had suddenly been called home, so was unable to pick up said Dodge car.

Time dragged on until the case was forgotten by all except the litigants when it suddenly came to trial. I had parked my car in front of the Mayer Hotel in Elko one forenoon, and was hailed by Judge Edgar Eather of Eureka.

"Come on up to my room," the judge invited. "I've a hell of a sore throat and I have to be in court in a few minutes. Got to gargle my throat." He mixed two whopping highballs of half whiskey, half ginger ale. We had "gargled" our throats for an hour when Billy Mayer came up with a message. "Judge," he said to Eather, "the lawyers have all their witnesses and have been waiting for you."

"My throat's still bad, Billy, so fetch us up another quart of my medicine—and tell 'em I'll be over in a few minutes."

The Old Yellowstone and ginger ale came up and we resumed the gargling as the judge received incessant calls from the courthouse. "Be there in a few minutes," he would tell them. "Throat's pretty bad but I'll be there."

"How come," I managed to ask, "they're having you try this case when you're from Eureka County?"

"Elko judge dish-qual'fied himshelf," Edgar said thickly. "Close friend of the defendants."

"Well, so'er you," I observed. "Better you get over there. But you're in bad shape, Edgar. Yuh won't know what the trial's about."

At this point Billy reappeared. "Christ, fellows," he ordered, "pipe down! Sounds like a Tong War up here! And," he added, "do you know it's *two o'clock* and the lawyers and witnesses are damn well fed up with sitting there since ten?"

"Tell 'em Judge Eather is on his way. C'mon Harry."

As we headed the four blocks across town, I recall the judge saying, "I'm keen t'day. Give 'em d'cision right from bench! Just like that!" As he snapped a thumb and finger the recoil sent him on his back. Retrieving his hat—which he jammed crosswise—he threw back his shoulders and, with both of us trying to act sober, we carefully climbed the courthouse steps.

I dimly recall seeing Edgar rocking back and forth, looking like a pigmy in that monstrous chair. Court was in session. I viewed the proceeding as if looking through the wrong end of a telescope and I believe our local James Dysart represented the defendants.

As the plaintiff stated his case the judge appeared to be sleeping, but when some remark brought a roar of laughter, the judge shot up like a jack-in-the-box and said, "Be no levity in my Court! Furthermore, stick to facts."

The "facts" must have been a jumble of contradictions from the way the judge would say, "Either blow hot or blow cold," or, "Strike all that out. Mere hearsay!"

Then a mechanic followed Simcox to the witness chair and just as it had been with the garage owner, there followed a barrage of "Objections!" from the attorney for the plaintiff, only in turn to bring a sleepy "Overruled!" from the judge.

Then the judge was half lying down on the bench as he scratched away with his pen. However, he did manage to straighten up as he went through a rigamarole of stating something about the "law of limitation and the Court finds in favor of the defendant." His gavel banged and "Court adjourned!" brought a howl of sarcasm from the plaintiff's attorney.

"We're giving Notice of Appeal!" he shouted as he shook a fist at His Honor. "And when this case comes before the Appellate Court, we'll get a reversal so quick it will make a jackass of you! Thank God we still have a few judges who aren't suffering with chronic constipation of the brain like you are!"

As the audience and principals went their respective ways, Judge Eather was being thanked by the defendants for a good job well done, but Simcox saw fit to add, "But, Lord God, Edgar, when we saw you coming in I said to Sam, 'Oh, oh, our judge is so damn drunk he won't know the law from a razorback hog! That fellow's attorney will make an idiot of him!' You see, Edgar, our case had become so complicated, I was sure you wouldn't be able to figure out just who *did* have a right to that automobile."

"Nothin' complicated about it!" Eather replied (after inviting us up to help him gargle his throat). "Just a plain case o' good ol' horse sense! Justice boils down t'just that. Plain horse sense."

Guess he was right, at that. The Appellate Court upheld Judge Eather's decision. ■

New Year's Eve at the Rand Ranch

Good neighbors can pull you through anything.

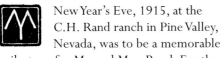 New Year's Eve, 1915, at the C.H. Rand ranch in Pine Valley, Nevada, was to be a memorable milestone for Mr. and Mrs. Rand. For the first time in years all their children except one married daughter were home to celebrate the New Year in a big way.

The C.H. Rands were free of debt and worry. The mortgage on the ranch had just been cleared, the check from the few head of horses recently sold assured the family of a year's supply of food and not a dime owed to a soul. Yes, the Rands felt they had the world by the tail and a down-hill pull.

Their sons, Bill and Dan, had pulled in from Elko long after dark with a six-horse team and two wagons (the lead one being a new Peter Schuttler just purchased in Elko). It was loaded above the sideboards with supplies and some folderols for the women folks—a big drum-type washing machine and a gas engine to power it.

With the wagons pulled along the west side of the ancient two-story home near the kitchen door, it was decided to wait until morning to unload them. Even though it was twenty below at nine p.m., there was no danger of anything freezing as the cases of canned goods were on the bottom of the lead wagon with near two ton of flour, sugar and sacks of oatmeal on top to protect them.

As it was related to me by members of the family that fateful New Year's Day, and many times thereafter during the years, the family had celebrated that midnight with a couple cowbells, much laughter and a few pistol shots by Dan. Distant neighbors were like that. We didn't need a

ballroom, crazy fools' caps and an ocean of "John Barley Corn" to welcome in the infant year.

All except Bill had retired in the spacious upstairs, for after the long haul Bill decided he needed a bath. So, with a copper boiler of water on the roaring kitchen stove and after a bath in a washtub on the floor, he too was soon in bed. A bit later, Mrs. Rand awakened to the smell of acrid smoke and on opening the door at the stairhead she was met by a sheet of sparks. Fortunately, she had the presence of mind to slam the door shut, but her cry had unleashed pandemonium as everyone tried to save whatever they could.

"Save the tin box, Mollie!" C.H. ordered, and Mrs. Rand tossed the box of papers and nine dollars out the south window. It was, "save this, save that!" and articles were shoved or flung out windows.

Dan was trying to push his duck-down feather bed through a pane he had kicked out, then kicked the whole window out to get the bulky "tick" through. C.H. ran down the opposite stairway with an arm of bedding as he shouted, "Save my shoes!" Rachel, who had come up from the University of Nevada in Reno, was in the larger living room below screaming to the boys, "Save my piano! Save my piano!"

As sheets of flame broke through into the bedrooms, Bill and Dan (who had been trying to find their clothes in the darkness) dropped everything and rushed down to aid Rachel and Mary who were trying to push the new piano across the floor. With the four behind it, the piano was skidded into a run only to wedge tight in the east doorway. They had forgot-

ten that in bringing the piano in, they had to remove the door casing. Mr. Rand, in haste and with his arms full of bedding, missed the top stairway step and rolled to the living room floor.

As flames broke through the door between kitchen and living room, it took but seconds for the living room to become an inferno, and the family, unable to get over the wedged piano, exited through smashed windows. It was only then that Mr. Rand remembered the wagons. His shout of "The wagons!" was accompanied by an explosion, and as they rounded the house the flaming wagons greeted their eyes. Two ten-gallon cases of gasoline for the washer engine had been put in the trail wagon and blazing embers and the heat of flames had set the oily gasoline boxes afire, resulting in exploding gasoline spraying both wagons.

One can easily visualize that shocked-dumb family as they stood in the snow on that starlit twenty-degrees-below-zero New Year's in night clothes or a blanket, watching the home disintegrate before their eyes. By sunup, all that remained was a mess of twisted iron bedsteads, cookware and warped stoves. They had one thing in their favor: a ten-by-twelve shack used as a bunkhouse, and in this the women could stay and the men could sleep in the barn hay. Food? There was none.

Their neighbor Bill Yates on getting up in the morning was worried over the valley smoke, so he quickly saddled up and galloped the two miles to the smoldering scene. "My God, Charlie," he greeted them, "this is awful!" Without preamble

Bill Rand

↑ ↑ Charles + Mollie Rand Sr. Dan Rand

All members of the C.H. Rand family. Photo a few years after the old home burned. ← Mrs + ↑ Mr. Rand Sr. on their 50th Wedding Anniversary. Photo By Harry Webb. Dan Rand

he asked, "How you fixed for money?"

"Had nine dollars in a tin box," came the reply, "but when it hit the ice it flew open and all we can find is three dollars."

"Well," said Yates, "have the boys hitch onto your hay rack and all of you come to our place. We'll find some duds for you and the folks and after breakfast you and I are heading for Elko to buy lumber and supplies."

"With what?" C.H. dolefully asked. "Three dollars?"

"With ten thousand if it takes that much!" Yates replied. "I owe nobody, and I

have that much in the bank. Get moving, boys."

"That's mighty nice of you, Bill," C.H. said, "as I don't know if my credit in Elko would cover lumber and money to rebuild and see us through. But Mollie and I will give you a mortgage on everything we own."

"No mortgage, Charlie," Yates all but snapped. "I'd never feel right again if I took a lien against a neighbor. Some day, in years to come if we're both still alive, who knows but that I may have to call on you for help."

Neighbors were like that in those days, and as I watched a far better home evolve from those ashes and rubble, Mr. Rand gave me a laughable footnote to this disaster.

"The funny part was that while we stood watching the wagons and winter's grub burn up, the clothes and bedding we had shoved out windows burned up, too. Mollie had saved some of my shoes, alright, but the only ones that didn't burn up were all for the left foot." ∎

The Transmutation of Herbert Brink

Bad blood between cowboys and sheepmen wasn't just in the movies.

 If anyone had intimated to us at the M Bar that Herb Brink would someday become a vicious, trigger-happy killer, we would have laughed him off the outfit.

Herb was just about the jolliest and finest all-around cowboy it would have been possible to find in the Big Horn Basin, in fact, the whole state of Wyoming. Not the so-called rodeo cowboy of today, but the embodiment of everything a real range hand should be: one hundred and sixty pounds of hardworking, laughing cowpuncher with plenty of cow know-how and a crack bronc rider.

Herb was never mean to a bronc and was equally kind and considerate of the human race. But let some bulldozer try running a whizzer or some spoiled horse get tough and Herb would soon show them they weren't so tough after all.

Herb was especially considerate of some stove-up elderly cowhand who was past the bronc-fighting stage. Or should some green rep (who admitted to not being much on setting a bronc) join the roundup wagon and have a bad actor in his string, Herb would say, "Better let me warm him up for you. I know that horse and you have to knock the nonsense out of him every now and then. He never cottons to a saddle when you first mount him."

Warming him up a bit meant setting the bronc for a hundred yards or so while he sun-fished and bellered and did his best to jar Herb's liver crosswise. But that was duck soup for the laughing Herb. "He'll be jake now," he would say, "until it's his turn on circle again." Herb was just that sort of cowboy.

Herb was an A-one roper, too, be it necking or heeling a calf. He was also a crack shot with the nine millimeter long-barreled Luger he all but wore to bed. I believe he and I were the only ones in the whole Big Horn Basin who had these fine German automatics, and when Herb first came to the M Bar from a broncbusting job at the Pitchfork Ranch, we had many a shooting match at tin cans or a running lobo wolf. Herb liked to gallop past a tin can atop a fence post and put a bullet through it.

One thing about him, if the boss sent him out on some job you could be sure the job was properly done. As our boss, George Pennoyer, said, "One thing about Herb, ask him a question and you'll sure as hell get an honest answer." Like, for instance, one day in August on the beef roundup Herb and I ran across a Hereford bull standing under a lone juniper tree out on a broad mesa. The bull had had the pinkeye for weeks and was long past help.

We had started to leave when Herb galloped back and put a bullet in the bull's forehead, which was observed by our boss half a mile away. Pennoyer met us on a run, red-eyed and cussing.

"Who the hell shot that critter back there?" he demanded. "Just because some cow gets on the prod you up and shoot her, huh? Well, by Christ…"

"I did," Herb replied softly, "and it wasn't a cow but a bull, and the goddamn maggots had eat his eyeballs out. He would have died for lack of water anyway, and I couldn't see him suffer."

"Well," Pennoyer said, "in that case, you did just right."

Herb was in one way different than most cowpunchers. He was building up a little cow business of his own over on the Ten Sleep Range east of the Big Horn River. Over there one needed neither a ranch nor hay. Although there were several little cow ranchers in the Nowood and Ten Sleep Valley, no one bothered about hay. The range was so lush all cowmen needed were a few saddle horses for branding calves and gathering beef.

It was a cast-iron rule among the big cow outfits that no cowboy could work for them if he owned any cattle. Experience had taught them that too many little cow owners had become big cattlemen that way.

But George "Kidney Foot" Merrill and his partners Pennoyer and George Phelps were the exception to the rule. They even sold some cows to Bill Hilcher, a nearby homesteader, just to let him get a start, and Bill went on punching cows for the outfit, paying for the cows out of his wages. So nothing was thought about letting Herb Brink ride for them. After all, Herb's cattle range was sixty miles away across the Big Horn.

Although the M Bar was still known throughout the state under that brand, the outfit since buying the huge holdings from Colonel Torrey in 1903 now used the milliron brand. After the beef roundup and fall work, such as moving stock from one ranch to another, we riders would each carry a "half" milliron on our saddles and cover the entire roundup territory branding any big calves missed on the spring roundup—and there were always lots of them.

That was the ideal part of the year for us. We were on our own. Plenty of roping practice which we didn't consider work, and it was downright fun.

Through the latter part of November and forepart of December in 1908, five of us had been ranging the countryside at will, working out of the various company-owned ranches that were strung from the M Bar on Owl Creek to the Z Bar T (that lay between the Pitchfork Ranch, above Meeteetse on the Greybull) to Cody.

George Mullison was to work down the Gooseberry to the Big Horn. Herb's territory was up the west side of the Big

Horn from the Greybull south to Owl Creek. The "Galloping Swede" and I were to search the range from the M Bar north to Grass Creek. Matt Brown was to work down the Greybull to the Big Horn.

By the middle of December the Swede and I had finished and were back at the ranch, leaving Matt Brown, Brink and Mullison yet to come in. To say that branding "slick-ears" was the finest job of the year would be putting it mildly. On running onto a slick-ear it would find a loop built onto it and while it bucked and bellowed on the end of our "tied fast" rope we would build a sagebrush fire for our branding iron. Then we would drag Mr. Calf close, hogtie it, and soon (if it was a bull calf) he'd be branded, an ear cropped and castrated. These days were the apex of fun after a hard summer of twenty-hour days with the roundup wagon.

There were times, though, when something happened that wasn't funny until we compared notes back at the bunkhouse. I was slapping a hot iron on a bellowing critter when the long-horned mother hit me in the rear, knocking me in the flame. My coat and angora chaps caught fire but Mrs. Cow cared nothing for my predicament and gored and rolled me about until my duds were near burned off. And what the fire didn't consume those horns ripped to shreds besides gashing up her calf's tormenter aplenty.

In the bunkhouse, though, it was hilariously funny. As was an instance the Galloping Swede related. The Swede was a rough, tough cuss and wouldn't take a good rope-horse for the job. He selected a spooky mount from his string, saying, "He'll be a rope-horse by the time I latch onto a few long-ears."

According to the Swede he was getting along "fine as frog hair" until his horse straddled the rope while he was building a fire out on the Zimmerman Spring flat. After bucking and falling down a few times, the spooked horse had taken for the hills as it yanked the calf along followed by its bawling mother. The Swede ran and walked several miles before he could catch the runaway outfit. All of which brings us to the crux of our narrative.

The Galloping Swede and I had been back at the M Bar two days when Kidney Foot Merrill pulled in from the Pitchfork,

which was his own headquarters, just at dinnertime.

"Herb hasn't showed up yet, huh?" he asked.

"Not yet," Pennoyer said, "but he should be dragging in any day now. He had a lot more territory to cover than these others."

The two partners exchanged talk of winter and range conditions and Kidney Foot laughed uproariously over the Swede's and my set-tos while branding, and casually asked how many big ones we had tallied.

While we were still at the table someone said, "Whatcha know; there's Herb now!"

Watching out the window we saw Brink unhooking the bed-straps on his bed-horse and slide the tarp-covered bed to the ground. This done, he led both horses toward the feed racks.

"Toss some more eatin' tools on," Pennoyer called to seventy-year-old Pete Sharp, the cook. "Another hungry hand just pulled in."

Herb came in smiling as always with a "Hi, everybody," and got a "Hi, Herb," in return, with Merrill's greeting as warm as the rest.

"How's things look along the river, Herb?" Merrill asked as smiling and amiable as two friends might.

"Looking extra good," Brink replied. "Never saw stock looking better and the feed's great. Of course that little storm we had a couple weeks ago pushed a lot of 'em down along the river, which give my horse and me a real workout. Looked like we hadn't had a spring roundup at all."

"Lots of long-ears, huh?" Merrill said. "The other boys say the same thing. Hope you didn't tangle with a panicky cow like Webb did, or our Galloping Swede."

"How come?" Herb asked, looking at the Swede, then eyeing my bruised and peeled-up face, Kidney Foot reared back laughing as he retold our experiences with a few embellishments.

Herb slapped his legs and roared along with the rest. "Thought maybe his Nibs here had run through a dead juniper or tumbled down a rimrock. I'm tellin' yuh, Kidney Foot, that's what yuh get for

sendin' boys out to do a man's work." And so went the ribbing as we waited for Herb to finish his meal.

Since George Merrill was known throughout Wyoming by the undignified moniker of Kidney Foot, it might be well to explain how the moniker came about: When he started the long drive north from Texas with a trail herd, his boots were already badly worn but nowhere along the trail could he find a boot large enough to get a foot in and when the drive reached Buffalo, Wyoming, there was little left but the uppers.

On going into a store that advertised, "We have boots to fit any man," Merrill demanded of the young, bespectacled clerk, "Let's see your boots, young fellow." Merrill was inordinately black-skinned

'Not bad,' Merrill said. 'How many did you put your own iron on?'

and of mean visage and the long-barreled six-shooter at his hip had the youth almost afraid to serve him.

"Wha-what size, sir?"

"Never mind the size you skim-milker!" Merrill roared. "Just trot out a number as wide an' as long as they come!"

After hauling out several of the largest size—which were far too small—the timid clerk said, "I'm afraid that's it, sir."

Letting out a string of oaths Merrill said, "Well what the hell kind of a store you running here, anyway? That sign out there says you'll fit any man! So you better get fittin' or by God…"

But the scared youth was already retreating out the back door. Turning, he shouted, "We can fit any man, alright, but not a kidney-footed gorilla!" Merrill's sense of humor spread the story and when he had become one of Wyoming's barons, Kidney Foot was a far better-known name than George Merrill.

We were all lounging in the office part of the huge ranch building when Merrill casually said to Brink, "About how many slick-ears did you brand this trip, Herb?"

"Tell yuh perzactly, in a minute, Kidney Foot," Herb said, getting out a book of cigarette papers. "Got 'em all down right here, uh huh, twenty-one. Eight bulls an' thirteen heifers. Pretty good haul, huh?"

"Not bad," Merrill said. Then in the same casual tone he went on. "How many did you put your own iron on?"

"Twelve, of course," Herb said, laughing. "You didn't expect me to take the short end of the cut, did you?" At this we all laughed as that would be the expected answer from any of us joking cowhands. But Merrill's next words, though spoken casually, froze the sound of laughter.

"Well, Herb, in the morning you take that horse you've used for a bed-horse and go across the river and stay there. If I ever hear of you on this side of the Big Horn again, I'll put you in the penitentiary. George will fix up your time right away. Everything clear, Herb?"

"Clear as mud," Herb said, not the least perturbed. Not another word was spoken regarding the incident, leaving us up in the air as to what had happened and the next morning Herb bid us a joking "so long" and went jogging off on his way to Thermopolis.

One thing that puzzled us most was why Kidney Foot had donated one of the outfit's horses, but after Herb was on his way Merrill soon cleared up this enigma.

"When Herb came to work for us last spring at the Pitchfork his bed-horse got away and went back to his home range, so naturally he had to have a bed-horse. That was the least we could do for any top hand like Herb had been."

That was mighty generous of him we conceded, but we were still in the cellar as to the why-for of sending Herb packing. It all sounded like a huge joke.

Merrill returned to the Pitchfork the next morning and it was Pennoyer who told us the why of things: When Matt Brown had worked down to the Big Horn he had decided to follow up the river a few miles before cutting back to the M Bar. He had run across George Mullison so they had stuck together, seeing a couple calves Herb had put the milliron on. But they also saw a milliron cow bellowing to an answering calf on the east side.

"Now how the hell did that critter get over there?" Mullison asked. "Cow must o' been on that side," Matt replied, "an' the calf was scairt t' follow her back."

Ice was frozen several feet out on both

sides of the river which prevented either the cow or calf from swimming to each other and also making it necessary for the riders to find a swift spot upriver, where the water wasn't swimming deep to cross.

On reaching the calf they found it wore Herb Brink's fresh brand and ear mark. That was Herb's undoing. After dragging the calf across they proceeded upriver and found the process duplicated. On account of slick ice on each side mother and weaner-size calf couldn't get together and only by dumb luck on Matt Brown's part, in choosing to ride up the river a short distance, by spring all telltale marks would have vanished and Herb would never have been suspected. He had

It was a grisly job the two lawmen had gathering what evidence they could.

also been truthful. Exactly twelve calves wore his brand.

Gathering all together, Mullison was left to push the cows and calves to the LU Ranch while Brown headed posthaste for the Pitchfork. With this evidence cinched Merrill lost no time in getting to the M Bar to face Herb.

It was April before we heard any more of Herb Brink. My brother's wife had gone to Nowood to visit her sister Ann and her husband Billy Goodrich at their ranch in the Nowood Valley on the east side of the Big Horn River. The Goodriches had a small cow outfit and while my sister-in-law was there, Brink had ridden in for a hurried talk with Billy.

"Did you know Joe Allemand and his partner Emge have two bands of sheep headed this way?" Herb asked. "They're saying come hell or high water they're going to cross the dead line and sheep us out of the Ten Sleep!"

"Yes, I've heard the talk," Goodrich said, "but I guess there's nothing we can do about it, Herb. It's public domain, so we'll just have to make the best of it. Uncle Sam's bringing action against some of the big layouts for fencing land they don't own, and we don't own this range. So we haven't a leg to stand on."

"The hell we haven't!" Brink said. "Once they get a foothold our goose is cooked so far as us little fellows are concerned, and you know it, Billy!" He turned to Bill Arrison, an old cowboy who happened to be at Goodrich's. "Ain't that right, Bill?"

"Looks that way, alright," Arrison agreed. "But what's anybody to do about it? Nothing. As Billy here says, just plain nothing!"

"The hell we can't!" Brink retorted. "I'll tell you what Al Keyes says we can do about it! He asked me to ride like hell and get every rancher to get on the punkin line [the one-wire ranch-to-ranch telephone line] an' warn all those we can't contact personally. By God we'll stop 'em! So if you want to have some fun an' save the Ten Sleep grass for your cows you better be ready to grab a gun an' get your rumps in a saddle."

"But how can we stop them?" Goodrich wanted to know.

Brink patted the Luger in his chaps pocket. "A dozen of us can kill a few hundred of their goddamned stinking sheep if they set foot across the dead line, that's how! So you fellows better think it over an' fast."

"Yes," Goodrich said, visualizing what the beautiful Ten Sleep range would look like in a couple of years. "You're dead right. Let these two open the gate and others will swarm in like bees to a honey pot. So I'm with you providing we just gun up on their woollies."

"That's all it'll amount to," Herb said.

"Count us in then," Arrison said, laughing.

"Okey doke," Herb called over his shoulder as he hurried away. "But," he added, "if they wanta get tough that's a horse of another color."

The so-called dead line was a posted line with no more legality involved than claiming the Big Horn River. But every few miles, posts with cross-arms proclaimed this territory taboo to sheep. Aside from the few small ranches strung along the Nowood Valley and a few cowboy cow owners, including Brink, a couple Thermopolis residents also ranged their cattle on this lush grass.

Sheriff "Irish Tom" Walsh and a Mrs. Brown (whose husband had been gunned down in his swank Thermopolis home by, according to gossip, someone Mrs. Brown had hidden in the basement) also ran several hundred head of cattle just south of this so-called dead line.

With the Emge and Allemand sheep wagons were Pete Cafferal and a helper boy, Jake Helmer's young son Bounce, with one wagon, and Joe Emge, Joe Allemand and a herder by the name of Lazier with the other. Each had a sheep band of two thousand head. When they had headed northeast for "dead line" territory the owners had received veiled warnings but they let it be known they feared no trouble from the few dinky ranchers and cowboys. They were breaking no law except a moral one and sheepmen and cowmen had always been at odds so threats were nothing new to them.

In the blackness of a young April 1909 night, the Greet brothers awoke to a sound they had hoped not to hear—the crackle and boom of gunfire. Bouncing out of bed in their log house on Spring Creek, one hurriedly lit a lamp (he never knew why) before dashing out to observe many flashes from the guns that rent the

darkness, but only for a moment. A bullet splintered a log by a window sending one in to douse the light. That bullet carried a warning for them to stay on their own "dung hill."

Peering around a log corner they soon saw flames from the burning wagons lighting the landscape. They had observed the two wagons and sheep bands in early evening and had hoped they would reach Joe Allemand's ranch, farther on, without incident. Now the night had been turned into a bleating, thunderous hell. Later that summer a ranch wife told this writer of a bullet piercing her window a mile and a half from the scene of the holocaust and dropping on the floor. The bullet was later introduced as coming from a 30-40 box-magazine Winchester belonging to one of the raiders but due to lack of ballistic testimony it was promptly squelched.

Although the valley telephone wire had been cut, it was later repaired and humming with the chatter of ranch wives who had been warned by their husbands and neighbor men to keep their "traps shut." But too much gossip and names had already trickled to the ears of the law and

long before any actual action was taken Sheriff Felix Alston was not lacking in suspects.

Herb Brink, it was said, had been unable to keep his own trap shut and had named names after dropping into the Goodrich's following the raid. Loose talk had soon put every cowman in the valley in a precarious position, and especially Goodrich and the old cowboy Arrison, as developed later on. By a fluke of rare good fortune they had been stricken "very sick" the afternoon before the raid but, nevertheless, it put an onus of suspicion on them.

It was a charred, gory mess that met the eyes of Sheriff Alston and County Attorney Percy Metz when they viewed the scene of carnage around sundown almost twenty hours after the raid. Joe Emge and herder Lazier were burned until their bodies popped open as they lay among twisted rifle barrels, tinware and cookstove in the remains of their wagon. One body, Allemand's, had not burned. It lay nearby with the throat shattered by a high-powered bullet. Carcasses of sheepdogs and sheep littered the ground near

the wagons while the sheep bands after mixing were scattered far and wide.

With all the carnage, it was a grisly job the two lawmen had gathering what evidence they could. Empty shell casings of various calibers were the main point of interest to the searchers, several being of nine-millimeter caliber. It was easy to determine that they came from a German Luger such as Brink always carried. When the news of the raid reached the M Bar one of the cowboys said to this writer: "It's a damn good thing you weren't in the Ten Sleep country at that time or you'd have sure been up Skunk Creek without a paddle or compass!" How right he was! Our Lugers were identical.

Once a grand jury was called, things happened thick and fast. Billy Goodrich and Bill Arrison were hauled in against their wishes to testify, a move that set the whole cow industry agog with suspicion. Friend turned against friend. Who next might spill their knowledge of the affair? Neighbor gave neighbor the "dog eye" and cattle barons from all over the state hopped into the fray by retaining every top-notch legal mind they could muster, and on learning this the sheep industry followed suit. This was to be a court battle to the finish.

When it was learned that two of the raiders, Keyes and Farris, had made a deal with the prosecutor and turned state's evidence an aura of hate and fear enveloped the entire community. To liven speculation and suspicion, a few hours after testifying Old Bill Arrison went off by himself and blew his brains out. To this day it is doubtful if there lives a person who could fathom the reason.

Bill had nothing at stake, he was simply an old cowboy, owning not a hoof of cattle and liked by everyone. At least until he repeated to the grand jury words Brink had told him. But the crowning puzzle was that he had killed himself with Herb Brink's Luger. Perhaps the finding of those nine-millimeter shells worried him, as he had been seen with the gun. Perhaps guilt over testifying against a friend suddenly deranged him. Who knows?

So tense was the feeling throughout the Nowood Valley when Billy Goodrich reluctantly told his story, Billy's tenure as a little cowman rancher was at an end

around those parts. Likewise a few others. Warrants had been issued for Ed Eaton, Tom Dixon, Milt Leander, George Saber, Herb Brink, Charley Farris and Al Keyes. But when these last two decided to jump to the law's side it left but five in the calaboose at Basin to face their accusers.

Speculation ran rife as to what had become of Pete Cafferal and the Helmer boy Bounce who had been with the Emge wagon and miraculously escaped the massacre. In the turmoil and confusion of grand jury proceedings they had been whisked away by the district attorney for safekeeping until trial date. Bounce had recognized one of the killers. Farris and Keyes had also been spirited out of the country. Where to, no one but the law knew and they weren't talking. These four were far too important to let the cattlemen lay hands on them.

Some said the men were cooped up in Sheridan, others maintained it was more likely they had been hidden away in Cody.

"Alston and Metz wouldn't take a chance on either o' them places," another said. "They wouldn't last as long as a snowball in hell in them cardboard jails! I'm bettin' they ain't even in the state. These sheepmen are out for blood an' I don't mean maybe. And what about the cowmen? With them four dead the state's case would be a blowed up sucker."

When the trial got under way in October, the feelings and open threats by opposing factions were so tense that several members of the state militia were brought in, a wise move. Basin was dangerously represented by angry cattle and sheep interests, who poured in from all parts of the state, so anything could happen.

It seemed half of Wyoming's male population were either housed in the little town or camped around its perimeter. We of the M Bar, the Pitchfork, the T.A. and many lesser west-side cow outfits were among the milling crowds that taxed the town's hostelries. This case was far more notable and controversial than had been that of Tom Horn's after the dry-gulching of Willie Nickell. Now there were two factions involved instead of just cattlemen hiring a "nester" killed.

One affluent cowman was heard to say, "It won't be healthy for any god-

damned jury that convicts them fellers! You can bet your bottom dollar on that!"

And the sheepmen were openly vowing, "If those five murderers don't hang, by Christ the jury will!"

It was the hardest fought case ever to be tried in the state, but the evidence was so overwhelming that on November 17 the fearless jurors brought in the verdict "Guilty." But not quite the sentences the prosecution had demanded. Only one, Herbert Brink, was sentenced to be hanged. (It was proven that the sheepmen had offered no resistance and Brink had shot Allemand as the latter stood with his hands up.)

The other four's sentences ran the gamut from three years to life at hard labor. But at that time we had a cattleman governor and not one of the five remained behind bars for very long. Brink was one of the first ones to be out and within a short time all had scattered to the four winds. Gone were their ranches, their cattle—everything they had once owned and been so proud of had been swept from under them.

Three score and two years have slipped away since that heinous killing and the Ten Sleep and Nowood valleys have long known tranquility. New generations of cattle and sheepmen have learned to abide with each other. The hatreds of the past are now but a memory.

But in looking back over the intervening years, I like to think of Herb Brink not as I last saw him, pale from being denied a summer's sun and slumping a bit as Judge Parmelee pronounced sentence, but sitting a bay mount with one leg crooked around the saddle horn as we compared our Lugers with the heavy guns others packed. Why Herb suddenly turned cattle thief none of us could say. Unless as Kidney Foot once said, "I guess Herb envied us owning over a hundred thousand head and him less than a hundred."

But whatever the reason, Herb was one cow waddie it was good to know and work with, and only for the sudden quirk that caused him to "run" his own brand on calves belonging to bawling milliron cows, the finest cowboy in the land and I would no doubt have shared many more jolly times on the old M Bar. ■

An Extraordinary Mule

Someone once said mules never buck. True, maybe with ordinary mules, but I had a varmint that was crookeder than a sack full of snakes.

 In the early twenties a sheepherder's pack burro, which happened to be an unaltered critter, ran off with our range horses and the next summer I noticed one of my mares had a buckskin something that was all ears and legs.

I figured it must be a mule, but a mule was one breed of critter I didn't need any more than I needed fourteen toes and all of them webbed at that. But three years later I ran in a bunch of horses and there's this buckskin mule with my brand on his shoulder. The black stripe running over his high withers, almost from knee to knee, and rangy legs, gave me an idea.

"Now there," I says to my son, "is the makin's of a lollapaloser of a saddle animal. Think I'll break that booger."

I recalled hearing Buffalo Bill tell of a fast mule he rode when he was a "pony mail" carrier for Majors & Waddel, so that settled matters and a couple weeks after castrating this snuffy, wall-eyed critter, I was ready to start educating him. Or vice versa.

Someone had said mules never bucked simply because being hybrids they didn't know how. True, maybe, with ordinary mules, but I soon found out I had latched onto an extraordinary one!

Buck? That varmint was a wampus cat and crookeder than a sack full of snakes, and I found out those long limbs weren't stuck on him just for walking!

Bronc peelers at one time or other have run afoul of some broncs that would kick their spurs or boot heels off while turning wrong side out, but this buckskin went 'em one better. His hind hoof not only ripped my spur off, he kicked my hat off while he was on his side six feet in the air. Leastwise I figured that's what happened while my head was floppin' down one side or the other. But one good thing about Buck, as I called him, was that his high withers and belly were built for a saddle. Also, anyone who ever had dealings with mules knows they're smart.

Well, this critter was a regular Einstein. When he found out he couldn't unload me in the corral he quit trying and took to neck-reining like a seasoned cow horse.

That's where he had me fooled. Thinking it safe to take him outside I decided one afternoon to ride out about a mile and see if I could run in a bunch of my work and saddle horses on him. On the way to the bunch, Buck acted as though he knew just what I wanted of him, but the moment the dozen or so horses headed down a steep ridge, Buck cut loose with a batch of bucking that had me riding him from ears to tail. I didn't want to get piled and have him take off for parts unknown with my saddle so I went for the old nubbin like I was trying to pull it out by the roots.

Then he quit bucking and sailed after those horses like a real mustanger's mount. But when he got among them, scattering them every which way, he shot on past them and there was no stopping him. That was when I found I had a cold-jawed stampeder on my hands!

With his chin against his brisket, I'm sure he knew there was a cliff ahead and decided to take me for a ride over it. At the speed we were going, the wind was sucking the air out of my lungs, but knowing how smart mules are I was sure he'd put on the brakes at the cliff's brink and was all braced for a sudden stop. Stop? He never slowed up, and the next thing I knew we were airborne.

Now, it's as natural for a rancher or

teamster to yell "Whoa!" when anything happens as it is for a dog to chase cats, and something was sure happening now! When we went off into nothingness, then headed straight down towards a bushy, green juniper, I was yelling "Whoa!" with all my lung power. Landing in the top of that green juniper tree sure saved our lives but very little of our hide and skin.

On seeing Buck tearing down the road minus his "pack," my son ran out in time to shoo my peeled up, blood-streaked mule into the corral. Me? When I came crawling in, most of my clothes and skin were trailing behind me and half my vertebrae were dislocated. I was groaning something that was somewhat stronger than "Now, isn't this provoking?" when my son asked what had happened.

"Tried to kill me!" I managed. "He's a natural born stampeder an' figuring the only way to kill me was to jump off a cliff."

"Well," young Harry said, "if I was you, Pop, I'd get rid of him."

My groaned answer to that was, "I ain't givin' a tinker's damn whether you was me or me you, Bill Rand's gettin' a mule free gratis for nothin' for his mowin' machine!"

When I was able to get to town I was relating my high-dive experience in Martinelli's saloon when a hobo, who was swapping funny sketches for drinks, called for a sheet of paper. In a jiffy I was handed the accompanying sketch captioned with some real mule-skinner rhetoric. ∎

Black Angel

The endless affection from and for Nigger George.

 George Bratten was the son of slave parents and, since he preferred being called "Nigger George," few in our town of Steamboat Springs, Colorado, knew or cared about his surname. "Jus' call me Niggah Geo'ge" he would say with an infectious grin that won him everlasting friends wherever he went.

As near as George could "recollect," he was born around 1858 but in the minds of us kids in 1896 he was as old as Methuselah, an age when kids sit bug-eyed as they hang on every word uttered by these old storytellers. George had learned to read only by studying the labels on cans and bottles but, oh, what a wealth of stories and knowledge came from within that ebony skin. The ideomatics he continually resorted to went far in enhancing his narratives, as we kids hunkered around him at the McKinley barn on the grassy, south shore of Soda Creek.

"When I was a stripplin'," he once told us, "I got tired hoein' and weedin' on that Tennessee fa'm of our Massa's an' had an awful itch t'roam an' see what laid in them fah off places. I'd heard o' Dodge City with its fun and cowboys an' I says look out Dodge Town, heah come Niggah Geo'ge! Then some fraidy cat tries t'scare me. He said 'You won't las' fifteen minits theah among white folks! You'll done catch lead-poison an' don't you fo'git it!'

"Our Massa was just a small plantation man, not big like most, an' when I wants my folks, who was free by then, t'come with me, my mammy says, 'Hush yo big mouf, son! Who'll take care of our Massa John if we leave him?'"

Here a look of sadness had crept into George's soft brown eyes. "Massa John was a good man," he said almost to himself, "a fine man."

George hadn't caught lead-poison in Dodge City, where he labored with other negroes on the railroad for seventy-five cents a twelve-hour day. Then the "itch" further smote him and he landed in Denver. Here he met a Mr. William McKinley, who gravitated between two homes, one in Denver, the other in Steamboat Springs.

A mutual attraction immediately welded these two and George had come to work for Mr. McKinley doing chores and attending to the fine bay buggy team. This was George's past history as he told it to us kids and, just as he had been drawn into the McKinley household, that same magnetic something drew us kids to him; not only the young sprouts but the elders as well. George had become a "chattel" to everyone. Be it an emergency or just a slight "fix-it" chore, and some kid would be sent running for Nigger George.

It seemed the whole town depended on George. And it wasn't because his services were always gratis, for any offer of pay was sure to be negated by his famous laugh and a waving of his outward palm. Although he was one of the family, George received twenty-five dollars a month—the usual wage at that time—and all but two dollars of this always went to a crippled sister back home. His corncob pipe and doing for others was his world, a world he called "hebben."

Whenever the opportunity arose we kids would head for Nigger George's. To us that name spelled everything in the decalogue; wonderful stories and watching him make, or perfect, some contraption we continually found it expedient for him to handle. It got to where we relied more and more on his knowledge and deft hands. To us, no problem or situation was too difficult for him to solve and ours embraced just about everything under the sun.

No one could saw out wood wheels and axles for our wagons, build finer sleds or "snowshoes"—no one called them skis in those days—or whittle out a beanie crotch like George could. When we lacked the dime for a pair of wide rubber bands for our beanies, and had searched the lots and wagon roads without success for saleable whiskey bottles, we could usually rely on George's tobacco-sack pocketbook to remedy our insolvency.

Be it to our credit, though, the giving was not always one-sided. Once when the McKinleys were away in Denver we found George sitting in forlorn meditation. Not only was he out of tobacco, but he had broken his corncob pipe and lost his pocketbook. This called for action, and scattering out we went in search of whiskey bottles. These would bring five cents for the pints and the same amount for two half pints. Naturally, in an emergency like this, the bottle crop would have to be nil so we resorted to trickery.

Sneaking in the open back door of Lee Miller's saloon we purloined several empties where he kept them, then going around front we entered the batwings and sold them to their owner. Hurrying the thirty cents to our friend we proudly told him how we had put one over on the saloonkeeper. But our ego was punctured when the coins were handed back as if they were hot coals and greeted with a lecture that probably influenced most of us through the rest of our lives.

"You git right back there with that money," George scolded, "an' tell Mista Lee 'zactly what you done t'him! Ise 'shamed o' you! Now git!" We got.

When we shamefacedly laid the coins on the bar it was with plenty trepidation that we stammered out our apologies. But instead of our expected execution, Miller seemed angrier with George than with us. "Now, why didn't George come to me in the first place? He knows he can have anything I have, even if it's the buttons off my coat and you tell him so!"

Handing us two packages of tobacco, and a briar pipe he said, "Give him these

and tell him I said not to be so all fired independent from now on. As for you kids, I ought to cut your ears off, but I'll let it go this time."

As we delivered Miller's gift and message George's eyes misted with emotion. "It's jus' like my poor ol' mammy used t'say t'my pa, 'Money haint ev'thin' an' so long as we don't got no ails an' have th' love o' th' Lawd an' folks like Marsh John an' otha white folks we got ev'thing a body needs. Th' Lawd meant fo' all his chillun t'be good t'each otha an' work fo' what they gits. So don't let me heah no complainin'.'"

Fondly eyeing and rubbing his newly lit pipe, George went on, "'An' that goes fo' you, too, George Washin'ton Bratten!' she says t'me. 'Be hones an' nevah let yoh han's take nuthin' yuh' h'aint wuked fo'.'"

So, George said to us, "Let that lesson be fo' you, too, an' don' take no mo' bottles you h'aint earned. An' so long's Ise heah, Mista Lee don' got t'clean his saloon agin."

During the few years I had the good fortune to be around him, we kids, as well as the town's adults, grew to love him to the point of idolatry. Not only was he our arbiter when we kids got into mischief but in times of sickness or danger George was always there to help. When some of us shot out half the windows in old man Phillips' planing mill with our slingshots, it was George who saved our scalps by interceding and replacing the panes.

When half the town's doors had red scarlet fever cards on them, it was George who delivered groceries and loaves of bread baked by the more fortunate ones. Nitre was the only known remedy for allaying fever, but George had something far better. He gathered white sage for a brew that did the job in a hurry without the nitre damage to kidneys. And when One Eyed Griff, in shooting up the town, put a slug through a young man's stomach, George was there, relieving the crippled mother and town wives as they helped and sat watch. When the end came, George's tears were as copious as were those of others.

Folks said it was uncanny how George always seemed to be in the right place at the right time, and proof of this came on three occasions when lives were at stake.

In Steamboat Springs, six feet of snow was a normal winter and, after a heavy snowfall, several of us were jumping off the high peak of a barn and plunging neck deep in the fluffy stuff. Then someone suggested diving off, which I did. The impact of my shoulders wedged the snow so tight around my neck it was impossible to wiggle loose. The frantic wriggling of my exposed feet only added hilarity to the scene so far as my comrades were concerned and, as the last breath was leaving me, I was yanked free. George had seen the foolish antic from two hundred yards distant and wallowed through the snow none too soon. Then he gave us a lengthy lecture on avoiding danger and especially on being alert for the least sign of distress of a playmate.

Another lifesaving performance of George's also concerned me. I had been left to watch over my three-month-old brother, strapped in the baby buggy out in the sun while my mother attended a quilting bee. I hadn't been too watchful and the buggy had rolled downhill and plunged over the cliff that formed the east bank of Soda Creek. George happened to be watering his team when the buggy hit the deep water, stampeding the team. After retrieving the buggy, he hurried down to the bridge and came toting the buggy and squalling baby up to our house. George's lecture, though calm, carried a quality I never forgot.

"Now you promised yo' mammy you'd tend this little fellah, didn't yuh! An' you didn't done it! Now when a body promises somethin', a body should nevah bust that promise even iffen he busts a leg t'keep it. 'Sides maybe drownin' that little shaver yo' done made my team run off and I begin t'think my words ain't no good."

Another George-as-savior-story involved Skinny Smith, the town's nineteen-year-old "character." What Skinny lacked in average sense though, was more than offset by visions of man's future. He strongly maintained that man would someday "be flyin' around like birds," and set out to prove it by making himself a pair of wings.

Secretly he planed and shaved two wide boards almost paper thin at the broad part, fitting the base like a crutch for the armpits. After he had secretly proven to himself that he could fly, he would then give a public demonstration of his ability. Selecting a sixty-foot tree in a remote part of Soda Creek, he climbed to the top, fitted his wings and jumped. But the force of air against the two-foot-wide wings yanked both shoulders out of their sockets, dropping him like a rock.

George, fishing along the stream, came on the unconscious Skinny crumpled there with both legs and most of his ribs broken. Exhausted and breathless, George came toting Skinny into town and it was he who sat many a night attending the suffering Skinny while many said, "The town would be better off if the witless lug died."

The Fourth of July was our big day in Steamboat and I well remember one when George surprised the residents by riding a bronc in the bucking contest. Two half-drunk bronc riders, Bob Gray and Johnnie Vigtoe, just for a gag, gave George two dollars to ride one of the broncs.

At that time, this event was held across the river from town in a sagebrush flat and when folks saw a cowboy earing down the meanest bronc of the lot for

George, Mayor Crawford yelled, "Those fools will get Nigger George killed! Stop 'em somebody!" But he was too late.

That bronc had a hide full of tricks but not enough to cope with George, whose left hand had a death grip on the saddle horn and the rear saddle strings wrapped around his right hand. Unlike today, the bronc had all outdoors to buck in and after going hog wild among buggies and spectators it went over the bank into the deepest hole in the river.

When the gasping George was fished out and being lauded for his fine ride, his only comment was, "I don' know 'bout no fine ride, folks, but I know that ol' man river strangled me 'til I was black in the face!"

It is an old saw that those whom we like best are the recipient of most of our jokes. So it was with George, not drastic or harmful, but some gag the men enjoyed pulling on him for a laugh, with George always laughing the loudest. George had been loaned by Mr. McKinley to camp-cook for two Denver men who had come to prospect an old mine up at Hahn's Peak north of Steamboat, and on his return a crowd was waiting in Judge Danfield's store for George to come in and, as usual, give a detailed account of his outing.

The loungers usually sat around discussing all subjects from the weather to mines as they munched crackers, oatmeal, or any item in the open barrels along the counter. As George talked and ate crackers, Danfield handed him several heavily laden with a new batch of butter Mrs. Woolery had fetched in that day. But instead of being butter, the spread was a new, amber-colored brand of axle lubricant known as Mica Axle Grease.

"Tell us how you like this new butter, George," Danfield said in all seriousness.

Finishing the stack of crackers George said, "Well, Judge, much as I hates runnin' down anybody's product, an specially that nice lady's, Ise got t'say she musta let it lay 'til it's got a mite ransom."

On looking back over those sixty-nine years since I last saw George, I am

reminded of my last knowledge of his honesty and intuition. Those two whom George had accompanied to Hahn's Peak had returned with ore samples running four thousand dollars a ton in gold when tested in our local assay office. The peak and its ore pockets had long been known to Denver mining men and the new find in this thought-to-be-worked-out mine came as no great surprise.

Mr. McKinley, being affiliated with the Colorado Fuel and Iron Company in Denver, soon had a buyer prepared to make a sizable offer for the property. An expert came, sampled the tunnel's face, and found the assays even better than those of the prospectors. That was all the prospective buyer needed to know and the deal was near being consummated when George, even though promised a bonus on the sale, meekly stated his opinion to Mr. McKinley.

"I hates t'butt in, Mistah 'Kinley," he said, "but I done got a look at that rock an' it smells fishy. Ise seen gold outa them Black Hills an' outa Leadville an' they ain't no two 'zactly alike. I'd say that gold in them samples nevah come outa Hahn's Peak. So that gen'man better shoot a few shots in that mine befo' he buys."

Valuing George's peculiar insight, this was done. The mine had been "salted." Nuggets and fine gold had been shot into the tunnel face with a shotgun.

All through the years we have found the negro as a whole imbued with the ideals that placed George high up the human ladder; judged not by our color but as individuals and by our individual traits. And if today's humans of every race could only have known lovable and loving George Bratten, embrace his idealism, practice his philosophy and cherish these as he did, the world would indeed be the ultimate of his "hebben." As those whom he lent succor to in times of sickness and stress often said, "If the good and righteous do become angels in heaven, Nigger George will surely be there." ∎

Training Charley

Charley Pratt's career with the railroad was uphill all the way.

From the time Charley Pratt was old enough to remember how Lola Montez had brought "civilization" to the fighting mining camp of Nevada City, California, by her golden voice, he had wanted to be a railroader. But after he and his mother moved to the state of Nevada, Charley spent most of his life following knife-blade streaks of silver in his mine below Palisade. There was a single exception: his short stint—a very short one—as a fireman on a woodburning, narrow-gauge locomotive.

As the years passed, his mother, "Grandma Pratt," became known to every generation of Palisaders as well as the trainmen on the Southern Pacific and Western Pacific as she sat on the lower step of her little house puffing smoke from her clay pipe, waiting for their shouts and waves.

But getting back to Charley's railroad job. His chance came after weeks of badgering the Eureka-Nevada's general manager for a job. In those days hundreds of tons of freight were trundled across the depot platform bound for Eureka, and the narrow-gauge was bringing back thousands of tons of ore from Eureka's bustling mines.

With the road's carpenters busily building gondolas and freight cars, the general manager suddenly found himself short of crewmen. "Now kid," he told Charley, "this first day is going to be a tough one for you as the engineer will have to be the whole crew to get this train through. Sudden illness of some of the crew has me behind the eight ball, so I'm depending on you two."

At last Charley was in the cab, being instructed by the engineer how to feed the three-foot lengths to the firebox while watching the steam gauge. And when they stopped at the foot of the Garden Pass, how to pile all the wood possible on the tender as a long steep grade lay ahead. Charley was making mental notes of his duties when his mother brought down his lunch bucket and stood watching as the two-crew train got under way.

Looking back and waving, Charley proudly grabbed the whistle cord and held it down until they were across the long, curved river bridge, when he was yanked down from his happy reverie.

"You damn lummox," the engineer yelled, "you've whistled me out of steam. Now get heaving that wood!"

Sixty years later, in relating that episode to a group of us bench warmers on Frank Martinelli's porch, Charley said, "You fellows have no idea how much cord wood that dinky locomotive could consume! When we pulled into the wood and water station at the foot of Garden Pass, the engineer told the wood handler and me to 'stack it extra high' because we had an awful heavy train this trip and might run short on the long grade below Eureka. He also stressed a fear that the little locomotive might stall on the long grade ahead. 'I sure don't want that to happen,' he told us, 'and roll back down and crack up in the gulch.'

"After a mighty effort, that little engine put us over the pass, and the engineer wiped his brow with his red bandanna as if it had been him done all the work.

"'Charley,' he said, once we were humming along, 'for a minute back there, I thought we were going to stall, but thanks to you keeping a full head of steam for me, by God the old girl made it! But I was scared and no fooling!'

"Him calling me Charley made me feel pretty sure I was due for a steady run. I felt good. 'Yes,' I told him, 'your talk with that wood fellow about maybe stalling and us cracking up had the pee-waddin' scared out of me, too. That's why I went back and tightened down all the brakes I had time for before we tackled that summit.'" ∎

THE "SLIM PRINCESS" ABOUT TO LEAVE PALISADE FOR THE LAST TIME AFTER MORE THAN FIFTY YEARS OF SERVICE. I TOOK THIS PICTURE AND PALISADE'S ENTIRE POPULATION TURNED OUT FOR THE OCCASION.

Cigarette George

**It was a mystery where he came from, who he was, and where he'd got
that endless supply of gold coins.**

 Most small towns have their share of peculiar characters, but Palisade, Nevada, had the oddest of all in a five-foot, 120-pounder known only as Cigarette George. If George had a surname he never divulged it during the twenty-six years he trod Palisade's single street.

Cigarette George was an enigma from the moment he stepped off a Southern Pacific train until his death. In fact, the skein of his life became more tangled after his death.

His first puzzling move was when he edged up to old John Swan's bar, his huge cowboy hat barely topping the bar, plunked down a twenty-dollar gold piece and meekly said, "Will you gentlemen join me in a little drink?"

The gentlemen, or otherwise, all agreed it was a good idea as an early May blizzard was howling up through town.

That was the beginning of the town's acquaintance with this little man from nowhere. Folks didn't ask questions and aside from saying, "Just call me George," the newcomer volunteered nothing except to ask if there was "any little house or cabin that might be for rent."

There being no such commodity in this town where the Eureka-Nevada narrow-gauge was the chief succor for the town's few citizens, George paid ten dollars for an old "popcorn wagon."

Then with the help of a few of his newfound friends, a heavy trunk and the wagon were deposited near a pint-sized spring that furnished the narrow-gauge and half the townsfolk's water supply. The Southern Pacific owned every odd-numbered section twenty miles each side of its tracks from "here to there," and since Palisade was on an odd section, anyone and everyone had built a home, store or saloon where they pleased.

With George established in his pop-corn wagon he soon became the town's most popular citizen, though his popularity stemmed mostly from the gold coins he used in lieu of "rag money," and there seemed no end to his gold wealth. Just who dubbed him Cigarette George made little difference, but at least it was appropriate. He was seldom seen without a Bull Durham in his mouth or rolling a fresh one.

Equally as odd as his supply of gold was the five-gallon black hat he wore. Under this enormous, fuzzy headgear he resembled a small boy with an expensive velour umbrella over him. That hat was like a trademark. For twenty-six years he was never seen without it as it became floppier and floppier.

Folks thought him eccentric and in many ways he certainly was. Although gold money was common in our towns in those days, no one had any such supply as Cigarette George. In buying drinks or groceries he would be given greenbacks in change, but it wasn't until the last couple of years of his life he tendered anything but gold. He could reach in a pocket, even a pocket of his perennial vest, and slap down a twenty- or ten-dollar coin.

As year after year wore on, the steady use of his gold was so unorthodox folks began saying, "That darn little booger must have a couple five-gallon cans of that money buried some'eres around his shack! But what the hell does he do with the paper money he gets?" This mystery was compounded as Cigarette George worked like a beaver building a wide rock foundation for his five-by-nine home.

It was queer alright, and George's eccentric doings were discussed not only in Palisade but on far-out ranches and towns. Hundreds of folks who never saw this nonconformist knew all about him, although we who were close to him actually knew nothing. Nothing, that is, except

that "that crazy galoot has more money than old man Carter has pills!"

As the years grew, it was obvious George was growing shorter and shorter and blacker and blacker. Folks believed— and rightly so—that his cramped quarters and the fact that he burned coal in his one-room abode accounted for the shriveling and pigmentation process.

George's friends made no secret of declaring him peculiar, but when he took to cutting the tall bluegrass alongside the S.P. tracks and building a haystack, we felt he had gone off his rocker for fair. His closest neighbor, Emmie Hawkins, had given him a big bed tick, and mornings and afternoons he would scythe down a few swaths of grass. Then after it had cured a few hours, he would stuff the tick full and be seen carrying mountainous packs across town and depositing them inside a wire fence he had put up. Day in and day out during summer he worked at his haying, sloping his haystack from one end so he could walk up it to empty the tick. And those watching from saloon benches would laugh and shake their heads.

Although Cigarette George hadn't as much as a goat, summer after summer he piled a new crop on the old until his stack required a ladder for him to dump his tick-load of hay. Then at the end of each season's haying he was particular in narrowing the stack's crown to keep out rain and melting snows, and the loungers would remark, "By God, ol' Cigarette sure knows how to build a good stack!"

Watching those ponderous bundles go by with nothing but George's feet showing was a comical sight and folks would say, "Now who but a lunatic would work like that when there's no reason for it?"

But time was gradually taking a toll on George, and one hot day he had set his balloon-size bundle down in front of Martinelli's saloon, wiped his brow with a grimy bandanna, and said, "Come on fellows, let's go wet our whistles."

We all wet our whistles and as our host pocketed a gold piece and some bills Bill Hammond said, "George, for Christ's sake tell us where the hell you got all that gold! The whole town's goin' to be as nutty as you are if you don't! For fifteen years or more you've done nothin' but plunk down double eagles. So how come?"

At the door Cigarette called back, "I make 'em, Bill. But my old Pappy always said, 'Never teach another man your trade, son, or he'll put you out of business.'" Cackling over this he rolled and lit a cigarette then got under his bulging tick and left us to wonder further.

"Ol' Cigarette's sure failing," Martinelli remarked as we watched the huge bundle weave on its way. "Be hell poppin' if he set that bundle on fire, wouldn't there?"

"Might just as well," Bill Hammond put in. "Been storing up that hay for five solid years and not a damn thing to eat it. But that gold is what gets my nanny! Some day he'll kick the bucket and Palisade'll see the biggest gold rush since the one to the Klondike. Everybody'll start diggin' up ol' Cigarette's yard for them cans he must have planted."

Weeks later several of us ranchers were shipping our beef, and after the last car door was slid shut and bolted we headed for Frank Martinelli's thirst emporium where Cigarette George had just "decorated the mahogany." Not with gold, but with a ten-dollar bill. "You damn fellers must've smelled this greasy bill," he said through a cigarette. "But come on, I'll buy."

"Well, look at George!" Bill Blair

exclaimed. "He's down to dirty ol' rag money! Run outa gold, George?"

"You better keep abreast of the times, Bill," Cigarette replied. "Didn't you know Uncle Sam made us turn in our gold for this bung-fodder a while back?"

"Yeah," Bill laughed, "but I supposed you were exempt. You know anybody that's lost their buttons ain't responsible in the eyes of the law." At this the crowd began cracking jokes about Cigarette George having the biggest haystack along the Humboldt River. "What yuh go'nta do with it, George? Eat it yourself?"

After taking their good-natured razzing for a while, George said, "That's all right fellows, but I'm not like a lot of you. I'm no I.W.W.; I was born to work, so I put up hay just to keep busy. Besides, some of these winters a lot of you cow fellows would give your eye teeth for that little ol' stack of mine."

We hadn't long to wait for George's

words to bear fruit. It caught us all unawares. On November 12, 1931, it started snowing, and one howling blizzard swept in on the tail of another without letup until March. It was what some called the old equalizer. It reduced big cowmen to ex-cowmen as their cattle starved to death by the thousands.

George Goodfellow was the first to run short of hay and made arrangements to ship five hundred head of his strongest cattle to the San Joaquin Valley in California. But how to get the cattle to Palisade was the problem, though a start had to be made and the sooner the better. A trail was broken by several strong horses wherever possible and men with scoop shovels made a path through the ten-foot drifts.

Three days after starting, the cattle, now weak, had made the twenty miles to Palisade where Goodfellow received bad news from the S.P. agent. "Not a chance, George, to get stock cars here for at least three days."

"Three days!" Goodfellow exclaimed. "These cattle have already gone three days without feed! Another three days and they'll be too weak to ship!"

Cigarette George had made the three hundred yards from his house to Martinelli's saloon on snowshoes made from barrel staves, and on hearing of Goodfellow's plight he said, "If you can get your cattle down near the slough where I got that stack of hay, you're welcome to it. I got plenty pitchforks."

Half the town turned out with trail-shoveling scoops and the Goodfellow cattle were soon "in clover," so to speak. But the queer part of the transaction was, even though hay had zoomed from five dollars a ton to fifty dollars—wherever any could be had—Cigarette George wouldn't accept a penny for his lifesaving stack of bluestem.

"You're the biggest damn fool this side of hell!" George was told as he bought hot-toddies for the crowd.

Each year as his haystack had grown he had been razzed aplenty, but now that it was no more and the cattle were rolling to a less inclement climate, the remarks were out of the joking stage.

"You could have shook Goodfellow down for any price you asked! Talk about crazy! You're even crazier than crazy!"

"Well," George began meekly, "I never claimed to be bright, but I've always had a soft spot for animals besides liking to treat folks when they're in trouble just as I'd like to be treated. And Goodfellow was in plenty of trouble. As for the money, I don't recollect ever hearing of anybody taking any of it with 'em when they shuffled off. Let's have another round, Frank."

Had it not been for killing a raccoon one fall day as I rode into Palisade for mail, it is doubtful if I would have ever learned one whit more of Cigarette George's past than had any other of his friends. He lived but a few yards from two members of the Hawkins family and was largely dependent on them for little favors.

He was a daily visitor at Mrs. Bill Hawkins' for a cup of coffee and depended on Mrs. Nat Hawkins to take a train to Carlin, nine miles distant, and fetch him a loin of pork. In those days a two-foot loin cost but a couple dollars, yet in handing her a ten-spot he would always say, "And get yourself something with what's left!" Under the circumstances if George confided anything of his former life it would have been with these two. But if he did they certainly kept their lips buttoned.

George all but lived on fat meat, which brings us to the raccoon in question. On spying the pelt tied behind my saddle he said, "Where in tarnation did you get the coon? They're better eating than the best hog that ever grunted. Tell me where you left the carcass and I'll go get it."

The upshot was I went back two miles and retrieved the carcass that was white with fat. The old saying, "The way to a man's heart is through his stomach," proved true with George. "Come in," he invited, "and have some coffee and beans

while I wash the gravel out of this fellow. Haven't had a taste of roast coon since I left California." As I had never been inside his domicile, I accepted his invitation.

His mentioning California was an opening wedge, and as I sat on the narrow bed, blackened like everything else from coal soot, George unfolded a tale that was as tragic as it was humane.

"Believe it or not," he related, "I once owned one of the finest dairy farms in Marysville, California, besides having a prosperous butcher shop business in the heart of town. But when a man's family turns on him, well—but you don't want to hear about family fights. Now if you ever want to cook a coon, always roast him…"

I got George stopped on how to cook a raccoon and asked what became of his Marysville business.

"She still has it, I reckon," he replied. "Yessir, my wife was the meanest woman God ever put breath in! Two daughters wasn't any better. They always sided with their mother no matter how much to blame she was. So when I couldn't stand her jawing any longer I went to a lawyer and signed over every stick and critter to her and…" George held up the carcass that now resembled an overfat lamb. "There now, I'll have me a roast coon tonight that will make your mouth water."

He continued, "Well, we had a good-sized joint account in the bank so I drew out $20,000 which left a little more than that for her. Then I went home and told her to have at it. She's all yours, I says, and wished her luck. When I walked out that house she threw her head back and mocked me and says, 'When will you be back, George?' and I says 'By God, never!' And that's the way it's been. I was never a drinking man and outside of a sociable drink I've stayed that way. Money means nothing to me, but I've enough to last from here on out."

I pondered this all the way home, trying to make myself believe his bizarre tale. Was his mind playing tricks on him or had he been spoofing me? I decided to keep mum on the subject and let the town go on wondering.

A year later, I had been north of the Humboldt looking for a horse of mine that had gotten away with a saddle on

him. I had sold the bronc and saddle to a young fellow who promised to pay me the fifty bucks "in a few days." But the kid was sparking a neighbor Mormon girl and in the interim had gone over one afternoon to the Pace homestead to visit her.

The numskull had tied the bronc to Mrs. Pace's clothesline post when the line was filled with dresses and Lon Pace's underwear, and on hearing a commotion outside she had run out in time to view an exasperating sight. The horse was headed north up the canyon with her line of laundry hooked under the saddle horn. The young fellow had received such a bawling out from Allie's mother he left the country and I was out a horse and saddle.

All day I had been searching the hills north of Palisade. As I came back through town I stopped at Nat Hawkins' house. "Nat around?" I asked his wife, Myra. Nat was the deputy sheriff.

"He's up at the jail," Myra replied, and I noticed she had been crying. "Cigarette George died this morning, so Nat and some of the folks have him laid out at the jail waiting for the undertaker to get here from Elko." This was an unexpected shock, as George had been plenty active two days before. In the forepart of the jail which served as a polling place, I saw George, looking smaller even than in life, laid out on a two-by-twelve plank resting across a couple chairs while Nat and his son-in-law sat at a table playing cards.

"What happened?" I asked.

"Heart attack, I guess," Nat replied. "Maybe he et too much raccoon. He had stopped in at Emmie's for coffee and wasn't feeling good. So after a while Emmie went over and found him on the floor by his bed."

The talk turned to George's hidden "five-gallon cans" of wealth.

"Find any money around?" I asked.

"Not a dime," Nat said. "But he must have it buried because we sure as hell gave that shack a real shakedown." We were discussing this puzzle when the undertaker and coroner arrived.

"Who's handling the funeral arrangements?" the undertaker asked as the coroner began examining the corpse.

"Far as I know," Nat answered, "it's up to the county. I've phoned to Edgar Eather in Eureka and he and Sheriff Jim

CIGARETTE GEORGE LIVED IN THIS POPCORN WAGON.

Ratattzi'll be down. Eather's our district attorney and said we'd bury George here on the hill."

An exclamation from the coroner brought our attention and we saw him untying a large tobacco sack. "Had this pinned inside an undershirt," he told us. "He had two undershirts on." At the table he began counting bills as our eyes bugged out further with each counted hundred.

"Seventeen hundred and fifty dollars!" the coroner said. "Have you any way," he asked Nat, "to keep this money until your district attorney gets here?" He was told the money could be kept in the safe at the narrow-gauge office, so Nat signed a form and George's earthly remains were on their way with the undertaker.

"Now ain't that one hell of a note!" Nat exclaimed. We knew exactly what he meant and agreed that it sure as hell was! If finding the money pinned to George's coal-blackened underwear was a revelation, it was nothing in comparison with what was unearthed when Sheriff Ratattzi pulled the lock off a tunnel door in back of George's domicile which he had dug for a cellar and storeroom.

"Lord!" Ratattzi exclaimed. "Where do you suppose Cigarette George got all this stuff and how did he ever cart it here? Talk about a pack rat!" At this I couldn't resist telling him and Nat what George had revealed to me. "Well," Ratattzi said, "that accounts for all that money he had, but all this stuff is a damn sight more puzzling!"

"Puzzling" was the understatement of the age. It appeared that any item in the line of hardware and whatnots was repre-

sented in George's cache. Yet there was scarcely an item among the tons of brand-new articles that George had, or ever would have had, any use for. But the queerest part was that no one had ever seen George bringing it there!

Months later, as the sheriff and district attorney stood among us ranchers and townspeople on a hillside that looked like a junk dealer's dream, Ratattzi said, "Now folks, here's the proposition. We've been in touch with a couple of women who claim to be George's daughters, so they think they are entitled to their dad's estate, which they think must be enormous as he was once rich. But from what we've learned, they're the last persons on earth poor old George would want to get a dime. But we haven't liked the tone of their sarcastic letters so we're going to see that his estate isn't worth a postage stamp. Get what I mean?"

We well understood what Jim meant, and we all laughed when he added, "So you better all have a wad of money because this sale is cash on the barrel head!" We savvied a hidden meaning there also.

"Alright, then," he began, "each of you pick out what you want and when I auction it off I don't want anyone to raise another's bid. We'll start with that grindstone."

Dan Rand was the only rancher with an engine to turn the thirty-six-inch stone that would normally cost forty-five dollars. "Fifteen cents," Dan said. "Sold!" said the sheriff, as Edgar Eather kept books.

Dan bid ten cents on a dozen new irrigating shovels and divided them among us. Frank Yates said, "Ten cents!" when a hundred-pound anvil was auctioned. Three kegs of assorted horseshoes fetched two bits and were divided between three of us. Three bundles of pitchforks of five to a bundle put another thirty cents in Eather's sale book and a dozen long-nosed spike-

mauls went to C.B. Sexton, manager of the Eureka-Nevada Railway for a quarter.

Monkey wrenches, Stillson wrenches and claw hammers were lumped off to Sam Zunino at a dime for two dozen or more and divided among us ranchers and himself. Fourteen six-pound sledgehammers, with S.P. stamped on them, went back to the Southern Pacific agent for free.

Wendel Jones bid ten cents on a complete set of bronze fireplace tools, screen, and gargoyle andirons. Not that he or anyone around had a fireplace but, as Wendel said, it was for "speculation." That and one other item were the puzzlers of all Cigarette George's hoard—a magnificent chandelier. That was a thought provoker.

A two-hundred-foot coil of steel stacker cable was knocked down to Bill Blair on his magnanimous bid of thirty cents. Two new wheelbarrows put another twenty cents in the estate's coffers.

Then came the crystal teardrop chandelier, which was the envy of all. This went to our postmistress for her exorbitant bid of fifty cents. A fancy grilled electric heart brought a quarter from Tony Demale even though he was fifty miles from electric power, and some wag said, "You'll have to plug that into your Coleman lantern, Tony!"

And so on down the line as *objets d'art* and whatnots went for a dime each including a two-foot-high Turkish vase. George's Winchester pump shotgun brought a whole quarter from John Craig, the narrow-gauge's boilermaker.

"Now," Ratattzi said, "I think the proceeds of this sale and that found in Cigarette George's shirts will just about cover the funeral and other costs. Don't you think so Edgar?"

"To be explicit," our district attorney replied, "I don't think so, I damn well know so."

So ended an era of a once-prosperous individual's life. No doubt the authorities had learned the name of the deceased but if it was used anywhere no one remembered it. To us he was just Cigarette George. In life he and his gold coins had been a deep enough mystery but it was nothing in comparison to what his death had left behind for us to ponder over. ∎

"Challenge at the Water Hole" © J.N. Swanson

HARRY'S RANCH WAS IN WILD, OPEN COUNTRY, AND IT WAS ALWAYS SURVIVAL OF THE FITTEST. THIS LITTLE BAND OF MUSTANGS IS LED BY A MARE WHO CHECKS TO MAKE SURE IT'S SAFE TO DRINK FROM THE CREEK. AS SHE SMELLS LION IN THE AIR AND THE MOUNTAIN LION GIVES A FAKE ATTEMPT AT BEING BRAVE, THE YOUNG BUCKSKIN STUD ROARS IN FROM BEHIND TO PROTECT HIS MARES AND COLTS. THE STUD ROUTED THE LION OFF THE ROCK AND CHASED IT ACROSS THE SAGE-BRUSH. MOUNTAIN LIONS ARE NOT COWARDS BUT THEY ARE CAREFUL. IF THEY GET A PAW HURT OR KICKED, THEY WILL FIND IT TOUGH TO SURVIVE.

Them Damn Cats

Sheepmen don't mind critters killing when they're hungry, but these two bobcats ate the liver out of one lamb and killed the rest just for meanness.

 With eight years of government trapping behind me, and over five thousand coyotes—and almost that many bobcats to my credit—I thought I knew all there was to know about predatory animals and especially "cats."

Any trapper would tell you that coyotes—some coyotes—could outsmart the brainiest fox that ever lived, but as for cats it required no more know-how to trap them than to shoot suckers in a rain barrel. Since cats depend as much on sight as on smell, a feather stuck in the ground or a small piece of red cloth on a bush was as good a lure as most scent.

To be a good trapper one must think like that particular animal. Yes, bobcats might be the stupidest of all predators but, as sheepmen knew, also the most expensive to support. It was several years after I had quit trapping for the government that I discovered I didn't understand all I knew about cats.

It was in late August 1929 that Isadore Sara—a Basque sheepman—came to my ranch with a problem that neither he, his camp mover nor three herders could handle. He was "topping out" the lambs of three bands of ewes on a mountain east of my ranch.

"It's the cats!" Isadore began. "I tell you if you don't get them damn cats they'll ruin me. They've killed sixty-eight lambs in two weeks and it's still two weeks before we can start for the shipping pens."

I didn't blame Isadore for being on the prod. We've had about two hundred ewes and lambs on the ranch in pasture and Isadore's loss of all those "black face" ninety-pound lambs, at twelve cents a pound at the railroad, was enough to make a saint swear.

"Doesn't sound like cats to me," I told him. "I'd rather think it's the work of an old coyote that's lost two or three legs in traps or it's a lion." (A mountain lion will slip among a band and kill a dozen sheep in five minutes.)

"Hell, no!" Isadore fumed. "It's them damn cats! Two whoppers. My herders have seen them. I don't mind critters killing when they're hungry, but these cats maybe eat the liver out of one and kill the rest just for damn meanness. It's like they was trying for a record or something. And don't tell me to try setting off bombs, either. My herders have set off enough bombs and dynamite to blow that mountain up if the powder was under it. And they set all day and half the night with their rifles, but the cats make a joke of them. No matter where the herders are the cats know it. They're human, I tell you, just plain human! If they wasn't they wouldn't walk right in any time of day and kill and kill."

Although we were crowded with work on the ranch, I promised to take a look-see around and try to figure out what could be done. But knowing that mountain as I did the palm of my hand, I could already see difficulty. With quaking asp trees scattered about the high ledges, along with two huge rockslides on the north slope, my dogs would be useless. A cat could dodge into those slides at any spot and come out hundreds of yards away. Rock slabs up to the size of a house had been thrown up and left in two long streams by some giant upheaval that had all but ripped the mountain apart.

When I reached the nearest band I found the herder, his carbine handy, making bombs. This is done by placing a layer of black powder in tomato cans, then a layer of sulphur, alternating powder and sulphur until the cans are full; the last layer being sulphur. When night comes, the herders place them about the bed grounds and light the sulphur. This burns slowly and later ignites the layer of powder and so on. As many as four explosions occur at long intervals from each can and are usually very effective against marauders.

"No good here," the Basque herder said, "but I make 'em anyway. Oh, scare ky-o-tee some, but not them cats. They prob'ly over there now someplace making big laugh at us."

When the lambs are being topped out, the bands must range wide and are never close-herded, so it was a problem setting traps where sheep didn't walk into them. With six thousand ewes and lambs roaming all over the mountain the herders and I were kept busy taking sheep out of traps, and while a #3 Newhouse didn't bother the ewes too much, it often splintered a lamb's leg. I made sets in the rockslides with scent but it was only wasted effort.

Before two days had passed, I too was convinced that those cats were part human. At least they thought like humans. Being determined to outwit them, I brought my best trail dog and, like the herders, sat with my carbine and the patience of a housecat at a gopher mound. I kept my eyes peeled in all directions, only to see sheep suddenly scatter. Sometimes this happened a quarter-mile away, other times but a few yards. But a cat's color blends with that of a sheep so closely nothing could be seen to shoot at and my bellowing dog tearing through the band only added to the damage by piling sheep end over end.

And while my dog worried himself to the panting stage fighting that boulder slide, the herder would be "dressing out" one or two fat lambs that had spilled a quart of blood from their opened throats. Ordinary cats being partial to fish I placed poison capsules in fish deep among those slides (so as not to poison a herder's or my own dog), but these two hellions were the most unorthodox cats I'd ever run up against. It was a cinch they never ate the fish baits or they'd have been dead.

During the two weeks I spent being educated by those furry sheep killers, I lowered the predator population by shooting two coyotes and trapping one cat some distance from the sheep bands, even though I was certain they were innocent of the carnage that went on without letup. And while Basque sheepherders prefer mutton to lamb, the cats kept them, as well as my outfit, eating high on legs o' lamb until we all craved a good old feed of beefsteak. Finally time ran out and the sheep, minus one-hundred-and-thirty-four lambs, were on the trail to the railroad and, with all my know-how, I had nothing to boast of except that I would get those cats if it took me all winter.

October came dry and cold, which made heavy-furred pelts and ideal trapping conditions. And with prime furs it held promise of being the highest price in years. Better yet, I had seen enough coyote sign

on the flats west of the high-cliffed mountain just north of my ranch to promise a bumper crop of pelts in jig time.

We had shipped our wether lambs, keeping about fifty ewe lambs for breeding. The ranch work was caught up, so I set out with a batch of traps to set along the nearby cattle and mustang trails that were literally padded down with coyote tracks.

As I started over this trapline two days later, I fully expected to have quite a skinning job, but I hadn't visited half a dozen sets than I knew I was in trouble. Every trap, except two with coyotes in them, had been dug up and were lying on top of the ground. What was worse, most of the squares of overalls I had placed over the trap pans and under the jaws were gone. Coyotes in traps often chew up the rag coverings, but this wholesale disappearance had me stumped.

On my next trip, I met with the same luck; traps exposed and minus their cloth coverings. In two weeks the overall squares I lost would have made half a dozen patchwork soogans and I was getting mighty few coyotes, although on other lines nearby I was hauling in the pelts. Every trapper has run up against some educated coyote, usually an old one, that would uncover every trap, but not a rag-stealing one. And since overall material was just the right texture to keep the covering of dirt from clogging the pan, I was searching ranch bunkhouses for old overalls until folks must have thought I had lost my buttons.

Sheep are predominately brush eaters and when I started trapping we would turn our small bunch out each morning below the high cliffs just north of the ranch where there was lots of buck-brush below the ledges. In the evening, either my stepson George or I would bring them in. Once, when we had left them out overnight, the coyotes had killed several ewes. A long, hard winter had decimated the millions of jackrabbits so the coyotes had to turn to sheep when their bellies got empty.

One evening, as I came in from my traplines, I was greeted with news far more disconcerting than my trapline troubles had been. George had been attracted by magpies to seven of our big lambs and two ewes, scattered in a radius of a few hundred yards. Three coyotes had run away as he came up. The peculiar part of it was that the slaughter had occurred late that day. Five lambs bore no marks except torn throats.

"I'll fix the coyotes!" I said. Waiting until any crows or magpies had gone to roost, I placed strychnine baits made with tallow in and under the carcasses. Coyotes had long since fought shy of the smell of cyanide or strychnine directly in carcasses so all government hunters had long been placing strychnine in small cubes of tallow.

Keeping the sheep and also my dogs penned up the next day, I yelped with joy when I found four poisoned coyotes. None had made it a hundred yards from the carcasses. "We'll have no more killings now," I said, though a bit puzzled over the fact that the sheep had been molested in the daytime.

Two evenings later, George had gone to fetch in the sheep and saw them running and tumbling down the steep slope and glimpsed two big bobcats hightailing it for the ledges above. What was more, he found three of the best lambs scattered about, their throats ripped open from ear to chest but no sign of the flanks being opened up.

"Do you suppose…?" George began thoughtfully.

"You're damn right, I suppose!" I said, along with some first-class cussing. "Those two cats have moved in on us, that's what! But they've picked the wrong territory this time, and I don't mean maybe! Tomorrow…"

"What about those ledges, Pop? The dogs have run cats in there dozens of times and we've never got one out yet."

"I didn't have my dander up then," I told him. "That's why."

The next morning, I was elated to find a skiff of snow had fallen during the night so hurriedly putting some hay in the browsed-out pasture for the sheep, we whistled up the dogs and took off. First I would see if I had anything in my "hard-luck" trapline, as I called it, then we would explore those ledges for cat tracks.

"If we could just be lucky enough to jump those cats out in the flat," I said, "their name's mud."

We were still half a mile from the first trap when the dogs picked up tracks and from the tonguing chorus and drawn-out bellow of our redbone hound as they headed toward the top of the mountain and the ledges, I knew they were on the red-hot trail of those cats.

But we were just a bit late. By the time our panting horses had reached the top of the ledges, the dogs were running up and down above the deep fissures where we had lost cats time and again. However, we made a discovery that made me stare in disbelief. The mystery of the disappearing trap coverings was solved. Under an overhanging ledge, where cats had long bedded down, lay my trap coverings. All had plenty of teeth marks and many had been chewed to soggy balls. Those cats had been the culprits that had put the kibosh on my coyote catching as well as making me a candidate for the booby-hutch.

"You know what?" I said, a sudden thought striking me. "You hightail it to Old Tommy's and see if he still has his pet bobcats around! While you're doing that, I'll go over one of the traplines and tomorrow, or whenever we catch these blasted cats off base, we won't let up until they're our meat."

"I don't think it's Old Tommy's cats," George said. "He's had them since they were kittens and they never bothered anything of his. So what makes you think it might be them?"

"All these rags," I snapped. "Besides, the old hermit never had anything for them to bother. Get going."

Old Tommy Jewell had been a bit queer for years, but since we'd had some "words" over my trapping within a mile of his place, he had gotten the idea I was laying to kill him. He had told sheepmen—who supplied him with grub and clothes so they could water their bands near his cabin—that he often saw me waiting behind bushes for a shot at him. Before we had fallen out, his two bobcat kittens had given me many a laugh as I watched them glom onto the cuffs of Old Tommy's overalls and hang on like bulldogs as he shuffled around. They still did it when they had grown to thirty-pounders and could all but drag him around. So it just could be they had succumbed to their wild instincts and taken to the hills. Tommy had castrated them when they were kittens and had been sure they never would leave.

That evening, as I was putting three coyote skins on stretcher boards, George came in all excited. "You hit the nail square on the head, Pop," he said. "Old Tommy's cats started staying away in the spring for two or three days at a time, and finally for good. He hasn't seen them since the middle of August so it must have been these same cats that worked on Isadore Sara's lambs. So we've got to get 'em now or we won't have any lambs by spring."

Thinking the cats would probably go back to the trapline for what appeared to be their favorite pastime—although I had ceased bothering to reset the traps—we circled the country without the dogs, picking up any tracks until we were back along the ledges. But since the cats could be holed up anywhere in them, we didn't bother to investigate.

On returning home in the late afternoon though, we were attracted to the sheep pasture by two crows, and on investigating could scarcely believe our eyes. There lay a lamb, still warm, its throat and flank laid open, entrails exposed and the liver eaten.

We examined the woven-wire pasture fence and found cat hairs where they had climbed over. If slipping in while we had every dog off looking for them wasn't adding insult to injury, I didn't know what was. In a jiffy we had the dogs on their trail, and in a short time we knew from the sounds the cats were holed up.

When we arrived at the ledges, we found the dogs trying to get back in a sloping, narrow cleft in the bottom of the hundred-foot-high cliff.

"Get up on top as quick as you can with two of the dogs," George said, "and I'll keep Old Mose and try to crawl in here a ways. Then, if the cats come out above or down here, we'll get 'em."

"Better yet," I said, "we'll burn 'em out! You stay here and start pulling any sagebrush and grass you can while I beat it to the ranch for a batch of hay."

With those instructions, I was already on my way. Night would be closing in to defeat us if we missed this chance. We both knew the cats could only come out of this one way below, although directly above this sort of cave they might be able to squeeze through one small opening. The cats would no doubt stay put, though, while the dogs were making a howling fuss below.

George already had considerable brush and grass carted back in the narrow slot when I arrived with four gunnysacks of dry hay. With this stuffed in behind the brush we were ready for business—that is if the cats hadn't already gone out above. On reaching the top, I was sure they hadn't. Some feet down the hole was clogged with a big rat nest. With two dogs on the alert, I sat with my Parker shotgun cocked and the safety off. I wasn't taking any chances of missing if the cats should leap out of some exit I hadn't seen.

"Set 'er afire," I yelled down and in a few seconds wisps of smoke began trailing out, then fed by a hundred-foot updraft was belching smoke and flame with a roar as if a volcano had let loose. A minute of this and I decided the cats had found another way out. No animal on earth could stand that inferno.

"See anything?" George yelled up.

"Nothing but a hell of a lot of smoke," I shouted back. "They must have…"

A sharp crack, followed shortly by another from George's Luger cut my words. Old Mose was sounding off his snarling, fighting bellow that sent my two dogs and me racing to where we could get down through the ledges. Then George was shouting a litany of "We got 'em! We got 'em! We got 'em!"

One monster lay by George, its fur still smoking. What had been a beautiful pelt was singed to where it was now worthless. The cat down the hillside that Old Mose and the other dogs were milling around only had his nose whiskers burned off. He had leapt through the flame and received the slug from George's Luger in his chest in midair. The second one, on seeing George, had paused on the slanting wall and let the flames roar around him until a bullet had toppled him forward.

Although triumphing over these two hellions called for a lot of backslapping, I was stabbed with a twinge of remorse as we loaded those two bodies behind our saddle cantles. Now that the exasperating siege of trying to outwit them was over, I couldn't help but look back on their antics and envision them as two beautiful, spotted kittens growling, chewing and clinging to Old Tommy Jewell's overall cuffs. Even their monkeyshines in upsetting my traps and purloining the cloth coverings suddenly far outweighed the lamb losses we had suffered.

There would be hundreds, yes thousands, of bobcats to follow and, no doubt, thousands of lambs killed by them. But I felt sure there would never again be cats with such a passion for killing or the ingenuity for downright cussedness and deviltry that these two had possessed. ■

The Mysterious Stranger

It was just another quiet night in the ghost town of Buckhorn until the young drifter burst through the door.

 The entire populace of Buckhorn, Nevada, was gathered round Judge Van Laningham's kitchen table for an evening of pinochle and arguments over the present status of this once roaring mining camp.

"She'll come back," said Polish Mike. "She's come back three times and'll do it again! When spring comes those capital fellers will come lookin' for some place to invest their money."

"Yes, siree," Bob Jarsen agreed. "Then Van here can be our real judge again and rule the roost."

"By God," Judge Van said, "I still run things around here, and if you fellows don't believe it just get outta line. We still have a solid jail down the gulch, you know."

Good-natured banter went on as they plunked down cards and listened to the howl of the wind that whistled down from the crown of the Cortez Range. A blizzard was showing its fury, but that hadn't stopped the nightly gathering of these three men who firmly believed in the resurrection of the old camp.

"Hey," Jarsen exclaimed, "did I hear a banging at the door?"

The noise came again and, on opening the door, snow and a stranger were blown in with the blast of air. With the collar of his sheepskin coat around his ears and snow plastered on his whiskers, it was hard to guess his age or looks—but no matter. The welcome mat was always out to strangers in Nevada and doubly so on a night like this.

The stranger had noticed what looked like a barn near Van's light. He was told to put his horse there as there was a bale of hay, or should be, and then supper would be fixed for him. Once the door was shut behind him, the three men began speculating as to who he was and what in the first place was he doing way up here?

Bob Jarsen thought he had the right answer. "We all know one of the Baby Face Nelson gang was seen by the Merrill brothers only a few days ago. In fact he barged in on them and they fed him."

The stranger's return stopped that theory short. But the seed of suspicion was planted even though Judge Van poo-pooed such wild conjecture.

The code of Nevada being against prying into strangers' affairs, the three learned very little as their guest appeared careful of what he said. However, as he devoured Van's stew like a starved pup he volunteered a few words. He had been working on the Dean Ranch (only a couple miles from the Merrill brothers' prospect cabin) when he heard his brother had been in a bad wreck, and he was now on his way to Eureka.

As the evening wore on, Jarsen and Mike decided to get to their own quarters before the snow got any deeper. Besides, they couldn't seem to learn anything from the stranger anyway.

Morning dawned clear, and after a fretful night, plagued with a premonition that something at Van's was amiss, Mike hurriedly got into his clothes. At Van's he found the place empty, cold and—worst of all—with bloodstains all over the house. But where was Van's body? Mike went first to the barn and then on to Jarsen's cabin, where he chattered a few garbled words that sent both ploughing through deep snow to the puzzling scene.

"Damn wonder he didn't murder us too," Mike said as they searched for "poor ol' Van." There was no chance to get Van's car through such snow so Mike, being the strongest, volunteered to head for the Winzell Ranch twenty miles down in the valley where there was a phone. "You keep lookin' around," he said to Jarsen, and with two cold biscuits in his pocket he was on his way.

Jarsen was probing a mound near the house when yells jerked his thoughts and eyes elsewhere and Mike came into view. "Git a crowbar," Mike gasped as he floundered forward. "He locked Van in the jail!" This added to the perplexing problem of blood, but at the jail they found bloodstains all over the lock and door and a raving Judge Van inside.

With the hasp pried off and the irate judge freed, he gave a generous cussing account of happenings. "I didn't want that jasper sleeping with me so I told him if he didn't mind being in jail he would at least be comfortable there. That was okay with him, so while he was digging the wood from under the snow just outside the door, I was trying to light a fire in the stove, as I always kept 'er ready to light in winter. But every time I lit a match the damn wind would bang the door shut and I was running out of matches. I yelled at that lunkhead to hook the hasp over the staple until I got the fire going and the damn fool not only done like I told him but he hooked the lock in it and snapped it shut!"

The judge took time to describe "that half-wit…"

"Can't see why he left yuh there, unless like we told yuh," Mike put in, "he was the Baby Face fellow, but why all the blood?"

"Because," Judge Van said, "I must have scared the daylights out of him by cussing him and telling him I'd blow his damned head off when I got out. Must have got a bad cut trying to tear that lock off with just his fingers."

Back in Judge Van's kitchen the three were discussing the mysterious event while Van stirred up his famous sourdough flapjacks. "I maintain we should get to a phone and get 'em on the trail of that feller," Mike said. At this Judge Van turned on Mike as if he had committed an unforgivable sin.

"Now you fellows listen to me," he roared. "I'm not giving a tinker's damn who he was—even if he was Baby Face himself!" Then he mellowed. "Remember now, keep this under your caps." Raising his right hand, he had them raise theirs and exercised his pseudo office to swear them to secrecy.

"If this got out," he warned, "we all might be pegged as damn fools." ∎

Waiting for Mary

Why couldn't Tommy get on the westbound train?

 A crony, "Gaspipe" Mullison, was the cause of my being in Nevada. He had written such a glowing account of the state I was hooked. Why, the winters were so mild ranchers turned their cattle on the range in February and the cowboys went around in shirtsleeves. To cinch matters, a job awaited me helping him break horses for the war. He and the boss would meet me.

Ha! So this blizzard was Gaspipe's fabled Utopia, huh? Hugging my pink silk shirt and light coat to my shivering carcass I bunted my way against the storm. That's when I bumped into the individual who was to become a close friend and plays a role in this narrative. With his sheepskin collar held tight against his ears, I shouted, "Any place around this burg where a fellow can get a drink and warm up?"

"Follow me," he shouted back, "and I'll show you." I catalogued him as just another old "sourdough" who hadn't two nickels to rub together. As we headed for the town we couldn't see, he said, "The Eberts Hotel is just up the slope and John Swan…" but the wind erased the last sentence.

As we bent elbows and exchanged names I learned my drinking pard, Tommy Jewell, was a well-known character in Palisade and Pine Valley to the south and was also in for a lot of ribbing from those I had invited to join us.

"How's your love life these days?" one laughed, and the hotel's owner, who appeared to know a Mary White and her parents better than most, asked, "Mary still in San Jose, Tommy? Last time we heard from her folks, Mary was working in a doctor's office, but that was years ago. What's the latest about her, Tommy? We

hear you correspond but it's a wonder she hasn't dumped you years ago and got hitched up."

Tommy was about to reply to some jokester when a hand gripped the collars of my coat and shirt and I was jerked backward. Thinking it was Gaspipe, I was wishing his greeting was not so rough, but instead I was being yanked and cussed by someone who thought I had let my sheep get in his meadow. A moment later, John Swan had come from behind his bar and had given my attacker the bum's rush down the hillside.

I was viewing my torn shirt and as Swan refilled our spilled glasses he said, "Crazy as a loon. He must have escaped from some institution 'cause he sure ain't from around here."

I was wondering if I wouldn't be wise to take the first eastbound train back to Elko, where I had left my wife until I took a look at this Hat outfit, when Gaspipe and the ranch owner, Bob Raines, blew in on a gust that shook the building. Naturally, this called for drinks and a new start on the kidding. Seemed Tommy's love affair with Mary White was a popular subject as he got a "Hi, Tommy, how's the world's greatest lover cutting it these days?" from Gaspipe, a "Howdy Jewell," from Raines and a remark about the affair that set the drinkers guffawing.

Turning to me, Gaspipe gave my shirt an extra rip and said, "Any damn cow waddie who'd come on a job in a silk shirt oughta be mailed back to his mama!" Then, looking around, he said, "Where's Kitty?" As I explained, Raines said, "We'll send for her tomorrow. We need some female cooking for a change."

The Hat Ranch lay seven miles up Pine

Valley I was told and somewhere along the road, Raines said, "Here we are, Jewell." As Tommy got out, he said to me, "So long, pard. I like you." A simple statement but it had a sincere ring that made me feel good and I was glad I hadn't joined the ribald laughter that told me he would never live down the jokes about his love affair.

It was only a short distance on to the fabled Hat (their brand) Ranch but in that space I learned that old Tommy was sitting tight on the Jewell Ranch as he claimed an interest in it. His aged father and uncle claimed the whole works and Tommy's claim was holding up sale of the property.

Thus matters stood with every rancher and hired man telling jokes—manufactured or otherwise—cracking jokes about "old Tommy's" love, and yet knowing nothing of the real depth of that love as I was to learn as the years sped by.

With my wife cooking at a dollar a day and my forty dollars a month, we planned on staying a couple months then going back to Sheridan, Wyoming. What I had seen of Nevada was too hilly and steep for my liking.

"This blasted country," I told my wife, "all stands on edge! Even the badgers can't dig a hole, they have to tunnel in the hillsides!"

"You just got out of the wrong side of the bed this morning," she said. "I like it here. The people are all friendly and helpful. This just happened to be a wet spring, which they needed."

"Might be okay for you," I snarled, "because you can listen in on that sixty-mile punkin line and hear all the news, but mostly of old Tommy's love affair, I suppose?"

But as I met more and more of the

natives, I began to see Nevada in a different light and began to like this up and down vicinity and its people. There is something about Nevada that bores under the skin and burrows into your heart and envelopes your every fiber. It worked that way with us and the "couple months" ran into forty years.

The Jewell Ranch sale enriched Tommy by $2,000 and he moved into the Marialdo Boarding House and became the town dandy. We were on our own homestead by then, but Tommy often got up to visit us and share Mary White's letters—letters that revealed their all-consuming love for each other. In one gushing with hope she wrote, "Oh, Darling, now that you have that money I pray that you will come to California and after all these wasted years we can be married, or if you prefer I will come to Palisade. Remember dear, because of my watchful parents, we never had a chance to embrace each other until I was getting on the train. Oh Tommy, dear, why did you ever let them take me away from you?"

As I was reading on through two more pages, Tommy was pacing the floor when my wife said, "Tommy, I think you should go to San Jose. After all these years you two…," she got no further.

"I could never have the courage to meet her," Tommy broke in as he tried to roll a cigarette. "It wouldn't be fair to her. Look at me. I've just began to realize I'm an old man."

"You ought to know," my wife said, "that the years have probably changed her also." But Tommy was shaking with the fear that Mary might come to Palisade so all argument was useless. I was reading on where Mary voiced the same fears. "After analyzing my love for you, what if we met and you didn't like what you saw? Oh, Tommy, I must not harbor such thoughts, but let's face it, I'm not the slender girl as when you last saw me."

When Tommy's finances were getting low he told us he had filed a homestead on the spot I had shown him and asked me to haul lumber and help him build a shack. This I was glad to do and soon we had him settled in a ten-by-twelve slant-roof house. Furniture and cookware were no problem as we had plenty odds and ends of such. Food? Between the sheepmen and us he

didn't want for a thing—unless it was Mary White and he didn't dare have her.

Several times I had ridden up on the blind side of the house and hearing his voice supposed he had a visitor, only to find he was loudly daydreaming of his Mary.

When Tommy left the Jewell Ranch he had salvaged three objects, his saddle, a Winchester .22 and—above all things—a seven-foot-tall secretary which his mother

had brought from Missouri. This many-drawered antique, despite its incongruity, lent an air of elegance to the room and as Tommy said, "had strangers looking around for a woman."

After he had a small pasture fenced,

we gave him a gentle horse so he could go to Palisade which was fifteen miles from his abode, or to our mailbox down on the county road and to repay me for our help he told folks I was "a second Mr. God."

Then came a day when he rode past our ranch without stopping and on his return went right on by. This puzzled us as well as hurt our feelings until a sheepherder came down and, as he laughed, said, "I think the old man he go loco, bet-

ter you go see."

I went up and found Tommy planting some garden truck and even though he talked rational enough the sight of him gave me a shock. It was so hilarious it bordered on being tragic. From the top of his bib overalls to the bottom of one leg there blossomed a stretch of granny knots tied in strips of flour sacking. He explained that he had snagged his overalls on a tree and, not bothering with thread and needle, he punched holes with his knife and tied the rip together.

I knew there was no need for such frugality as the past two Christmases had brought large boxes from Mary with every conceivable item Tommy could ever use. She had anticipated his every need from sweets to heavy underwear and sox and woolen shirts as well as bib overalls and a carton of Bull Durham, as he may have been a smoker when she left the valley.

When I told my wife about Tommy's ridiculous raiment she saw nothing funny about it. "That sixty-year love of theirs is enough to make anyone a bit queer. Who knows, Mary may be getting the same way." Come to think of it, sixty years was one hell of a long time to carry on a romance! Well, one thing it had done was to see those who had been his avid jokesters gone, and the new crop had forgotten it.

Through the winter I kept pretty close watch over Tommy and one day he said, "I got some dandy Basque-style beans so stay awhile and eat beans with me."

He had heated a skillet-full with plenty onion and far too much garlic, and as we were washing up the plates, Tommy did something that caused me to think, "Mary should see this!"

As he finished wiping our plates and turning them upside down on the table, I noticed he had used the dishrag instead of the dishtowel. Then after wiping out the skillet he spent some time before the secretary's mirror as he meticulously smoothed his moustache with the greasy rag. To this I offered no comment as the

hills had several old recluse miners who showed signs of goin' queer in the head.

Winters and summers slipped by and one day a herder told me, "That old Tommy think cracking up. He says you hide behind a bush with your rifle laying to kill him."

That added to our puzzled thinking because, one day in the spring, Sam Zunino rode by and told me the same thing. Sam said, "He pointed out a bush where you hid with your rifle." This convinced me Tommy's mind had begun playing tricks on him.

It was evident he was avoiding us and one day when I took a couple letters up to him he placed them in the secretary instead of sharing their contents with me. Alright, I thought, "If you prefer shunning me after telling Mary and the world I was Mr. God, so be it!"

I still made it a habit to visit him as often as convenient and we would have him down for a woman-cooked meal, although it was evident he preferred being alone. One day, when passing, I found him as amiable as when we had raised glasses to each other's health so many years ago and, except for a bad cough, I saw no change in him.

A few days later, Adolph Berning and his deputy, Wilbur Phillips, drove into my ranch asking how to get to the Tom Jewell place. This had us worried and to our

questions Wilbur replied, "All we know is that a sheep outfit's camp-mover brought word to get to Jewell's, so here we are."

At Tommy's, we found him in bed gasping for air, so hurriedly got him on a mattress in the bed of Berning's truck and fixed him as comfortably as possible. After the rough jouncing to my place, the truck roared away as Berning said, "I doubt if the old guy lasts till we get to Carlin."

Anxious to hear how Tommy was after the long, rough ride, we went to Phillips' as we and Wilbur were close friends. "We had him in the doctor's office," Wilbur said, "and Dolph and I were talking about the mining claim you and he had as pardners and I happened to say 'Harry's sure a fine fellow isn't he?' and Dolph replied 'the best in the West' and somehow Tommy managed to say, 'He's a no good sonovabitch!' and damned if that wasn't his last breath!"

Some days later there came a frantic letter from Mary White to us saying she had written Tommy three letters without getting a reply and would I let her know if he was ill? If he was, she would come right up. That called for a studied answer. We had long known Tommy had his mail held in Palisade until he or some sheepman picked it up, but we hesitated to tell her so and we certainly couldn't tell her that her lover's last breath was cursing me. So to lessen the shock we told her of his short illness and closed with, "We were told by his Carlin friends that with his last breath he was calling for you."

We received a thank-you note from Mary in which she said, "I grieve yet I am content…and somehow, happy. God bless you."

I knew Tommy's house would have plenty inquisitive visitors so to keep Mary's letters from prying eyes I brought the carefully tied packets home. The last time I saw Tommy's beloved secretary it was the abode of the pack rats.

This closed the book on the most passionate though paradoxical romance of all time—unless it was that of Pygmalion's for the ivory statue of his own carving. ∎

Hoover's Visit

Carlin was a wild town, but nothing topped the day a "shoe and sox cowboy" caused an uproar that had President Hoover's Secret Service agents reaching for their guns.

 Folks in Carlin, Nevada, often said "excitement" should have been the town's middle name and they were sure right. Carlin could even boast of having one of its citizens, a Mrs. Potts, being taken to Elko and hanged because she shot and killed an old man for his paltry dollars.

We Pine Valley ranchers seldom went to Carlin, other than passing through it on our way to Elko, but it seemed every time we did, hell was popping.

One day the town was in an uproar because Dolph Berning, the town marshal, had killed a "boxcar passenger" when he insisted on coming downtown to buy a loaf of bread.

Another time found the town in a frenzy when the murderer of four Elko citizens calmly snoozed in Max Sperlich's saloon while the law combed a dozen states for him. His undoing came when the murder weapon fell out of his inside coat pocket and Marshal Berning snapped the cuffs on him. Shortly after that, Berning was shot dead when he stopped a car thief, and we found the armed citizenry taking off in hot pursuit, though some said, "Dolph got his today and it's good riddance!"

But for unadulterated excitement, nothing topped the day President Hoover was making a speech from the rear platform of his palatial car while the train made its Carlin stop. Mr. Hoover was in deep trouble with cattlemen, sheepmen and railroaders alike, so he was out doing some political fence mending. We ranchers had been apprised of his Carlin stop, so we were on hand to see how he was going to talk himself out of this jam.

Now comes the cause of said excitement in the form of Winn Griffin. Winn was termed by some as a "shoe and sox cowboy" because he never wore boots, though that didn't hinder his bronc riding ability. Winn liked to get soused to the gills on Frank Lightner's gulch-perked firewater, ride a green bronc into town, and have it knock down folks as it bucked all over the street and store fronts. Winn had also heard of the president's arrival and decided to give the folks something to remember the event by.

The president was having difficulty in driving home the good points of his tenure due to the catcalls and boos from his disgruntled audience when, as if that weren't enough distraction, our drunked-up Winn rounded the corner of the depot

With a bucking, squealing bronc among them, the people lost what little interest they had in Hoover platitudes.

with a war whoop and hung in the spurs.

With a bucking, squealing bronc among them, the people lost what little interest they had in Hoover platitudes and were trying to save being trampled as someone shook his fist and made a disparaging remark. That did it, bringing a shouted piece of advice from the red-jowled Hoover: "If you won't respect the man, you should at least show respect for your president!"

With Winn whooping like crazy, the bronc slammed into the side of the moving presidential car, went down in a heap, and was dragged along as the passengers and the crowd shouted, "Stop the train! Stop the train!" Somehow, the bronc had got to his feet and was mowing a path through the crowd on its way out of town. As Winn was being hauled from the rail, the air brakes took hold and passengers were catapulted from their seats by the dead stop.

But the pandemonium in the cars was lost by the shouts of "Don't anybody leave this spot!" by half a dozen Secret Service agents with drawn guns. As they circulated among us, the agents plied the question that appeared to be of prime importance: "Which one of you shook his fist at the president and shouted bush-wah?"

Apparently they believed the bucking act and ensuing commotion had been a planned cover-up for an assassin to gun down the president. It is hard to say how long the interrogation would have gone on among the stilled crowd had it not been for an agonized female scream of "Oh, my God. The train cut that man's foot off!" Then she fainted.

"Sure enough did," someone exclaimed. "I can see the bone sticking out of his shoe there!" Winn was streaked with blood from his face to his one good foot and blood was oozing through the leg of his Levi's. Also, the severed foot was so spattered with corpuscles it was hard to determine the extent of the mayhem.

"Poor ol' Winn," a drunk said. "I knowed them damn broncs would someday cripple him worse than he already was." Eager hands were steadying Winn as he sat flat-bottomed on the ground.

Bill Arthur, co-owner of the Rutledge-Arthur Garage, picked up the begrimed shoe and took it to its owner. "You okay, Winn, or shall we get ol' Doc to look you over?"

"Hell, yes, I'm okay," Winn mumbled as he tried to screw the damaged foot back onto his metal stub.

Many watchers showed signs of getting sick as Winn fumbled with the gruesome foot until Bill Arthur said, "It's only Winn's wood and leather foot, folks, so there's nothing to get excited about. Years ago I saw him staggering along in Battle Mountain with his foot screwed on backward. Sure looked funny to see one spur pointing ahead and the other like it should be."

As the president's guardians climbed aboard the palatial car, one was heard to say, "Now, by God, I've seen the world's eighth wonder!" ∎

A Horse Called Satan

This outlaw bronc was considered a man-killer from the first time he was saddled.

 Had it not been that I swapped a top saddle horse for an outlaw bronc, I wouldn't have experienced the scariest hours that could befall any cowpuncher. But looking back on it, that night's episode is laughable.

I had gone back to the Grand River in Colorado from Wyoming's Big Horn Basin for a short look-see at my old home and was heading north again when Tim Mugrage mentioned a certain horse the locals termed an "outlaw." Tim said the owner, an Englishman by the name of Dick Panting, was going to shoot it. Dick had had various bronc busters breaking horses to ship and sell back East but one particular horse was so unbreakable he rated nothing but a bullet. "And," Tim went on, "a horse has to be a stem-winder if Mickey McFarland or Bob Gray couldn't break him."

This aroused my curiosity and soon Dick and I were sitting on his corral sizing up thirty head of horses. "When my help comes," Dick said, "we're loading them out for the East tomorrow."

"You still got that outlaw bronc folks have been telling me about?" I asked. "I heard you couldn't break him so was thinking of killing him."

"That's him with a bar on his shoulder—that chestnut sorrel over there. Yes, I intended to kill him before he killed someone but changed my mind. I've decided to ship him. He's such a fine looker I might get a hundred for him just on his looks," he said, giggling. "Then somebody back in New Jersey can have the honor of shooting him."

"I hear he's been fooled with until he's spoiled beyond breaking," I said as I sized up the beautiful animal that looked even more docile than many of the others.

"Not spoiled," Dick snorted. "He was a man killer from the first time he was saddled! Damn near got Bob Gray a few days ago. After he bucks you off he's on top of you with all four feet and his teeth! Must be part grizzly bear from the way he goes after a man."

"Sounds like a bad-actor alright," I conceded.

"Got the war sign on every rider I've had," Dick resumed. "Starts off like he was going to jump the corral then maybe before he hits it he comes uncoupled, bucking seven directions at once."

"You say he's like a grizzly bear," I ventured, "so I suppose you call him Grizzly."

"Worse than that," Dick replied. "One of the boys named him Satan and I can't think of a more appropriate name for the bastard."

The more I studied the animal the better I liked his springy action. And the small, well-shaped head and short underlip told me he was of fine Morgan stock. "I think I'll take a settin' at Mister Satan," I said, "so let's cut him in that corral and we'll see if he can live up to his reputation."

Dick looked at me as if he thought I was an escapee from some mental institution. "Got a pretty big opinion of yourself, haven't you?" he finally said.

"Nope," I shot back, "but I think you fellows have overestimated Satan's ability is all."

"Be ready to slam that gate on the others then, because he'll be the first one through." Dick was right. The sorrel slithered through when I had the gate barely cracked and it was good to see him circle the high corral as if hunting a hole in it. I'd already made up my mind Satan would never be gunned down here or any other place, even if I had to walk and lead him clear to the Big Horn Basin.

Something about him had gotten under my skin and I vowed I'd own him. If I could break him—or rather, ride him—I'd have a top-notch saddler. On the other hand, if he was the wampus cat that Dick thought he was, I'd make wages just enter-

ing him in bucking contests, same as Old Steamboat was then bringing in the sheckles for his owner. Hell, I couldn't lose!

"What's his age?" I asked.

"Seven," Dick answered. "Started to break him two years ago, but the more my riders worked on him, the meaner he got and he's too old now to change his tactics."

Going to my horse, I unbuckled my rope. "When you rope him," came Dick's warning, "do it from on top of the corral when he comes by. And don't you dare get down in the corral until we have him snubbed tight against these poles or he'll jolly well take a chunk out of your leg or skull!"

"My God!" I said. "What's the matter with all you fellows? He doesn't act bad to me. Just scared more than anything else. But give a dog a bad name," I paraphrased, "and he'll sure as hell bite yuh. But what I'd like to know is what those bozos did that would make a green bronc so vicious a man doesn't even get in the same corral with him?"

As the horse shot by us I laid a loop on him and was taking a dally around a post when he hit the corral at my feet, squealing like a stuck pig.

"Take up the slack!" Dick yelled. "We got to choke him down before we can get a hackamore on him!"

Of all the broncs I'd handled, I'd never run up against such a peculiar, fighting critter as this one. No wonder he'd acquired the name Satan. Dick finagled the hackamore on with a forked stick, which I also thought a dude stunt, bar anything I'd come across. But I'd seen enough to know that here was a spoiled horse and one a fellow better watch mighty close or he'd come out the loser.

Since he had gone through the initial process many times of being Scotch-hobbled, I soon had a hobble running past his left shoulder to the off hind foot and back under his belly to the neck rope. Crosshobbling, we called it. That way the bronc stomper could administer the "blanket lesson" and slide around on a bronc without danger of having his teeth kicked out.

With my saddle on the sorrel I mounted and dismounted several times, then let him hunch around the corral, sliding his hobbled foot that barely touched the ground.

"He won't do anything as long as that hobble is on," Dick said. "He's gone through that plenty times the past two years."

"Sure springy on three legs," I said, "and I'll bet a fellow'd have a real saddler if he could get the meanness out of him."

"Can't be done," Dick vowed. "He's too old now and it's seven years too late. Born that way. But you go ahead and tinker around with him while I go take a look at a pot of beans I'm cooking. But I'm warning you! Don't take that hobble off and try to ride him until I'm close by! You hear?"

"Yep," I told him as I talked to Satan, letting him camel-walk around the corral as I patted his neck. "That old fuddy duddy must have had some damn poor bronc busters around here," I said aloud to myself and Satan as Dick disappeared in his shack.

Getting off and on several times, with no sign of the horse making a crooked move, I carefully untied the hobble rope and let it drop. A Scotch hobble is a pretty exhausting thing for a horse and a green bronc wouldn't realize his foot was free for a while. Perhaps Satan would react the same way if I didn't let a spur touch him off.

I was nudging him into a walk when he reached around, sunk his teeth in a chap leg then shot across the corral like a racehorse. I thought he was going to smash into the heavy poles but instead he swapped ends and went into the worst sun-fishing gyrations I'd experienced. His grunts and squeals were enough to scare the Devil himself and before I knew it I was rolling on the ground with Satan doing a good job trying to make mincemeat of me with hooves and teeth.

Luckily, I rolled under the corral poles while Satan made the stirrups pop as he bucked and squealed as if he hated the

world. I was yelling, "Hop to it old boy!" when I heard a shout and saw Dick set down his bean pot on the run and grab an ax as he passed the woodpile.

"Damn, damn and damn again!" he panted as he took in the situation. "I bloody well told you not to take that hobble off 'til I come back! Now our dinner is shot to hell! So take that gun of yours and kill that blasted horse. If you don't, I will!"

"I can ride that sonovabitch," I said, every bit as mad as Dick was, "an' show him a thing or two!"

"Yes," Dick snorted, "and you can also raise hell and jolly well put a block under it from what I've seen so far! So he's just scared, eh?"

"Caught me nappin'," I alibied, as I

I was rolling on the ground with Satan doing a good job trying to make mincemeat out of me with hooves and teeth.

tossed a loop on Satan and had him hit the poles under me as I snubbed him close. Crawling in the saddle from atop the corral was no trouble as this was probably a routine performance to him.

With two fingers through my quirt loop we were working to get the rope off when Satan swapped ends and headed for the opposite side of the corral. The two turns of the rope were burning grooves in the pole when the end tangled and Satan was whip-cracked so suddenly I'm sure sparks flew off his tail, and only for the corral meeting me I'd have been catapulted so far it would have taken me an hour to crawl back.

Oh, I was bunged up, no mistake about that, but some philosopher said, "There's good in every evil," or vice versa, and it proved true with Satan. That hoolihan taught him more in two seconds than those bronc busters had in two years. When I got able to stagger around, he let me walk up to him and take the rope off his neck without so much as kicking me.

"Well, bronc rider," Dick smirked, "have you any more brilliant ideas?"

"You're damn tootin'," I snapped. "For ten dollars to boot I'll swap horses!"

Almost before I knew what I'd said I was pocketing ten dollars. Then someone was saying, "Where the hell'd you come from?" and there sat Fred McGee on his horse. I had known Fred since I was a pup and went to school with his cousins.

"That your hull on Satan?" he asked and started laughing.

"Yeah," I said, "and it's by God go'nta stay on him 'til I hit northern Wyoming!"

"You'll never make it!" Fred offered by way of advice. "I hazed for Dick's last bronc stomper and saw him get piled four times in two miles. You'll be goin' along and all of a sudden Satan takes a good run at it then turns wrong side out an' down comes your meathouse! You're afoot an' wonderin' what happened. I wouldn't swap this briar pipe of mine for that critter. He'll buck you off and get away from you if you try ridin' him outa this corral!"

"I'm stuck with him now," I told Fred, "so if I manage to ride him maybe I won't get off him for five hundred miles or so. But come hell or high water I'm headin' back for Wyoming this afternoon. So why not go along so you can catch him if he piles me?"

"Like to," Fred mumbled through his pipe, "but like a damn fool me an' Mattie Mather is figurin' on gettin' hitched come spring. Tell you what I'll do though. I'll ride a piece with you an' catch him when he dumps yuh."

Fred didn't know I'd learned a lot since he last saw me as a gangling miner's kid.

No use wasting words on preliminaries but, as I said, that tail popping taught Satan a lesson he never forgot! At least I could walk up to him and mount without getting kicked in the belly or feeling his teeth. But during the few miles Fred stayed by me, Satan put on enough bucking acts to equal all the broncs I'd ever tackled! If he'd bucked straight ahead we'd have been well on our way out of Colorado.

But I discovered he was about the easiest bucker I'd set on or been piled from. He was like a rubber ball and even though he went crookeder than a gunnysack full of snakes there was no jar when he hit the ground. Don't misunderstand me! I hung an' rattled plenty times but under the circumstances I didn't dare get bucked off because Fred's horse didn't look like he

With fiddle case under one arm, all I had to do was to barely touch Satan with a spur and he'd down his head and put on a show.

could outrun a tumblebug!

After I was on my own Satan loosened up, and when I let him into his easy, ground-covering lope I watched him close and stayed screwed down tight and took no chances. Even after we put sixty miles behind us one day when most broncs would be dead tired, he put on a bucking act that evening, and again the next day, which brought me to the harrowing experience I mentioned at the beginning.

I had stayed overnight at the 71 Ranch on the Sweet Water and vowed I'd ride the tail off this ornery horse that day so, like a fool, pushed on in the face of a snowstorm as I wanted to make the fifty miles to Shoshoni on the Big Wind River that day. Traveling as the crow flies, I had reached some 'dobe buttes and (due to the swirling

storm) couldn't tell south from north. For hours I must have traveled in a circle.

Then with over half these miles behind him Satan had come uncorked when a jackrabbit jumped out near him. My main thought now was, what a hell of a spot to get bucked off in or have Satan slip while bucking and find myself afoot. Not a pleasant thought.

We had come to a flat just as darkness closed in on a he-man blizzard and, smelling smoke, was soon accosted by a pair of dogs and a band of blatting sheep bedded around a sheep wagon. Working for a cow outfit I had been taught to hate sheepherders, but when that lanky fellow said, "Tie your horse in the lee of the wagon and get in here," I felt like hugging him.

While he was cooking supper I learned his name was Jim and was herding for Johnnie Love whose ranch lay about ten miles to the north. The man had a peculiar voice and I noticed when he talked he placed his thumb over a dime-sized hole in his Adam's apple. If he failed to do this, the words whistled out through this hole sort of like the sound of a fife.

But that didn't bother me. What did bother me later on when Satan had been fed some oats and the wagon being rocked by the storm, was the way Jim kept eying my chaps and six-shooter which hung on a wall hook. His eyes would change to pin points as we talked sheep for hours and I was beginning to wish for morning so I could get the hell out of there.

I won't go into all the uncomfortable feelings that shot through me as every now and then Jim would whet a butcher knife up and down on the stovepipe and prattle, "Jimmy cut the cat! Jimmy hix the ball tosser!"

I was sitting on the bed in the rear of the wagon when he suddenly whirled and screeched, "You cowmen are trying to catch me and tie me on an anthill, aren't you?"

I stammered that I was no cattleman and was just on my way to the Big Horn Basin.

"Oh yes you are!" he hissed through that hole. "You're a spy! So I'm going to have to cut your throat!"

As he reached for me, I ducked past him, yanked the door open, tumbled down over the steps and stood there with the blizzard cutting through me. "If this isn't one hell of a mess I don't know what is!" I said aloud as Jim stood in the doorway coaxing me to "come in out of this storm and let me cut your throat."

How long this went on I can't say, but it seemed like hours. "Christ," I groaned, "if I only had my chaps and gun!" But I didn't, and was about to mount and take off anyway when Jim started whimpering and begging me to come back in. "I won't hurt you," he said. "I don't want to hurt anyone. Please come in or you'll freeze. See, I'll hide my knife under the stove."

Considering the blizzard I had little choice, so after watching him hide that long butcher knife under the stove, and having nothing to lose but my head, I ventured inside, leaving the door open. Once inside I lost no time retrieving my .45, but it wasn't needed. Jim had become as meek as a lamb and talked intelligently and coherently of his past. When he was eighteen at home in London he had cut some pretty wild capers for a Britisher and his father had shipped him off to Australia as a "remittance" man, receiving ten pounds every month from his dad just to stay clear of the family and no longer disgrace them.

Needless to say, daylight found me vacating Jim's hospitality, storm or no storm, and on reaching Love's ranch I related my night's experience.

"Yes," Mr. Love said, "we knew Jim was batty but he's a good herder and we believed him dangerous only to himself. A year ago, while our camp tender was out to Jim's flock, something might have cracked in Jim's head while Scotty was off getting a load of wood for him. Man, that was a mess. When Scotty got back he found the wagon full of blood and Jim with his throat cut from ear to ear."

"Come to think of it," I put in, "I heard about that but it went in one ear and out the other. I've heard of herders going nuts like that just from loneliness."

"It wasn't being alone caused his trouble," Love said. "He had a bad love affair and went on a two-month bender over it. It was the girl's mother who put the kibosh on the marriage though. Then some damn cowboys got Jim to write the girl a letter when he was half sober saying he had fallen heir to his folks' estate in England and asked her to come to Lander and marry him.

"Jim's well educated and I guess that letter was a classic because the old lady and daughter hopped a train in Cheyenne and couldn't get to Lander fast enough. Guess they thought the girl would be a princess or something. God, what a disillusionment that was! From what I heard it was awful. Those women lost no time getting to hell away."

"What happened that was so awful?" I inquired.

"Oh, those cowpunchers got Jim dead drunk before the train pulled in and laid him out on the platform near where the coach would stop, and there he laid in the hot sun with a jug cradled in his arm. That wouldn't have been so bad but he had vomited all over his chest, even his face, and was covered with blowflies. One hell of a sight I guess. Shortly after that is when he tried to whack his head off with a butcher knife."

"I can't see how he managed to pull through," I put in.

"No, nor can anyone else," Love admitted. "Scotty saw Jim was still gurgling so he loaded him in the wagon and damn near killed my team racing to Monita and a doctor. Juniper berries, oats, and rocks and God only knows what all had been sucked into the windpipe but the booger survived as you saw for yourself."

Here I'd started off to write about a horse and somehow got sidetracked with a crazy sheepherder. So back to Satan: For some unknown reason Satan appeared attracted to me, just as I'd been to him. Oh, he'd buck at the drop of a hat and I had more fun with him during the three years I had him than I could have had with those two monkeys Lon Leathers had in his saloon down in Shoshoni.

While working for the M Bar and afterwards, I often fiddled for dances and I could always cause a scatterment of people and rigs on mornings after a dance broke up. With my fiddle case under one arm, all I had to do was to barely touch Satan with a spur and he'd down his head and put on a show with all the accompanying bellering and squealing of a green bronc. Folks would think I was about to be harpooned by a buggy tongue or slammed against a tree and would be yelling advice, but Satan loved this and was careful never to smash into any object. When I thought we'd put on show enough all I had to do was pull up the reins and say, "That'll do, Satan," and he'd walk off as though nothing had happened. Yes, it was as though we spoke the same language—a language that one day got me in a fight.

Being a good-natured hombre all during my adult life I had avoided fighting because as a kid around mining camps, bloody fights were a common diversion, but twice I got mad enough to fight, once over my dog and once over my horse. (Oh, as a kid at school I licked the preacher's son every recess until his younger sister took me on one evening and knocked all the fight out of me.)

In August 1909, when the beef roundup was to start and a couple hundred of the top cow horses were run in from the pasture for our strings, the cowhands' private saddlers were among them. A big-mouth rep for the Antler outfit was bragging about his bronc riding when Sam Cremer said, "I'll give you five dollars to see you ride that Satan horse of Webb's."

I told the fellow I was sure he could ride Satan but since I had never seen Satan buck with anyone but myself it was okay. I noticed a pair of star rowels on his spurs so said, "But please don't spur him. He'll buck without it and those rowels will cut him up. He's hog fat and thin-skinned."

I had thought Satan was out of his old running trick before breaking in two but he double-crossed me. When Big Mouth drove those hooks in the blood flew and, instead of bucking, Satan shot halfway across the big corral then all but turned wrong side out and the fellow went rolling. When Satan, panting like a lizard, wound up near me and the group, the fellow rushed over and yanked the reins out of my hands, saying, "I'll ride this bastard and cut his guts out!"

"No you won't!" I said. "You had your chance and I asked you not to spur him. Look at his sides, now!"

"I'm ridin' him," he snapped, "and you're barking up the wrong tree if you try to stop me!"

I jerked the reins from him and was saying, "I don't want him cut up," when I hit the dirt from a haymaker to my snout. Under ordinary circumstances he could have whipped me with one hand but this was something out of the ordinary and he and a corral-full like him couldn't have stopped me that day and I had the boys all whooping for me.

I guess I went berserk because after smashing his face 'til it looked like a buzz saw had struck it I proceeded to stomp a few teeth out. George Pennoyer, our roundup boss, then said to him, "Now stick your hull and bed on your horses and get to hell off this outfit!" I never saw the fellow again and it was probably well for me I didn't. I might not have had a horse to fight for.

A few dozen instances as those at dances, or in the street down in Thermopolis, and Satan was known far and wide. Those not knowing I was having fun put me down as the greatest rider in the land and would also say, "I'd shoot that damned horse if I owned him!"

There came a day in early April 1910 when all that frippery with Satan backfired on me. I was about to leave for the East to join Buffalo Bill's Wild West Show and knew Satan and I had to part company. It was a tough decision to make but I had a strange premonition of never returning to Owl Creek—a prophecy that has to this day remained fulfilled.

But could I sell Satan? I couldn't give him away! Even though there was a ready market for saddle horses among the ranchers, every contact I made would bring, "Say, isn't that the so and so critter you call Satan? Not on your tintype! I need a saddle horse, not an outlaw!"

By the evening before I was to leave I was desperate. I not only wanted all the money I could get my hands on, as venturing three thousand miles away to ride broncs which maybe I couldn't set was a scary proposition to say the least. Time was also of the essence now, and as much as I loved my horse, I had to dispose of him somewhere, somehow.

As a last resort I went to the M Bar where my old friend Fred McGee and wife Mattie were working. During supper, Fred and I talked like Dutch uncles to a big lug of a ranch hand who'd never heard of Satan—at least not the horse named Satan—and wanted "that beautiful horse" and wished he had the fifty dollars to buy him.

That's when old pal Fred saved my bacon. "I'll give Harry the fifty," he said, "and you can pay me when you get the money."

To say I felt like bawling when I patted Satan a quick "so long" would be putting it mildly because I knew from the way he nuzzled me he knew our parting was for keeps. I lost no time getting away from the ranch before that fellow decided to ride him because time had proven Satan to be a one-man horse. (I had once loaned him to a cowboy we called Sagebrush Bill who was no bronc rider, and later learned Bill

had led the horse ten miles simply because Satan wouldn't let Bill mount him.)

The next day, April 10, 1910, I was on the tri-weekly stage bound for the unknown and whatever lay before me thousands of miles away. It was a month later when a letter came from Fred telling me Satan had thrown the young fellow, breaking his back, and had been sold to some horse buyers who were there from Grand Island, Nebraska.

We stood laughing over the getup and Charley said, 'Christ, what a crowbait to be decked out like that.'

But, wait! There's a strange sequel to this story! My older brother Charley had followed me in riding broncs in Buffalo Bill's show and, like myself, had gravitated to Philadelphia and was working with me for the Lubin Moving Picture Company.

One day he, Smoky Warner and I were coming along Philadelphia's Market Street when a comical sight attracted us. Hitched to a battered junk wagon was a horse with his ears stuck through a straw bonnet and tethered by a long leash anchored to an iron weight dropped to the sidewalk.

We stood laughing over the getup and Charley said, "Christ, what a crowbait to be decked out like that!" We noticed many white scars on the bone-poor critter's head and his left knee was bowed like a barrel stave and knotted as if it had been broken or out of joint at some time. There also were numerous white scars on the dark-

sorrel ribs, attesting to the abuse he had suffered before he was beaten into submission.

Smoky and I had started on when Charley halted us saying, "Holy Jesus, fellows, it's old Satan!" Spitting in his hand he smoothed down the hair on the nag's forearm. One glance at that short Bar branded there and I could do nothing but lean against poor old Satan and beller like a whipped papoose. To worsen matters he gave a weak nicker of recognition as I stroked his muzzle, made by a farrier's twitch or a tightened rope.

Smoky and Charley were both good two-fisted cussers and they were doing a fine job of it now as they called down every available curse on everyone from Satan's owner back to whoever had clubbed a beautiful animal into the subdued derelict hitched to that wagon.

We waited and waited for the driver—a wait that was in vain—as we were due back at the studio. But whenever possible we haunted that spot and street in hopes of spying old Satan somewhere. I have used the word "old" but Satan was not old in years, only his abused, scarred body was old.

Charley had said, "By God we'll buy ol' Satan from that geezer if we find him and if he won't sell him we'll take him anyway! We'll put him to pasture at Louie Webber's farm!"

This fervent desire, however, was not to be fulfilled. We never saw Satan again. Though Dick Panting had vowed to shoot him, we three cowhands now wished Dick had made good his threat. I thought of all the fun I would have missed had he done so but a beautiful horse would have been spared the misery and manhandling those scars showed he had endured somewhere along the line since I had sold him just three years before.

I often wish we had never run onto him that day in 1913. Those moments beside him left an indelible, recurrent vision that will remain in a crevice of my memory for all time. ■

A Lucky Shot

If Eddie's citified bride ever goes hunting again, you can bet he'll load her gun with blanks.

 My rancher friend Eddie tells this one on his wife, but being as I don't want him goin' around with knots on his head, I'll leave his last name off. Now, every deer-hunting season Eddie always joined a couple of cronies and had fun in the high country away from the ranch for a few days' hunting. But this particular fall he had just gone in double harness with a cute little city girl from California and that sort of created a problem. She insisted on going along.

Kathy wouldn't take no for an answer, which time and again was "No!" But after she'd cried and sniffled awhile, Eddie threw up his hands and gave in.

Naturally he knew where the best deer spots in northeast Nevada were and also the easiest crags and gullies to prowl. But was Eddie about to take his bride to one of those easy hunting spots? Not by a long shot! The ornery cuss left his pickup a good mile from the worst spot he could think of. Oh, there were deer there sometimes, but no seasoned deer hunter would wallow through and fight the thick, shirt- and Levi-tearing brush for all the deer in Elko County.

"I'll teach Miss Smarty a lesson in deer hunting that'll cure her once and for all," he told himself. He handed her an eleven-pound Sharps and a couple of 45-90 cartridges. Then, holding his 30-06, a slight five or six pounder, Eddie said, "Let's git goin'!"

"Why don't you let me have the little gun and you take this heavy thing?" Kathy asked.

"This one'd kick your head off," he replied, almost busting inside he was so tickled at her complaint. He was even more pleased with his plan when at last they reached his chosen gully and he saw plenty of moisture running down her cheeks.

"Now, Kathy," he instructed, "you work down this side of the hill ["this side" being thick brush interlaced with mountain holly] and I'll be right over the ridge from you." Eddie then said he would meet her about half a mile down the gully.

"How do I put these brass bullets in the gun?" she wanted to know. "And when I kill a deer, what shall I do?"

Eddie almost felt sorry for his little wife, but breaking her of wanting to tag along when he went hunting called for drastic measures.

"By golly, that's right," he said grudgingly as he shoved a three-inch cartridge in the old relic. "Can't kill deer with an empty gun. But if you kill a deer I'll hear the shot and come a runnin'."

With this he mosied through the scrub mahogany where walking was easy. "No use to hurry," he told himself. "She won't get very far in that brush."

He was sitting on a rock scanning the lower reaches with his scope when he heard the boom of the Sharps. "Oh, Lordy!" he thought. "She's been packin' that gun cocked and maybe fallen and…oh, Lordy," he repeated and started running.

Of course, there was the slim chance that a deer had jumped out and she had fired. But that was grasping at any straw. As Eddie ran over the brow of the hill, he stopped short and breathed a "Thank God!" though it was hard to believe his eyes.

As Eddie tells it, "I was plenty happy to see her alive, and from her angry voice I was sure she had had beginner's luck and had got herself a deer. But backing away with his palms outspread was a young cowpuncher I knowed, an' I couldn't blame him. Kathy had the muzzle o' that ol' cannon rammed in Jim's belly a foot.

"O'course I was real proud o' that little wife of mine, but I was also scairt she

EDDIE AND KATHY IN DOUBLE HARNESS, "AND FOREVER SHALL LOVE ABIDE."

had somehow got another shell in the gun and might blow him in two.

"As he kept backin' away in that brush he thought the same thing, I reckon, because he kept sayin', 'Okay, okay, lady, if you say you shot it an' it's yourn, then it's yourn! But it looks like you ort o' at least let me take my saddle and bridle off his carcass.'" ■

Treasure of the Rio Tinto

Nobody believed the heavy-drinking Frank Hunt could hit it big, but he shocked us all.

Like every prospector this writer has known, S. Frank Hunt decided the formation he located his claim on four miles south of Mountain City, Nevada, was the apex of a huge body of ore. This is a timeworn theory prospectors cling to whenever a likely looking outcropping is discovered. Nothing to it now but "sink on it!"

Geologists have long shot this theory full of holes. What the prospector believes to be the apex of a vein or ore body may now be all that is left of what was once a mountain, eroded and washed away, carrying veins and ore bodies with it.

Frank Hunt wasn't a run-of-the-mill prospector. He had poured over many books on geology and studied rock formations. When he planted a four-by-four post in the leached gossan outcrop and nailed a Prince Albert tobacco can to it to protect his location notice, he was obsessed with the belief that by sinking on it he would unearth a copper bonanza.

"You just watch," he would tell anyone he could corner. "Some of these days you'll see Rio Tinto in inch-high type in every newspaper in the country."

In about 1913, Frank Hunt began sinking a shaft on his Rio Tinto claim. As the years rolled by he was still "sinking," but with every foot the work became harder and the footage slower. Frank's flimsy ladder had lengthened, and when a lone prospector starts sinking a shaft he has undertaken the hardest and slowest form of development work.

We once asked Frank if he had ever paused to estimate the number of trips he had made up and down his ladder. "Listen, Bub," he said, his massive shoulders shaking with mirth, "I never figured the trips, but if the trips down were added to those up and my ladder was long enough, I'd be exploring the moon by now! But don't worry, I've got a mine under me there."

The hills are never lacking in just such optimists, following the multitudes before them who left the thousands of deep, barren holes that clutter ghost camps and unnamed gulches.

But to all who are bitten by this get-rich bug, there is a must that faces them: how to obtain the necessary supplies for their development work? Beans, flour and coffee could usually be wrangled from some easy-touch storekeeper. But while such items kept a man's belly from rubbing his backbone, the key ingredients in shaft or tunnel driving are blasting material and the stamina of a Missouri mule.

Frank had so far furnished all the manpower, but at a depth of one-hundred-and-fifty feet the round trips had grown slower and ever harder. That was when a forty-year-old by the name of Ogden Chase entered the picture one evening at the back-room bar in the Commercial Hotel in Elko. Like all prospectors, Hunt was holding forth on the merits of his mine and his main problem.

"You're going at it the wrong way," the newcomer asserted. "Capital is what you need. Without it, you're butting your head against a stone wall. Never get anyplace without money. Big money."

"I agree with you there," Hunt said, accepting his umpteenth drink of Frank Lightner's moonshine. "But capital's a mighty big if right now, pardner. My face is good—at least so far—in this burg and Mountain City for a gunnysack of salt pork and beans, but that's all. Just try to raise some cash around this town to mine on and see how far you git! This town's got to where you couldn't raise a row with a hundred Irishmen and a barrel of Newt Crumley's whiskey. Ain't that right, Newt?"

"Right, Frank," the hotel owner agreed.

"Not when you got angles," the newcomer said, "and angles is what I've got the most of."

"Oh?" Hunt queried. "Let's hear just one."

"Incorporate," was the advice.

"Incorporate what?" an old prospector put in. "A hole in the ground?"

"Just a hole," the young promoter replied. "Show me your hole in the ground," he added, "and I'll show you how to drag in the money hand over fist."

Two days later, Hunt windlassed Ogden Chase to the surface. "What's she look like to you?" he asked, looking down the hole.

"Just like what she is," Case replied, "a hell of a big hole in the ground. But it's just what we need. Only remember this, just because we incorporate and start selling stock doesn't mean we can sit on our rumps and watch the money roll in. We'll have to keep digging a little, otherwise we'll be dining on bread and water in a federal hoosegow. It's not like it was thirty years ago. There's a Blue Sky Law now. Not only that but in this state any money raised for development work must be spent on development."

When Hunt complained that he couldn't buy feed for his cat let alone pay for incorporating, Chase said, "I've just about enough money for that. The laws of Delaware are so loose and cheap a person can even incorporate a company there to sell stock in a tomcat fight."

The Rio Tinto Company was thus incorporated with a capital stock of two million shares at five cents per share. Soon Elko was plastered with Rio Tinto stock, not that the home folks believed in it but because they knew old Frank and felt sorry for him. While some people might buy twenty, fifty or perhaps a thousand shares, most went to grocery stores and saloons. One Basque sheep and wool buyer took several thousand shares, but after two years of the Rio Tinto still just one more hole in the earth, he unloaded his gilt-edge paper on some gullible Easterner at a dime a share.

With the Depression at its worst, times were tough for Hunt and Chase. But they still could swap a few shares for groceries, booze and powder, and to keep out of the law's clutches they alternated their drinking visits in Elko with working the claim. Old Frank did the underground work, and the 225-pound Chase windlassed up the rock.

With Hunt not having to clamber up and down a ladder, the footage went faster. Chase could lower his partner in the bucket then go back in the cabin a few feet away, and read for an hour or two while Hunt drilled, or until he yanked on the long bailing wire that clanged a big cowbell at the top of the shaft.

But the ground had become increasingly dangerous. A soft shale had come in on the footwall that required timbering and any sort of timber was miles away. Stock sales were at a standstill. Elko and Carlin had long since reached the saturation point. It was even growing difficult to deal with the stores and saloons. Timber, that was the burning question. Then Chase had an idea.

"What about that stack of railroad ties Ray Hage left here? Suppose he'd sell 'em to us?"

"Doubt it," was the reply. "Ray had those ties hauled from Elko for a cabin he wants to build before winter."

"Then ask him to loan 'em to us. Tell him you're afraid to work down there unless we timber. You know him pretty well, don't you?"

"Sopped gravy from the same skillet, practically," Hunt said, "but that's not saying we can talk him out of his ties. If we could just get them ties, though," he said thoughtfully, "we'd be jake. It's worth talking to him, anyway."

Contacting Ray Hage was considerably easier than wrangling those forty ties out of him. "Christ, Frank," Hage said, "I hate to part with my ties. I worked like hell pulling them out of the river besides paying Fred Horn forty dollars to haul them up there. Still, I don't want to see you get killed, so guess I'll have to let you have them for what the hauling cost me."

"Bully for you, Ray. I appreciate that," Hunt said. "We can't give you the cash but we'll sure give you a batch of stock. Git him some stock, Ogden."

"Hell, Frank," Ray laughed. "Your stock isn't worth any more to me than an acre of post holes in Siberia. I've got to have the money."

"Money's what we ain't got," Chase said, reaching in Hunt's battered Buick for a bulky brief case. "We're gon'ta give you five thousand shares of Rio Tinto and you

can sell 'em."

"Damn it," Ray reiterated, "I've told you I don't want your stock! I'm behind in our rent and need the cash. So you sell the shares and fetch me the money."

"Wish we could, Ray," Hunt said, "but we've reached the point in this man's town where it would be easier to sell ice to the Eskimos than sell forty dollars worth of stock to these natives."

"Tell you what we'll do, Hage," Chase

FRANK HUNT STRUCK IT BIG IN 1932 AFTER NINETEEN YEARS OF WORK. THE COPPER MINE PRODUCED UNTIL 1948.

said in a business-like tone. "We're going to give you ten thousand."

"Make it twenty, Ogden," Hunt interrupted. "What's a few thousand shares to us? We've still got near two million of 'em left."

"Frank," Hage said resignedly, flinging out his arms, "I can't spend all day arguing with you fellows. Take the goddamned ties and if you ever get the money you can pay me for them."

"You're an angel, Ray," Hunt said, pounding Ray on the back. "But we'd rather give you a big block of..."

"Forty dollars, Frank," Ray said over his shoulder, then flung a parting shot. "If you ever see that much."

Weeks later, Ray's old Graham-Paige chugged northward on its way to Mountain City. Ray was making a hurried trip to see what was needed at his claim, which was a short distance over the hill

from Hunt's shaft in Copper Gulch. He'd also visit Hunt and Chase and then return to Elko for the necessary supplies for a couple months at his claim.

In the middle of Sunflower Flat he could see a black splotch several miles ahead and on coming up to it found Hunt and Chase in a heated argument with a stranger. The stranger's dilapidated Model T was beside the deep-rutted road heading north while Hunt's Buick stood in the middle of the road pointing south. Ray pulled up near the Buick's front end and got out.

"What's all the rumpus?" he asked, noting that Hunt and Chase were so drunk they could barely stand.

"Shombitch run us over!" Chase mumbled. "C'llided, tha's what."

"A hell of a place for a collision," Ray observed, surveying the miles of flatland, "here in a desert that's level for twenty miles in any direction and you collide. If that isn't something for Ripley, I don't know what is. Why didn't one of you pull out to the side?"

"Right of way," Hunt said. "Plain case of we had right of way. Uphill has right of way."

"Hill!" Ray exclaimed. "Show me a hill. Flat as a stove top here for ten miles!"

"Teck'nal point," Chase put in. "River runs north, so we comin' uphill."

"Owyhee River's miles away," Ray told him. "This whole thing's silly. You two are getting crazier by the week!"

"I was trying to climb my wheels out of these ruts," the stranger angrily explained, "when these lousy drunks tore that fender there off. But they'll pay me for it and by damn you can bet your bottom dollar on that; twenty-five bucks or by damn I'll know why."

"Offered him ten thous' Rio Tint'," Hunt sputtered from where his neck hung over the Buick's right door.

"Matter of teck'nality, that's what," Chase put in. "Matter of teck'nality. But we'll give the lubber twenty thousan' shares of Rio—no we won't either," he countermanded, "fifteen, 'cause teck'nality involved."

"Damn you and your stock!" the stranger shouted, getting out his car crank. "And that goes for your 'technicality' also! I'll have twenty-five dollars or take it out of your damned hides!"

Acting as mediator, Ray explained the partners' financial status, thus avoiding a pair of busted skulls. "Alright, then," the stranger said and increased his wrath by spending several minutes cranking his car. Still cussing, he shot it in a reverse circle.

"Hey!" Ray called. "I thought you were headed for Mountain City!"

"I was," the irate victim shouted. "Now I'm headed for Elko. I'll either have twenty-five dollars or by damn those two birds'll be in jail as soon as they hit town!" With the left rear fender and raggedy top flopping he bounced back into the rutty road and pulled the gas lever to the bottom of the quadrant.

"Looks like you fellows are in for it," Ray said, watching the dust-and-smoke trail left by the Model T. When he turned he saw Hunt sitting behind the Buick's wheel as if ready to leave. Chase lolled in the back seat nursing an empty Old Yellowstone bottle. "You're a fine damn pair of big-shot mining promoters," Ray said in disgust. "No wonder you can't unload your stock. Everybody's fed up on you—including me."

"Now, now, Ray," Hunt cajoled, "don't you go back on me. We're pals ain't we? We're old rootin' tootin' sourdough mixin' badgerin' buddies," he snickered. "Hey, back there!" he addressed Chase, now in an alcoholic sleep that a shotgun blast couldn't have roused. "Give our friend here a snort and throw in twenty thousand shares of gilt-edge for a chaser."

Ray afterward said although he was mad enough to wring the necks of those two drunks, he had to laugh. "Never mind the whiskey and the shares," he told Hunt. "What you fellows better do is either stay clear of Elko or if you're bound to go you better start rustling twenty-five dollars. That fellow means business."

"To hell with that feller!" Hunt shouted. "I ain't afraid of him. When he gets cooled off he'll be glad to take a batch of stock for that old hunk of tin. What's a fender or two, anyway? We'll all be tycoons soon as my mine comes in. We got 'er timbered now, Ray, and makin' footage like a badger in a black loam hillside."

"Okay, Frank. But I think you better turn around and go back to your cabin."

"I'm headin' for Newt Crumley's," Hunt said, his tone growing mean, "and you or nobody else is stoppin' me."

Back in Elko three days later, Ray heard that his mine neighbors were in jail. The justice of the peace was prejudiced against drunks in general and Hunt and Chase in particular. The "collision" occurred seventy miles out of his jurisdiction and was a civil case, but he had slapped the mining tycoons in a cell on general principles: "Thirty days and a

RAY HAGE WOULD HAVE BEEN RICH IF HE'D TAKEN RAY HUNT'S STOCK INSTEAD OF THE TWENTY-FIVE DOLLARS.

hundred dollars for disturbing the peace and directing abusive language toward this Court."

Again Ray was called on as peacemaker, but the chore wasn't as easy as it had been on the desert. The talk boiled down to a mere hundred-dollar fine which, so far as Hage and any of his close friends were concerned, might as well have been a million. Finally, a few days wheedling and his now-and-then boss, Emmet Bachman, could no longer withstand Ray's pleas and came through with the personal loan to Ray.

The years wore away and still Ray's erstwhile friends hadn't reimbursed him for but half the loan from Bachman. But Ray, needing money, had settled his forty dollars account for twenty-five dollars for the railroad ties. In the meantime, a disgruntled Utah holder of a few thousand Rio Tinto shares had heard of his company's escapades and the feeble progress in the mine. Rumors sifted to Elko in 1931 that an investigation was about to be launched.

An investigation of any sort could be

serious. The Blue Sky Law was not something to be sneezed at, and Hunt and Chase buckled down to a little work even if it interfered with their drinking bouts in Mountain City and Elko. But these trips were easily circumvented. Although Prohibition had been kicked out, there remained in most watered gulches a moonshiner and his still, so the partners could satisfy their needs right in their shack.

It was the evening of February 26, 1932, when news broke over telephone and telegraph that electrified not only Elko but most western states: "We've struck it!" the wire read. The huge body of copper ore Frank Hunt had for nineteen years stoutly maintained lay beneath his shaft had been struck at a depth of 225 feet. Elko went hog-wild, and two mad stampedes were on—one searching desks and sewing machine drawers, the other trying to get up to stake claims.

Even the snowdrifts and nigh-impossible roads could not deter the stampede. But Hunt's faith in his prospect had caused him to stake claims covering several thousand feet in length and width. Even though the hills soon bristled with location stakes, there was little chance of new claims lapping over the estimated ore body.

In Elko, barbers, bakers, beauty operators, saloon and storekeepers—in fact anyone who had been talked out of cash or merchandise for the five-cent stock—pawed through every cubby hole, searching for long-forgotten stock certificates. But alas and alack; to ninety percent of the holders the pretty, gilt-edge certificates had been just so much fancy paper and they had either thrown them away or palmed them off on some outsider as gullible as they had been. "Probably just a flash-in-the-pan, anyway," they consoled themselves.

But when the Anaconda Copper Company ran test holes and made an offer of $300,000 for the property, John Q. Public sat up and took notice. Ogden Chase was understood to have accepted half the offer for his share, but Hunt had been more cagey. He had not only held out for a larger amount but retained a "washtub" full of the stock as well.

Chase later explained how Hunt's

dream had come true: "It had been one hell of a cold day since early morning, blowing a gale with snow spears that would cut your eyes out. Frank had been in the shaft all forenoon, in fact to past one o'clock drilling for another round of shots. I had windlassed up all the muck from the shots the afternoon before and after we'd had a bite of dinner Frank went down to load the holes for shooting. We usually did that. After shooting, Frank never went back down until the next morning as powder gas all but tore his skull apart.

"But after the round had been fired that afternoon, Frank said he guessed he'd go down and take a look, as his three-foot drills had hit a soft strata and he was anxious to see if it was the same slide formation we had gone through twice before. I told him he better wait until morning to go down but when old Frank gets his neck bowed you might as well talk to a stump. He's been worried lately, too, over word from Salt Lake that our sales and expenditures were being looked into, so thought we better be Johnny-at-the-rat-hole and try to make a showing. Let a trickle of news get out that our company's being investigated and we'd be dead. We'd be able to sell the Brooklyn Bridge easier than a dozen shares of our stock.

"Anyway, I lowered him and went back in the cabin and was shoving some wood in the stove to keep a pot of beans boiling when the bell started ringing like crazy. My first thought was that Frank was passing out from the gas. I ran out and cranked that windlass faster than a hundred-horsepower engine. When I dropped the shaft lid Frank didn't wait for me to lower the bucket back on it. He simply tumbled out along with half a bucket of black copper, yelling, "We've struck 'er! We've struck 'er!"

Yes, they'd struck her, alright. They had uncovered a body of high-grade copper that sent their stock skyrocketing—two-fifty, five dollars, ten dollars…

As the Anaconda people sped up development, the stock continued to climb until it seemed the sky would be the limit. And as wealth rolled in, Frank Hunt devised ways to give it away. One hundred and fifty thousand went to a hospital in Honolulu. An endowment went to the

Mackay School of Mines in Reno for research and the financing of prospectors who could not otherwise explore Nevada's ledges. The irony of it all was that he had worn the spring of his life away digging for that which promised an easy, illustrious autumn. He had but a short while to enjoy his wealth. With a "poke" that boasted $2.5 million and much more to come, he cashed in life's chips in La Jolla, California.

There's a sequel to this narrative that were it not so tragic would be hilarious. Ray Hage, Hunt's mining neighbor and savior, and a man named Sills were working on a W.P.A. project in Elko, as one Republican critic phrased it, "raking leaves and snow from one street and dumping it on the next so they wouldn't run out of leaves." For two days Ray and Sills had been exploring every corner of their minds for a clue as to where they had met before. They knew they had, but where? Then one afternoon Sills was sure he had it. "I know now," he said. "It was in Ogden. Seems we…"

"Not in Ogden," Ray broke in. "I was never in Ogden in my life."

"Hmm, then it was in Denver."

"Nope. Never been there either."

"Well, by damn," Sills said, "it was some place!"

Ray was in hearty agreement with that, but where?

When the dump truck returned later, Ray couldn't wait for its driver to step down. That "by damn" had unlocked a memory cell. "You're the fellow Frank Hunt and Ogden Chase collided with up there in the desert a few years ago!" he blurted out.

"By damn, yes!" Sills exclaimed. "And you was the pacifier." Then he leaned back in the seat and laughed until tears flooded his face.

"I know just what you're thinking," Ray said as he, too, laughed until he had to sit down on the curb. Their pipes lit, they went back over the events that would have brought each of them a fortune.

"Look where we'd have been," Sills said, still unable to quash a laugh. "Here we are, working for forty dollars two weeks out of the month and I understand that stock is around forty dollars now. You know, Hage, the whole thing strikes me

funny now, but my luck has always been just like that. If I was starving to death and it started raining soup, I'd be caught out with nothing but a toothpick."

"Sure fits me," Ray said. "I finally settled with Hunt and Chase for twenty-five bucks for my ties, but never did get but half the money I borrowed to get them out of jail, and I've never had enough money to get more ties hauled to my mine. Besides that, when he made the strike and the whole town stampeded up there through a blizzard to stake claims, I like a damn fool joined them and tore all the guts out of my Graham-Paige before I was twenty miles on the road. I wrote to Hunt just a few months ago, telling him I'd appreciate any little help he'd care to give me, but he never had the decency to answer my letter."

"What about the grubstake laws?" Sills asked. "Couldn't you have hauled him into court and come in for a share in the mine?"

"Looked into that, too," Ray said, "but being as I'd settled with him for twenty-five dollars for the ties I was told I didn't have a leg to stand on."

"Well," Sills said, "I never got anything for my fender, either. A lawyer wanted fifty dollars to bring suit against them but I found I could get a good fender for three dollars at George Green's wrecking yard, so I called it quits.

"Oh well," he added, as if finding nourishment in the statement, "one thing's damn sure. The old buzzard won't be able to take any more with him when he kicks the bucket than you will."

Sills was so right. S. Frank Hunt's tenure as a millionaire was a short one. But when he went the way all prospectors must, his Rio Tinto millions remained here.

Today the hollow eves of the massive concentration plant and other weathered structures of the old Rio Tinto stare vacantly out over the flats where, for a quarter of a century, fleets of trucks sped seemingly unending wealth to the railroad in Elko. Yet people have long expected to rejuvenate the old workings by applying new processes and extracting techniques.

Yes, hope truly springs eternal in the breast of man—especially if he is in the mining game. ■

"WILD HORSE COUNTRY" © J.N. SWANSON

WHEN HARRY BECAME A COWBOY, HE WAS WORKING ON BIG OUTFITS IN WYOMING. COWPUNCHERS WOULD STAY OUT WITH THE HERD FOR DAYS OR WEEKS AT A TIME AND SOMETIMES NEEDED A PACKHORSE TO CARRY THEIR SOOGANS, BOVINE DOCTORING SUPPLIES AND GRUB——IF THEY WEREN'T WORKING WITH THE WAGON. THIS VAQUERO IS MOVING THROUGH NORTHWESTERN NEVADA'S MUSTANG COUNTRY LOOKING FOR RANCH WORK, AND HE SPOTS A BAND ON TOP OF THE NEXT HILL.

Old Mose

That old dog was worthless as a trail hound. He couldn't track cats and he always scared the horses. In fact, he failed every test I put him to—except one.

 My wife awakened me one bitter cold, stormy night and whispered, "It's out there again." I unsnapped my .38 Special from the "sheriff's underarm holster" hanging from the bedpost, and listened to padded feet on our ranch house porch.

Moving to the door, I yanked it open just in time to see a long tail disappear off the porch. But as I pulled the trigger I knew it wasn't the big bobcat that had been slipping in and killing our cats.

The bobcat, which I had twice glimpsed, had killed our old cat and all but one kitten. Several nights now, we had heard the dying squall of a kitten, and on hearing the padded feet on the porch a second time I was ready for Mr. Predator. But again I was too late to do more than fire in the direction of departing sounds.

At last sleep, then daylight came, and on hearing a slight sound I peered out a window, my six-shooter ready. But imagine my surprise when I beheld the shivering, emaciated form of a dun-colored hound dog lying with his back against the wall. Softly opening the door I spoke to him, but in one bound he was off the porch and around the corner of the house.

Hurriedly getting breakfast, we made a sourdough hotcake the size of our largest skillet and two inches thick. Breaking this in a big pan of milk, I tried to coax the hound up to me but he seemed to fear for his life. Where he had come from or why he was bone poor was a mystery. My Nevada ranch was several miles from the nearest neighbors and I knew they owned no such critter as this.

Leaving the pan of food I went inside, and presently we heard the slup slup of starved jaws. On going out I saw the pan was empty. That feed must have weighed all of six or seven pounds, and the dog's sides swelled out until it looked like his ribs would burst open. Still he was hungry and didn't run when I brought out more cakes and milk.

"This is the greatest thing that could happen to me!" I told my wife. "This is some sort of a trail hound and just what I need. He must have got lost and been roaming these hills for a month from the looks of him." I didn't care a whoop who he'd belonged to; he was mine, now. I was all but in raptures over finding him—or, to be more exact, him finding us.

I was trapping predators at the time for the government and after losing my last dog from strychnine baits, tossed carelessly about by neophyte trappers, this hound dog was a godsend. Not knowing any other name for him I naturally called him Mose and from the second pan full of breakfast Old Mose was my shadow. If I went to the barn, corrals, blacksmith shop or whatever, Old Mose went also. When I

I don't believe I ever saw another dog that could irritate me as Mose did.

was in the house he lay down by the door nearest me.

Oh, I had me a fine trail hound and no mistake. But from the looks of his sore feet it would be several days before I could take him on a trapline out to track and tree bobcats. For this I could hardly wait.

A week passed and a light snow had fallen during the night, which was ideal for seeing cat tracks, and I knew bobcats would be out hunting in the early morning. Giving Mose a feed of hotcakes and milk (no raw meat for a dog about to go on a trail as it lessens its sense of smell) and me full of breakfast and enthusiasm we set out for cat country about four miles north of my ranch. Lots of junipers and ledges over there and always some cats. Any time I had wanted to trail cats I always got one or two in those juniper hills. Now I had me a trail hound.

Out on a sagebrush flat, I saw where a big bobcat had caught and eaten part of a jackrabbit then headed for the juniper ledges. I put Mose on his track and expected to hear him give a bawl and take off. I didn't know what breed hound Mose was but from his color I judged him to be a redbone coonhound.

Mose didn't appear to know what I expected him to do. He'd sniff the fresh track then look at me as if asking, "What now, boss?" Getting off my horse I'd push Mose's nose down in a track then I'd trot along saying, "Go git him, Mose. Sic'im!" But Mose would only go as far as I did, then he'd stand and look on ahead awhile, then turn a questioning eye on me.

That cat track was so fresh I could almost smell it myself, but to Mose it was just a series of holes in the snow. It had me stumped. He was the first dog I'd ever seen that wasn't interested in cats.

"Mose," I said, "I don't know where the hell you've been all your life but I damn well know why you got lost and damn nigh starved to death! You ain't got brains enough to do anything but eat and only then when somebody hands it to you!"

As if I had just paid him a big compliment, Mose galloped around me making happy sounds then taking a snow bath by kicking himself along on his belly and plowing the snow with his long nose.

As I hurriedly followed the bobcat's tracks through juniper hills, I knew just about where he would halt for the day. A high, overhanging cliff lay ahead and my dogs had jumped many a cat from the tufts of ryegrass growing beneath an overhang. Perhaps if the cat jumped and Mose saw him he'd surely have brains enough to know it was a cat and his dog instinct would tell him to chase it.

On tracking the cat as it circled the ledges, going up from below, I could—from the opposite hillside—trace his tracks to a long overhang where they ended. No sign of tracks where he would have had to come out in the snow above, so he had to be curled up behind one of the grass tufts.

As I stood wondering where the cat could be I saw Mose looking up the cliff. Some fifty feet from the ground there was a large nest on a small projection which from the size of the sticks I knew had been built by an eagle, and in this I could make out a spotted form which could either be the cat or an owl.

If it were the cat and I drilled him in the head there was no way to get him out of the nest. On the other hand, I might be able to wound him. Holding low, I put a 25-35 through the nest and out leapt the cat, a front leg dangling. As the cat bloodied the snow as he all but fell on Mose, I yelled "Git him, Mose! Atta boy Mose! Go after him!"

Then I realized Mose wasn't after him, but flying down the canyon in twenty-foot leaps, yelping at every jump and leaving the cat and its bloody trail behind.

"If this isn't a hell of a fine note," I told the hillside as I scrambled up it to my horse, "I never saw one!"

In a few minutes I had the cat, and after skinning it I followed Mose's tracks, calling him as I hurried along. But it was wasted breath. From the looks of those splay-toed, twenty-foot leaps, that cussed hound was probably home before I had the cat skinned.

That settled my dream of having a fine trail hound. In fact, although I didn't

want him to follow me on my traplines, I often tried to coax him along but all I got for my efforts was to see him sit as immobile as a post and watch me leave.

I don't believe I ever saw another dog that could irritate me as Mose did. I hated him. And as time wore on my hatred increased. Yet, his faithfulness and adoring eyes as he dogged my steps while doing

I was mounting my horse to leave when Ed's two dogs came running, and the dogfight started.

chores kept me from killing him. If I chanced to be working cattle or bringing in a bunch of wild horses, Mose was sure to be sitting like a statue in the middle of the land, scaring everything back on me. Cussing and rock throwing couldn't budge him. But, worst of all, I would be such a screaming maniac my rocks always missed their mark.

As spring came and I would be irrigating, my shovel would near cut his feet off before he'd move. If I bellied down by a ditch for a drink Mose would also have a drink, but he was always careful to wade in the ditch just upstream from my face to do it.

"That damn hound dog is driving me plumb nuts!" I told my wife. I had run a bunch of broncs round and round a big pasture afoot until my tongue hung out, then as they neared the corral Mose outran them and squatted squarely in the gateway, causing them to break back.

Running to the house for my gun I said to my wife, "By God, I've had it! That dog's caused me trouble for the last time!"

"Maybe if you ever spoke one kind word to him," I was told, "he would learn what you wanted him to do. Look at him. His eyes never leave you. You can see he's begging you for a little attention."

"I'll give him some attention!" I said, grabbing my six-shooter. "But it'll be with hot lead!"

Then my son started whimpering, "Don't shoot him, Daddy! Please don't

kill him. We'll give him to somebody."

One day in Elko I was telling my dog troubles to Ira Goldsby and he said, "Say, the Chinese section foreman for the S.P. has two pups he's trying to give away! They're out of an Airedale."

"Let's go," I cut in. "Even if they've got but three legs they'll be better than that hound."

Those pups were just past the weaning age and were fighters from the start. When we'd thrown out a batch of food and Old Mose would be gobbling it down, those pups would tie into him and run him away. He could have swallowed both of them in two bites but there wasn't a spark of fight in him. And as time went on and Terry and Jerry got some real teeth, they slashed Mose up at every meal and often between meals.

I had intended to haul Mose far away and dump him out in some town, but decided to keep him so the pups would get lots of practice fighting. He knew I hated him but he still dogged my every step around the ranch and bedded down at night as near as he could get to me without coming in. One morning while I was stapling barbed wire back on some posts along the meadow, Mose suddenly showed signs of life by stopping dead in front of me. With his tail straight out and nose pointing he seemed frozen to the spot.

"Hears a rattlesnake, I suppose," I said to myself as I stood listening. Not a sound. Mose stood, scarcely breathing. With the hammer handy, I advanced a few yards, peering and listening for Mr. Rattler's warning. Suddenly, up flew a golden pheasant, the first I'd heard of in my section of the country. The pheasant had dropped to the ground near some willows and Mose galloped on ahead but on nearing the spot where the bird had lit he stood as if carved out of wood. Only then did it come to me that he was some sort of bird dog. But a bird dog was what I needed least.

I talked bird dog to everyone I met in and out of town, but no luck. Mose had taken to following me when I went four miles to a ranch on the stage road to our mailbox but after the rancher's two big dogs chewed him up badly, without his fighting back, he would wait back on a hill several hundred yards until I came back by. Nothing could persuade him to venture closer.

The two pups, Terry and Jerry, were now five months old and showed promise of being great trail dogs. They trailed everything from our lone house cat to rattlesnakes, which proved the Airedale stock was asserting itself. Also, the pups would by now go for Old Mose's throat whenever their one-sided fight took place, which was several times a day.

Then one day I got the surprise of my

damn dogs of mine," Ed said. "They jumped on every dog that came up the road and chewed them up. I'll bet they'll think twice from now on before bothering anybody else's dogs."

That evening I was lying on my back under our trees and, as always, Mose had flopped down a few feet away. I had been thinking about Mose tearing into those dogs and also of the many times I had tried to kill him with boulders and near doing it with my six-shooter, and it struck me I at least owed him a word of kind-

didn't mind being clawed or tooth-slashed.

On going over one of my traplines one day, I came to three sets where two coyotes and a bobcat had pulled up the trap pins and escaped. Yet, although the animals had been gone several days, those pups immediately took a trail yelping at every jump with Old Mose racing along with them. Terry, the female, ran as if on a radar beam. Running at full speed with head up, she would now and then swing from one side of the scent to the other while Jerry ran with his nose to the ground. Mose simply ran so as to be in on the kill. The cat hadn't gone far before it went up a pine and the trap chain tangled around the limb. But the two coyotes had covered several miles, zig-zagging back and forth, yet it hadn't fooled those pups.

Mose set up a furious barking alongside my head. It was the first time I had ever heard him bark.

life. Mose and the two pups had followed me when I went for the mail. The pups went to the corral with me where the owner and I stood talking. Old Mose sat on the hill at a safe distance. I was mounting my horse to leave when Ed's two dogs came running, and the dogfight started.

The pups were no match for Ed's two vicious dogs, and we were each shouting and kicking at them when Mose was among us like a whirlwind and sunk his teeth in a dog's kidneys, all but breaking his back. Yelping, the dog dragged himself away when Mose was on the other, and a real dogfight was on.

I was trying to break up the fight when Ed yelled, "Let 'em go!" and kept shouting, "Eat him up, Mose! Chew his guts out!" It was only when Mose had the dog by the throat, strangling him, that I grabbed Mose by the tail while Ed pried his jaws apart with a pitchfork handle. Once free, Ed's dog lost no time getting out of there.

I had witnessed many a dogfight but I had never seen a more vicious, adept fighter than Mose had suddenly become. Although I was proud of him, this sudden transformation had me all but stupefied. Here those pups had fought him half a dozen times a day from the day they arrived on the ranch and of late had left plenty gashes on him without Mose so much as snapping at them. Yet when his little tormentors were in trouble he had rushed to their aid with a vengeance.

"Best thing ever happened to them

ness. Rolling over I saw him stretched out on his belly, his lower jaw resting on his paws and his brown eyes on me.

"Mose, you worthless old bastard," I said, laughing, "you don't know it but you're not worth the powder to blow you to hell."

His reaction was so spontaneous it brought a lump in my throat. Making happy little sounds he wriggled along on his belly like a scolded puppy and began licking my hands as his nose continued making joyous little whimpers. I knew then I had cussed and thrown rocks at him for the last time.

A few days later Mose saved me from being bitten in the face by a big rattlesnake. I had parted some heavy grass by a swift-running ditch and had bellied down for a drink when Mose set up a furious barking alongside my head. It was the first time I had ever heard him bark. Raising up, I parted the grass with my shovel only to hear it struck with the rattler's fangs. There was little doubt but that Mose had saved me from a fatal bite in the face.

When fall came and I started trapping again, I found those two pups lived up to all my expectations. Animals often pull up a trap pin or break the chain and get away unless the trapper has a good trail dog. Those pups were as good right from the start as any of the seasoned dogs I had owned. But Old Mose gave me a real surprise. He not only took up the hunt, he wanted to do all the killing by himself and

One coyote had circled and crossed its tracks several times but Terry made but a few jumps before she came back and raced away on the freshest part of the trail. Jerry and Mose learned to rely on her judgment.

At the insistence of a skeptical friend, Ed Thomas, I once showed just how good those pups were. Locking them in the barn, Ed and I took saddle horses and with a dead woodchuck tied to my lasso we started out. I dragged that "chuck" more than a mile, crossed a stream several times, circled, and on coming back to the ranch dragged the frazzled chuck a few hundred yards along the starting trail. I lifted it up so it didn't touch the ground and on getting back I placed the carcass on a hayrack.

When we put the pups on the trail they were off yelping. But after going but a few yards Terry stopped, sniffed the air, and raced back to the hayrack and tried to climb on it.

"Well, I'll be damned!" Ed exclaimed. "All that dragging for nothing!"

There are very few dogs that can outrun an average coyote but by the time Terry and Jerry were two years old, given half a chance, Terry had out-run many a coyote and jerked him down. Her method was to grab a hind leg as she passed and down would go the coyote, perhaps to be on its feet and running the other way only to be met by Jerry and Old Mose. I had watched this game many times on some

big meadow after the hay was up and coyotes were looking for mice.

I had quit trapping for the government two years before, as the work interfered with my ranch work and, besides, I could make more money trapping for myself during October and November than in two years working for the government. I enjoyed trapping and to hear the yipping of Terry and Jerry—Old Mose had learned to yelp every few hundred yards—on a cat or lion trail was a thrill never to be forgotten. But all this came to a sudden end when disaster struck in the form of ill health. It was a case of a lower climate for my wife, and quick.

In September 1942, the ranch and cattle were sold to Judge Charles Cook of Beverly Hills, California, and my wife and son went to Los Angeles while I stayed on the ranch a couple months to gather cattle and start the judge off on the right foot. Terry and Jerry were later given to a trapping rancher friend but the judge wanted Old Mose left on the ranch to "keep the

coyotes away."

There is an old truism made famous by Senator Vest that "A dog is a man's best friend." It is equally true that dogs have an intuition so uncanny it is hard for a dogless person to believe. From the day Judge Cook and I made the deal, our dogs knew it—knew it was the end of something. Their whole manner changed. They didn't care whether they were fed or not. And when my friend came in his car to get the two young dogs it was pitiful. So pitiful I don't care to dwell on it.

After Terry and Jerry were gone, my real problem was Old Mose. I almost had to stuff food in his mouth, otherwise he wouldn't eat and no matter what I was doing he tried to keep his head against my leg. The new owners were kind to him and tried to make friends but he would have none of it.

My last day on the ranch was the worst. Back and forth, back and forth, Mose was against me as I loaded small possessions in my car. Mose's demeanor

added to my melancholy. I was parting with a beautiful ranch that thirty years had gone into building. And from watching other beautiful ranches go to rack and ruin in two years after City Dude money acquired them, I knew mine would go the same route.

At four o'clock in the afternoon I tried to say a cheery farewell to the Cooks, but my heart was heavy. I was never one who could pen a dog up in a city or I would have had Mose in the seat beside me.

Old Mose ran alongside the car to the end of the lane then sat on his haunches. Just before dropping over a hill I paused for a last look back. Dimly, I saw Mose still sitting there. In thirty minutes I was on Highway 40 heading into the setting sun. It was difficult to see where I was driving. But it was not the sun that blinded me. It was a vision of a lonely old hound—and memories. ∎

"Cutting Out Bulls" © J.N. Swanson

Bulls are put in with the cows on open range for two months during the year so that the cows will all calf at the same time, usually in early spring. These bulls have been taken out once, but managed to get back to the ladies. The cowboys use their romals to help push them away from the herd.

Glossary of Terms

BATWING—Tough, wide chaps, built with leather that will last.

BEANIE CROTCH—Slingshot.

BOSAL—Noseband on a classic hackamore, often made of braided rawhide.

BRONC BUSTER/STOMPER—A cowboy who breaks wild horses to the saddle.

BUCKBOARD—A four-wheeled wagon.

CAVVY—A large band of horses taken out on the range to work cattle. Some are good cutting horses, some circle horses, others greenbroke colts for the cowboys to train during the cattle drive.

CAYUSE—A native range horse.

CHAPS—Leather leggins worn over trousers. Protects a cowboy's legs from brush and rocks.

CHUCKWAGON OR WAGON—Carries cooking equipment, food and soogans for cowboys "out with the wagon" on open country for weeks or months. Staples would include beans, salted meats, coffee and sourdough starter for biscuits.

CIRCLE—A wide area where a cowboy trots out to pick up cattle that were missed on the first roundup. A circle horse needs to cover big country and a lot of miles in a day.

DEMIJOHN—A large, narrow-necked bottle usually enclosed in wicker and used to hold liquor.

DOUBLETREE—A crossbar on a wagon, carriage or plow.

DRY GULCHING—The act of killing by ambush.

GREENHORN—A dude or innocent cowboy who hasn't learned much.

HACKAMORE—A bridle with a loop capable of being tightened about a horse's nose, in place of a bit.

HANG 'N RATTLE—To hang on to a bucking bronc, sometimes suffering mightily.

HEADING—Throwing a lasso rope over the horns or neck of a bovine.

HEELING—Catching two back feet of a running bovine.

HOG-LEG—A six-shot revolver shaped like part of a hog's leg.

HOULIHAN—A loop on a rope used to catch cattle or horses. According to word-wizard.com, "the roper carries the loop in his hand, and when the chance presents itself, he swings one quick whirl around in front of him, toward the right, up over his head, and releases the loop and rope in the direction of the target. As it comes over, it is turned in a way to cause it to flatten out before it reaches the head of the animal to be roped. It lands straight down, and so has a fair-sized opening. It is a fast loop and is strictly a head catch, being especially used to catch horses in a corral."

I.W.W.—Industrial Workers of the World, a.k.a. the Wobblies.

LATIGO—A long strap on a saddletree of a western saddle to adjust the cinch.

MULE—A long-eared, sterile cross between a burro and a horse.

OUTFIT—Common name for a ranch.

PREDICATORS—Common name for predators in the early 1900s.

PUNKIN LINE—Name for rustic telephone line between ranches.

QUIRT—A riding whip with a short handle and a rawhide lash.

RAMROD—A boss on a cattle outfit.

REMUDA—A herd of horses from which ranch cowboys select their mounts. Selection is made depending on the kind of work they will do that day.

REP—A ranch representative working under delegated authority. The rep oversees gathering of his boss's cattle and horses.

RIATA—A lasso rope of hemp or braided rawhide.

RIDGELING—A partially castrated male animal, which still has the urge to mate.

RINGTAIL—A horse carrying its tail in a form approximating a circle.

ROMAL—Long quirt attached to a set of closed reins that are connected to a horse's bridle. To keep it out of the way, cowboys tuck it behind the saddle cantle.

SLICK-EAR—Range animal lacking an earmark.

SOOGAN—A bedroll or quilt.

SPARKING—Keeping company with.

WADDY—A cowboy.

W.P.A.—Works Progress Administration. It was started in 1935 to help provide economic relief to citizens of the United States.